Humorous Tales

Edgar Allan Poe

1st WORLD
LIBRARY
Literary Society

Humorous Tales
Edgar Allan Poe

© 1st World Library – Literary Society, 2004
PO Box 2211
Fairfield, IA 52556
www.1stworldlibrary.org
First Edition

LCCN: 2003195097

ISBN: 1-59540-423-6

Purchase *"Humorous Tales"*
as a traditional bound book at:
www.1stWorldLibrary.org/purchase.asp?ISBN=1-59540-423-6

1st World Library Literary Society is a nonprofit
organization dedicated to promoting literacy by:

- Creating a free internet library accessible from any
computer worldwide.
- Hosting writing competitions and offering book
publishing scholarships.

Readers interested in supporting literacy
through sponsorship, donations or
membership please contact:
literacy@1stworldlibrary.org
Check us out at: www.1stworldlibrary.org

Humorous Tales
contributed by the Charles Family
in support of
1st World Library - Literary Society

Contents

THE DUC DE L'OMLETTE

And stepped at once into a cooler clime.   Cowper

KEATS fell by a criticism. Who was it died of "The Andromache"? [1] Ignoble souls! – De L'Omelette perished of an ortolan. L'histoire en est breve. Assist me, Spirit of Apicius!

[1] Montfleury. The author of the Parnasse Reforme makes him thus speak in Hades:– "L'homme donc qui voudrait savoir ce dont Je suis morte, qu'il ne demande pas si'l fut de fievre ou de podagre ou d'autre chose, mais qui'l entende que ce fut de 'L'Andromache.'"

A golden cage bore the little winged wanderer, enamored, melting, indolent, to the Chaussee D'Antin, from its home in far Peru. From its queenly possessor La Bellissima, to the Duc De L'Omelette, six peers of the empire conveyed the happy bird.

That night the Duc was to sup alone. In the privacy of his bureau he reclined languidly on that ottoman for which he sacrificed his loyalty in outbidding his king– the notorious ottoman of Cadet.

He buries his face in the pillow. The clock strikes! Unable to restrain his feelings, his Grace swallows an olive. At this moment the door gently opens to the sound of soft music, and lo! the most delicate of birds is before the most enamored of men! But what inexpressible dismay now overshadows the countenance of the Duc?– "Horreur!– chien!– Baptiste!– l'oiseau! ah, bon Dieu! cet oiseau modeste que tu as deshabille de ses plumes, et que tu as servi sans papier!" It is superfluous to say more:– the Duc expired in a paroxysm of disgust.

"Ha! ha! ha!" said his Grace on the third day after his decease.

"He! he! he!" replied the Devil faintly, drawing himself up with an air of hauteur.

"Why, surely you are not serious," retorted De L'Omelette. "I have sinned– c'est vrai– but, my good sir, consider!– you have no actual intention of putting such– such barbarous threats into execution."

"No what?" said his majesty– "come, sir, strip!"

"Strip, indeed! very pretty i' faith! no, sir, I shall not strip. Who are you, pray, that I, Duc De L'Omelette, Prince de Foie–Gras, just come of age, author of the 'Mazurkiad,' and Member of the Academy, should divest myself at your bidding of the sweetest pantaloons ever made by Bourdon, the daintiest robe–de–chambre ever put together by Rombert– to say nothing of the taking my hair out of paper– not to mention the trouble I should have in drawing off my gloves?"

"Who am I?– ah, true! I am Baal–Zebub, Prince of the

Fly. I took thee, just now, from a rose–wood coffin inlaid with ivory. Thou wast curiously scented, and labelled as per invoice. Belial sent thee,– my Inspector of Cemeteries. The pantaloons, which thou sayest were made by Bourdon, are an excellent pair of linen drawers, and thy robe–de–chambre is a shroud of no scanty dimensions."

"Sir!" replied the Duc, "I am not to be insulted with impunity!– Sir! I shall take the earliest opportunity of avenging this insult!– Sir! you shall hear from me! in the meantime au revoir!"– and the Duc was bowing himself out of the Satanic presence, when he was interrupted and brought back by a gentleman in waiting. Hereupon his Grace rubbed his eyes, yawned, shrugged his shoulders, reflected. Having become satisfied of his identity, he took a bird's eye view of his whereabouts.

The apartment was superb. Even De L'Omelette pronounced it bien comme il faut. It was not its length nor its breadth,– but its height– ah, that was appalling!– There was no ceiling– certainly none– but a dense whirling mass of fiery–colored clouds. His Grace's brain reeled as he glanced upward. From above, hung a chain of an unknown blood–red metal– its upper end lost, like the city of Boston, parmi les nues. From its nether extremity swung a large cresset. The Duc knew it to be a ruby; but from it there poured a light so intense, so still, so terrible, Persia never worshipped such– Gheber never imagined such– Mussulman never dreamed of such when, drugged with opium, he has tottered to a bed of poppies, his back to the flowers, and his face to the God Apollo. The Duc muttered a slight oath, decidedly approbatory.

The corners of the room were rounded into niches. Three of these were filled with statues of gigantic proportions. Their beauty was Grecian, their deformity Egyptian, their tout ensemble French. In the fourth niche the statue was veiled; it was not colossal. But then there was a taper ankle, a sandalled foot. De L'Omelette pressed his hand upon his heart, closed his eyes, raised them, and caught his Satanic Majesty— in a blush.

But the paintings!— Kupris! Astarte! Astoreth!— a thousand and the same! And Rafaelle has beheld them! Yes, Rafaelle has been here, for did he not paint the ——? and was he not consequently damned? The paintings— the paintings! O luxury! O love!— who, gazing on those forbidden beauties, shall have eyes for the dainty devices of the golden frames that besprinkled, like stars, the hyacinth and the porphyry walls?

But the Duc's heart is fainting within him. He is not, however, as you suppose, dizzy with magnificence, nor drunk with the ecstatic breath of those innumerable censers. C'est vrai que de toutes ces choses il a pense beaucoup— mais! The Duc De L'Omelette is terror-stricken; for, through the lurid vista which a single uncurtained window is affording, lo! gleams the most ghastly of all fires!

Le pauvre Duc! He could not help imagining that the glorious, the voluptuous, the never–dying melodies which pervaded that hall, as they passed filtered and transmuted through the alchemy of the enchanted window–panes, were the wailings and the howlings of the hopeless and the damned! And there, too!— there!— upon the ottoman!— who could he be?— he, the petitmaitre— no, the Deity— who sat as if carved in marble, et qui sourit, with his pale countenance, si amerement?

Mais il faut agir– that is to say, a Frenchman never faints outright. Besides, his Grace hated a scene– De L'Omelette is himself again. There were some foils upon a table– some points also. The Duc s'echapper. He measures two points, and, with a grace inimitable, offers his Majesty the choice. Horreur! his Majesty does not fence!

Mais il joue!– how happy a thought!– but his Grace had always an excellent memory. He had dipped in the "Diable" of Abbe Gaultier. Therein it is said "que le Diable n'ose pas refuser un jeu d'ecarte."

But the chances– the chances! True– desperate: but scarcely more desperate than the Duc. Besides, was he not in the secret?– had he not skimmed over Pere Le Brun?– was he not a member of the Club Vingt–un? "Si je perds," said he, "je serai deux fois perdu– I shall be doubly dammed– voila tout! (Here his Grace shrugged his shoulders.) Si je gagne, je reviendrai a mes ortolans– que les cartes soient preparees!"

His Grace was all care, all attention– his Majesty all confidence. A spectator would have thought of Francis and Charles. His Grace thought of his game. His Majesty did not think; he shuffled. The Duc cut.

The cards were dealt. The trump is turned– it is– it is– the king! No– it was the queen. His Majesty cursed her masculine habiliments. De L'Omelette placed his hand upon his heart. They play. The Duc counts. The hand is out. His Majesty counts heavily, smiles, and is taking wine. The Duc slips a card.

"C'est a vous a faire," said his Majesty, cutting. His Grace bowed, dealt, and arose from the table en presentant le Roi.

His Majesty looked chagrined.

Had Alexander not been Alexander, he would have been Diogenes; and the Duc assured his antagonist in taking leave, "que s'il n'eut ete De L'Omelette il n'aurait point d'objection d'etre le Diable."

LIONIZING

all people went
Upon their ten toes in wild wondernment.

Bishop Hall's Satires.

I AM, that is to say I was, a great man, but I am neither the author of Junius nor the man in the mask, for my name, I believe, is Robert Jones, and I was born somewhere in the city of Fum–Fudge.

The first action of my life was the taking hold of my nose with both hands. My mother saw this and called me a genius:– my father wept for joy and presented me with a treatise on Nosology. This I mastered before I was breeched.

I now began to feel my way in the science, and soon came to understand that, provided a man had a nose sufficiently conspicuous, he might by merely following it, arrive at a Lionship. But my attention was not confined to theories alone. Every morning I gave my proboscis a couple of pulls and swallowed a half–dozen of drams.

When I came of age my father asked me, one day, if I would step with him into his study.

"My son," he said, when we were seated, "what is the chief end of your existence?"

"My father," I answered, "it is the study of Nosology."

"And what, Robert," he inquired, "is Nosology?"

"Sir," I said, "it is the science of Noses."

"And can you tell me," he demanded, "what is the meaning of a nose?"

"A nose, my father," I replied, greatly softened, "has been variously defined by about a thousand different authors." [Here I pulled out my watch.] "It is now noon, or thereabouts– We shall have time enough to get through with them all before midnight. To commence then: The nose, according to Bartholinus, is that protuberance– that bump– that excresence– that–"

"Will do, Robert," interupted the old gentleman. "I am thunderstruck at the extent of your information– I am positively– upon my soul." [Here he closed his eyes and placed his hand upon his heart.] "Come here!" [Here he took me by the arm.] "Your education may now be considered as finished– it is high time you should scuffle for yourself– and you cannot do a better thing than merely follow your nose– so– so– so–" [Here he kicked me down stairs and out of the door.] – "So get out of my house, and God bless you!"

As I felt within me the divine afflatus, I considered this accident rather fortunate than otherwise. I resolved to be guided by the paternal advice. I determined to follow my nose. I gave it a pull or two upon the spot, and wrote a pamphlet on Nosology forthwith.

All Fum–Fudge was in an uproar.

"Wonderful genius!" said the Quarterly.

"Superb physiologist!" said the Westminster.

"Clever fellow!" said the Foreign.

"Fine writer!", said the Edinburgh.

"Profound thinker!" said the Dublin.

"Great man!" said Bentley.

"Divine soul!" said Fraser.

"One of us!" said Blackwood.

"Who can he be?" said Mrs. Bas–Bleu.

"What can he be?" said big Miss Bas–Bleu.

"Where can he be?" said little Miss Bas–Bleu.– But I paid these people no attention whatever– I just stepped into the shop of an artist.

The Duchess of Bless–my–Soul was sitting for her portrait; the Marquis of So–and–So was holding the Duchess' poodle; the Earl of This–and–That was flirting with her salts; and his Royal Highness of Touch–me–Not was leaning upon the back of her chair.

I approached the artist and turned up my nose.

"Oh, beautiful!" sighed her Grace.

"Oh, my!" lisped the Marquis.

"Oh, shocking!" groaned the Earl.

"Oh, abominable!" growled his Royal Highness.

"What will you take for it?" asked the artist.

"For his nose!" shouted her Grace.

"A thousand pounds," said I, sitting down.

"A thousand pounds?" inquired the artist, musingly.

"A thousand pounds," said I.

"Beautiful!" said he, entranced.

"A thousand pounds," said I.

"Do you warrant it?" he asked, turning the nose to the light.

"I do," said I, blowing it well.

"Is it quite original?" he inquired, touching it with reverence.

"Humph!" said I, twisting it to one side.

"Has no copy been taken?" he demanded, surveying it through a microscope.

"None," said I, turning it up.

"Admirable!" he ejaculated, thrown quite off his guard

by the beauty of the manoeuvre.

"A thousand pounds," said I.

"A thousand pounds?" said he.

"Precisely," said I.

"A thousand pounds?" said he.

"Just so," said I.

"You shall have them," said he. "What a piece of virtu!" So he drew me a check upon the spot, and took a sketch of my nose. I engaged rooms in Jermyn street, and sent her Majesty the ninety–ninth edition of the "Nosology," with a portrait of the proboscis. That sad little rake, the Prince of Wales, invited me to dinner.

We are all lions and recherches.

There was a modern Platonist. He quoted Porphyry, Iamblicus, Plotinus, Proclus, Hierocles, Maximus Tyrius, and Syrianus.

There was a human–perfectibility man. He quoted Turgot, Price, Priestly, Condorcet, De Stael, and the "Ambitious Student in Ill–Health."

There was Sir Positive Paradox. He observed that all fools were philosophers, and that all philosophers were fools.

There was Aestheticus Ethix. He spoke of fire, unity, and atoms; bi–part and pre–existent soul; affinity and discord; primitive intelligence and homoomeria.

heologos Theology. He talked of Eusebius
s; heresy and the Council of Nice; Puseyism
ostantialism; Homousios and Homouioisios.

is Fricassee from the Rocher de Cancale. He mentioned Muriton of red tongue; cauliflowers with veloute sauce; veal a la St. Menehoult; marinade a la St. Florentin; and orange jellies en mosaiques.

There was Bibulus O'Bumper. He touched upon Latour and Markbrunnen; upon Mosseux and Chambertin; upon Richbourg and St. George; upon Haubrion, Leonville, and Medoc; upon Barac and Preignac; upon Grave, upon Sauterne, upon Lafitte, and upon St. Peray. He shook his head at Clos de Vougeot, and told with his eyes shut, the difference between Sherry and Amontillado.

There was Signor Tintontintino from Florence. He discoursed of Cimabue, Arpino, Carpaccio, and Argostino– of the gloom of Caravaggio, of the amenity of Albano, of the colors of Titian, of the frows of Rubens, and of the waggeries of Jan Steen.

There was the President of the Fum–Fudge University. He was of the opinion that the moon was called Bendis in Thrace, Bubastis in Egypt, Dian in Rome, and Artemis in Greece.

There was a Grand Turk from Stamboul. He could not help thinking that the angels were horses, cocks, and bulls; that somebody in the sixth heaven had seventy thousand heads; and that the earth was supported by a sky–blue cow with an incalculable number of green horns.

There was Delphinus Polyglott. He told us what had become of the eighty–three lost tragedies of Aeschylus; of the fifty–four orations of Isaeus; of the three hundred and ninety–one speeches of Lysias; of the hundred and eighty treatises of Theophrastus; of the eighth book of the conic sections of Apollonius; of Pindar's hymns and dithyrambics, and of the five and forty tragedies of Homer Junior.

There was Ferdinand Fitz–Fossillus Feltspar. He informed us all about internal fires and tertiary formations; about aeriforms, fluidiforms, and solidforms; about quartz and marl; about schist and schorl; about gypsum and trap; about talc and calc; about blende and horn–blende; about micaslate and pudding–stone; about cyanite and lepidolite; about haematite and tremolite; about antimony and calcedony; about manganese and whatever you please.

There was myself. I spoke of myself;– of myself, of myself, of myself;– of Nosology, of my pamphlet, and of myself. I turned up my nose, and I spoke of myself.

"Marvellous clever man!" said the Prince.

"Superb!" said his guests;– and next morning her Grace of Bless–my–soul paid me a visit.

"Will you go to Almack's, pretty creature?" she said, tapping me under the chin.

"Upon honor," said I.

"Nose and all?" she asked.

"As I live," I replied.

"Here then is a card, my life. Shall I say you will be there?"

"Dear, Duchess, with all my heart."

"Pshaw, no!– but with all your nose?"

"Every bit of it, my love," said I:– so I gave it a twist or two, and found myself at Almack's.

The rooms were crowded to suffocation.

"He is coming!" said somebody on the staircase.

"He is coming!" said somebody farther up.

"He is coming!" said somebody farther still.

"He is come!" exclaimed the Duchess, "He is come, the little love!"– and, seizing me firmly by both hands, she kissed me thrice upon the nose.

A marked sensation immediately ensued.

"Diavolo!" cried Count Capricornutti.

"Dios guarda!" muttered Don Stiletto.

"Mille tonnerres!" ejaculated the Prince de Grenouille.

"Tousand teufel!" growled the Elector of Bluddennuff.

It was not to be borne. I grew angry. I turned short upon Bluddennuff.

"Sir!" said I to him, "you are a baboon."

"Sir," he replied, after a pause. "Donner und Blitzen!"

This was all that could be desired. We exchanged cards. At Chalk–Farm, the next morning, I shot off his nose– and then called upon my friends.

"Bete!" said the first.

"Fool!" said the second.

"Dolt!" said the third.

"Ass!" said the fourth.

"Ninny!" said the fifth.

"Noodle!" said the sixth.

"Be off!" said the seventh.

At all this I felt mortified, and so called upon my father.

"Father," I asked, "what is the chief end of my existence?"

"My son," he replied, "it is still the study of Nosology; but in hitting the Elector upon the nose you have overshot your mark. You have a fine nose, it is true; but then Bluddennuff has none. You are damned, and he has become the hero of the day. I grant you that in Fum–Fudge the greatness of a lion is in proportion to the size of his proboscis– but, good heavens! there is no competing with a lion who has no proboscis at all."

TALE OF JERUSALEM

Intensos rigidam in frontem ascendere canos Passus
erat
            Lucan

- a bristly bore.
            Translation

"LET us hurry to the walls," said Abel–Phittim to
Buzi–Ben–Levi and Simeon the Pharisee, on the tenth
day of the month Thammuz, in the year of the world
three thousand nine hundred and forty–one– "let us
hasten to the ramparts adjoining the gate of Benjamin,
which is in the city of David, and overlooking the
camp of the uncircumcised; for it is the last hour of the
fourth watch, being sunrise; and the idolaters, in
fulfilment of the promise of Pompey, should be
awaiting us with the lambs for the sacrifices."

Simeon, Abel–Phittim, and Buzi–Ben–Levi, were the
Gizbarim, or sub–collectors of the offering, in the holy
city of Jerusalem.

"Verily," replied the Pharisee, "let us hasten: for this
generosity in the heathen is unwonted; and fickle–
mindedness has ever been an attribute of the
worshippers of Baal."

"That they are fickle–minded and treacherous is as true as the Pentateuch," said Buzi–Ben–Levi, "but that is only towards the people of Adonai. When was it ever known that the Ammonites proved wanting to their own interests? Methinks it is no great stretch of generosity to allow us lambs for the altar of the Lord, receiving in lieu thereof thirty silver shekels per head!"

"Thou forgettest, however, Ben–Levi," replied Abel–Phittim, "that the Roman Pompey, who is now impiously besieging the city of the Most High, has no assurity that we apply not the lambs thus purchased for the altar, to the sustenance of the body, rather than of the spirit."

"Now, by the five corners of my beard!" shouted the Pharisee, who belonged to the sect called The Dashers (that little knot of saints whose manner of dashing and lacerating the feet against the pavement was long a thorn and a reproach to less zealous devotees– a stumbling–block to less gifted perambulators)– "by the five corners of that beard which, as a priest, I am forbidden to shave!– have we lived to see the day when a blaspheming and idolatrous upstart of Rome shall accuse us of appropriating to the appetites of the flesh the most holy and consecrated elements? Have we lived to see the day when–"

"Let us not question the motives of the Philistine," interrupted Abel–Phittim, "for to–day we profit for the first time by his avarice or by his generosity, but rather let us hurry to the ramparts, lest offerings should be wanting for that altar whose fire the rains of heaven cannot extinguish, and whose pillars of smoke no tempest can turn aside."

That part of the city to which our worthy Gizbarin now hastened, and which bore the name of its architect, King David, was esteemed the most strongly fortified district of Jerusalem; being situated upon the steep and lofty hill of Zion. Here, a broad, deep, circumvallatory trench, hewn from the solid rock, was defended by a wall of great strength erected upon its inner edge. This wall was adorned, at regular interspaces, by square towers of white marble; the lowest sixty, and the highest one hundred and twenty cubits in height. But, in the vicinity of the gate of Benjamin, the wall arose by no means from the margin of the fosse. On the contrary, between the level of the ditch and the basement of the rampart, sprang up a perpendicular cliff of two hundred and fifty cubits, forming part of the precipitous Mount Moriah. So that when Simeon and his associates arrived on the summit of the tower called Adoni–Bezek– the loftiest of all the turrets around about Jerusalem, and the usual place of conference with the besieging army– they looked down upon the camp of the enemy from an eminence excelling by many feet that of the Pyramid of Cheops, and, by several, that of the temple of Belus.

"Verily," sighed the Pharisee, as he peered dizzly over the precipice, "the uncircumcised are as the sands by the seashore– as the locusts in the wilderness! The valley of The King hath become the valley of Adommin."

"And yet," added Ben–Levi, "thou canst not point me out a Philistine– no, not one– from Aleph to Tau– from the wilderness to the battlements– who seemeth any bigger than the letter Jod!"

"Lower away the basket with the shekels of silver!"

here shouted a Roman soldier in a hoarse, rough voice, which appeared to issue from the regions of Pluto– "lower away the basket with the accursed coin which it has broken the jaw of a noble Roman to pronounce! Is it thus you evince your gratitude to our master Pompeius, who, in his condescension, has thought fit to listen to your idolatrous importunities? The god Phoebus, who is a true god, has been charioted for an hour– and were you not to be on the ramparts by sunrise? Aedepol! do you think that we, the conquerors of the world, have nothing better to do than stand waiting by the walls of every kennel, to traffic with the dogs of the earth? Lower away! I say– and see that your trumpery be bright in color and just in weight!"

"El Elohim!" ejaculated the Pharisee, as the discordant tones of the centurion rattled up the crags of the precipice, and fainted away against the temple– "El Elohim!– who is the God Phoebus?– whom doth the blasphemer invoke? Thou, Buzi–Ben–Levi! who art read in the laws of the Gentiles, and hast sojourned among them who dabble with the Teraphim!– is it Nergal of whom the idolater speaketh?– or Ashimah?– or– Nibhaz?– or Tartak?– or Adramalech?– or Anamalech?– or Succoth–Benith?– or Dragon?– or Belial?– or Baal–Perith?– or Baal–Peor?– or Baal–Zebub?"

"Verily it is neither– but beware how thou lettest the rope slip too rapidly through thy fingers; for should the wicker–work chance to hang on the projection of yonder crag, there will be a woful outpouring of the holy things of the sanctuary."

By the assistance of some rudely constructed machinery, the heavily laden basket was now carefully lowered down among the multitude; and, from the giddy pinnacle, the Romans were seen gathering confusedly round it; but owing to the vast height and the prevalence of a fog, no distinct view of their operations could be obtained.

Half an hour had already elapsed.

"We shall be too late!" sighed the Pharisee, as at the expiration of this period, he looked over into the abyss– "we shall be too late! we shall be turned out of office by the Katholim."

"No more," responded Abel–Phittim,– "no more shall we feast upon the fat of the land– no longer shall our beards be odorous with frankincense– our loins girded up with fine linen from the Temple."

"Raca!" swore Ben–Levi, "Raca! do they mean to defraud us of the purchase money? or, Holy Moses! are they weighing the shekels of the tabernacle?

"They have given the signal at last!" cried the Pharisee– "they have given the signal at last!– pull away, Abel–Phittim!– and thou, Buzi–Ben–Levi, pull away!– for verily the Philistines have either still hold upon the basket, or the Lord hath softened their hearts to place therein a beast of good weight!" And the Gizbarim pulled away, while their burthen swung heavily upwards through the still increasing mist.

"Booshoh he!"– as, at the conclusion of an hour, some object at the extremity of the rope became indistinctly visible– "Booshoh he!" was the exclamation which burst from the lips of Ben–Levi.

"Booshoh he!– for shame!– it is a ram from the thickets of Engedi, and as rugged as the valley of Jehosaphat!"

"It is a firstling of the flock," said Abel–Phittim, "I know him by the bleating of his lips, and the innocent folding of his limbs. His eyes are more beautiful than the jewels of the Pectoral, and his flesh is like the honey of Hebron."

"It is a fatted calf from the pastures of Bashan," said the Pharisee, "the heathen have dealt wonderfully with us!– let us raise up our voices in a psalm!– let us give thanks on the shawm and on the psaltery– on the harp and on the huggab– on the cythern and on the sackbutt"

It was not until the basket had arrived within a few feet of the Gizbarium, that a low grunt betrayed to their perception a hog of no common size.

"Now El Emanu!" slowly, and with upturned eyes ejaculated the trio, as, letting go their hold, the emancipated porker tumbled headlong among the Philistines, "El Emanu!– God be with us– it is the unutterable flesh!"

BON–BON

Quand un bon vin meuble mon estomac
Je suis plus savant que Balzac–
Plus sage que Pibrac;
Mon brass seul faisant l'attaque
De la nation Coseaque,
La mettroit au sac;
De Charon je passerois le lac
En dormant dans son bac,
J'irois au fier Eac,
Sans que mon coeur fit tic ni tac,
Premmer du tabac.

                                    French Vaudeville

THAT Pierre Bon–Bon was a restaurateur of
uncommon qualifications, the cul–de–sac Le Febvre at
Rouen, will, I imagine, feel himself at liberty to
dispute. That Pierre Bon–Bon was, in an equal degree,
skilled in the philosophy of that period is, I presume
still more especially undeniable. His pates a la fois
were beyond doubt immaculate; but what pen can do
justice to his essays sur la Nature– his thoughts sur
l'Ame– his observations sur l'Esprit? If his omelettes–
if his fricandeaux were inestimable, what litterateur of
that day would not have given twice as much for an
"Idee de Bon–Bon" as for all the trash of "Idees" of all
the rest of the savants?

Bon–Bon had ransacked libraries which no other man had ransacked– had more than any other would have entertained a notion of reading– had understood more than any other would have conceived the possibility of understanding; and although, while he flourished, there were not wanting some authors at Rouen to assert "that his dicta evinced neither the purity of the Academy, nor the depth of the Lyceum"– although, mark me, his doctrines were by no means very generally comprehended, still it did not follow that they were difficult of comprehension. It was, I think, on account of their self–evidency that many persons were led to consider them abstruse. It is to Bon–Bon– but let this go no farther– it is to Bon–Bon that Kant himself is mainly indebted for his metaphysics. The former was indeed not a Platonist, nor strictly speaking an Aristotelian– nor did he, like the modern Leibnitz, waste those precious hours which might be employed in the invention of a fricasee or, facili gradu, the analysis of a sensation, in frivolous attempts at reconciling the obstinate oils and waters of ethical discussion. Not at all. Bon–Bon was Ionic– Bon–Bon was equally Italic. He reasoned a priori– He reasoned also a posteriori. His ideas were innate– or otherwise. He believed in George of Trebizonde– He believed in Bossarion. Bon–Bon was emphatically a– Bon–Bonist. I have spoken of the philosopher in his capacity of restaurateur. I would not, however, have any friend of mine imagine that, in fulfilling his hereditary duties in that line, our hero wanted a proper estimation of their dignity and importance. Far from it. It was impossible to say in which branch of his profession he took the greater pride. In his opinion the powers of the intellect held intimate connection with the capabilities of the stomach. I am not sure, indeed, that he greatly disagreed with the Chinese, who held that the soul lies in the abdomen. The Greeks at all events were right, he thought, who employed the same words for the mind and the diaphragm. By this I do not mean to insinuate a charge of gluttony, or indeed any other serious charge to the prejudice of the metaphysician. If Pierre Bon–Bon had his failings– and what great man has not a thousand?– if Pierre Bon–Bon, I say, had his failings, they were failings of very little importance– faults indeed which, in other tempers, have often been looked upon rather in the light of virtues. As regards one of these foibles, I should not even have mentioned it in this history but for the remarkable prominency– the extreme alto relievo– in which it jutted out from the plane of his general disposition. He could never let slip an opportunity of making a bargain.

Not that he was avaricious– no. It was by no means necessary to the satisfaction of the philosopher, that the bargain should be to his own proper advantage. Provided a trade could be effected– a trade of any kind, upon any terms, or under any circumstances– a triumphant smile was seen for many days thereafter to enlighten his countenance, and a knowing wink of the eye to give evidence of his sagacity.

At any epoch it would not be very wonderful if a humor so peculiar as the one I have just mentioned, should elicit attention and remark. At the epoch of our narrative, had this peculiarity not attracted observation, there would have been room for wonder indeed. It was soon reported that, upon all occasions of the kind, the smile of Bon–Bon was wont to differ widely from the downright grin with which he would laugh at his own jokes, or welcome an acquaintance. Hints were thrown out of an exciting nature; stories were told of perilous bargains made in a hurry and repented of at leisure;

and instances were adduced of unaccountable capacities, vague longings, and unnatural inclinations implanted by the author of all evil for wise purposes of his own.

The philosopher had other weaknesses– but they are scarcely worthy our serious examination. For example, there are few men of extraordinary profundity who are found wanting in an inclination for the bottle. Whether this inclination be an exciting cause, or rather a valid proof of such profundity, it is a nice thing to say. Bon–Bon, as far as I can learn, did not think the subject adapted to minute investigation;– nor do I. Yet in the indulgence of a propensity so truly classical, it is not to be supposed that the restaurateur would lose sight of that intuitive discrimination which was wont to characterize, at one and the same time, his essais and his omelettes. In his seclusions the Vin de Bourgogne had its allotted hour, and there were appropriate moments for the Cotes du Rhone. With him Sauterne was to Medoc what Catullus was to Homer. He would sport with a syllogism in sipping St. Peray, but unravel an argument over Clos de Vougeot, and upset a theory in a torrent of Chambertin. Well had it been if the same quick sense of propriety had attended him in the peddling propensity to which I have formerly alluded– but this was by no means the case. Indeed to say the truth, that trait of mind in the philosophic Bon–Bon did begin at length to assume a character of strange intensity and mysticism, and appeared deeply tinctured with the diablerie of his favorite German studies.

To enter the little Cafe in the cul–de–sac Le Febvre was, at the period of our tale, to enter the sanctum of a man of genius. Bon–Bon was a man of genius. There was not a sous–cusinier in Rouen, who could not have told you that Bon–Bon was a man of genius. His very cat knew it, and forebore to whisk her tail in the presence of the man of genius. His large water–dog was acquainted with the fact, and upon the approach of his master, betrayed his sense of inferiority by a sanctity of deportment, a debasement of the ears, and a dropping of the lower jaw not altogether unworthy of a dog. It is, however, true that much of this habitual respect might have been attributed to the personal appearance of the metaphysician. A distinguished exterior will, I am constrained to say, have its way even with a beast; and I am willing to allow much in the outward man of the restaurateur calculated to impress the imagination of the quadruped. There is a peculiar majesty about the atmosphere of the little great– if I may be permitted so equivocal an expression– which mere physical bulk alone will be found at all times inefficient in creating. If, however, Bon–Bon was barely three feet in height, and if his head was diminutively small, still it was impossible to behold the rotundity of his stomach without a sense of magnificence nearly bordering upon the sublime. In its size both dogs and men must have seen a type of his acquirements– in its immensity a fitting habitation for his immortal soul.

I might here– if it so pleased me– dilate upon the matter of habiliment, and other mere circumstances of the external metaphysician. I might hint that the hair of our hero was worn short, combed smoothly over his forehead, and surmounted by a conical–shaped white flannel cap and tassels– that his pea–green jerkin was not after the fashion of those worn by the common class of restaurateurs at that day– that the sleeves were something fuller than the reigning costume permitted– that the cuffs were turned up, not as usual in that barbarous period, with cloth of the same quality and color as the garment, but faced in a more fanciful manner with the particolored velvet of Genoa– that his slippers were of a bright purple, curiously filigreed, and might have been manufactured in Japan, but for the exquisite pointing of the toes, and the brilliant tints of the binding and embroidery– that his breeches were of the yellow satin–like material called aimable– that his sky–blue cloak, resembling in form a dressing–wrapper, and richly bestudded all over with crimson devices, floated cavalierly upon his shoulders like a mist of the morning– and that his tout ensemble gave rise to the remarkable words of Benevenuta, the Improvisatrice of Florence, "that it was difficult to say whether Pierre Bon–Bon was indeed a bird of Paradise, or rather a very Paradise of perfection." I might, I say, expatiate upon all these points if I pleased,– but I forbear, merely personal details may be left to historical novelists,– they are beneath the moral dignity of matter–of–fact.

I have said that "to enter the Cafe in the cul–de–sac Le Febvre was to enter the sanctum of a man of genius"– but then it was only the man of genius who could duly estimate the merits of the sanctum. A sign, consisting of a vast folio, swung before the entrance. On one side of the volume was painted a bottle; on the reverse a pate. On the back were visible in large letters Oeuvres de Bon–Bon. Thus was delicately shadowed forth the two–fold occupation of the proprietor.

Upon stepping over the threshold, the whole interior of the building presented itself to view. A long, low–pitched room, of antique construction, was indeed all the accommodation afforded by the Cafe. In a corner of the apartment stood the bed of the metaphysician.

An army of curtains, together with a canopy a la Grecque, gave it an air at once classic and comfortable. In the corner diagonary opposite, appeared, in direct family communion, the properties of the kitchen and the bibliotheque. A dish of polemics stood peacefully upon the dresser. Here lay an ovenful of the latest ethics– there a kettle of dudecimo melanges. Volumes of German morality were hand and glove with the gridiron– a toasting–fork might be discovered by the side of Eusebius– Plato reclined at his ease in the frying–pan– and contemporary manuscripts were filed away upon the spit.

In other respects the Cafe de Bon–Bon might be said to differ little from the usual restaurants of the period. A fireplace yawned opposite the door. On the right of the fireplace an open cupboard displayed a formidable array of labelled bottles.

It was here, about twelve o'clock one night during the severe winter the comments of his neighbours upon his singular propensity– that Pierre Bon–Bon, I say, having turned them all out of his house, locked the door upon them with an oath, and betook himself in no very pacific mood to the comforts of a leather–bottomed arm–chair, and a fire of blazing fagots.

It was one of those terrific nights which are only met with once or twice during a century. It snowed fiercely, and the house tottered to its centre with the floods of wind that, rushing through the crannies in the wall, and pouring impetuously down the chimney, shook awfully the curtains of the philosopher's bed, and disorganized the economy of his pate–pans and papers. The huge folio sign that swung without, exposed to the fury of the tempest, creaked ominously, and gave out a moaning sound from its stanchions of solid oak.

It was in no placid temper, I say, that the meta-physician drew up his chair to its customary station by the hearth. Many circumstances of a perplexing nature had occurred during the day, to disturb the serenity of his meditations. In attempting des oeufs a la Princesse, he had unfortunately perpetrated an omelette a la Reine; the discovery of a principle in ethics had been frustrated by the overturning of a stew; and last, not least, he had been thwarted in one of those admirable bargains which he at all times took such especial delight in bringing to a successful termination. But in the chafing of his mind at these unaccountable vicissitudes, there did not fail to be mingled some degree of that nervous anxiety which the fury of a boisterous night is so well calculated to produce. Whistling to his more immediate vicinity the large black water–dog we have spoken of before, and settling himself uneasily in his chair, he could not help casting a wary and unquiet eye toward those distant recesses of the apartment whose inexorable shadows not even the red firelight itself could more than partially succeed in overcoming. Having completed a scrutiny whose exact purpose was perhaps unintelli-gible to himself, he drew close to his seat a small table covered with books and papers, and soon became absorbed in the task of retouching a voluminous manuscript, intended for publication on the morrow.

He had been thus occupied for some minutes when "I am in no hurry, Monsieur Bon–Bon," suddenly whispered a whining voice in the apartment.

"The devil!" ejaculated our hero, starting to his feet, overturning the table at his side, and staring around him in astonishment.

"Very true," calmly replied the voice.

"Very true!– what is very true?– how came you here?" vociferated the metaphysician, as his eye fell upon something which lay stretched at full length upon the bed.

"I was saying," said the intruder, without attending to the interrogatives,– "I was saying that I am not at all pushed for time– that the business upon which I took the liberty of calling, is of no pressing importance– in short, that I can very well wait until you have finished your Exposition."

"My Exposition!– there now!– how do you know?– how came you to understand that I was writing an Exposition?– good God!"

"Hush!" replied the figure, in a shrill undertone; and, arising quickly from the bed, he made a single step toward our hero, while an iron lamp that depended over–head swung convulsively back from his approach.

The philosopher's amazement did not prevent a narrow scrutiny of the stranger's dress and appearance. The outlines of his figure, exceedingly lean, but much above the common height, were rendered minutely distinct, by means of a faded suit of black cloth which fitted tight to the skin, but was otherwise cut very much in the style of a century ago. These garments had evidently been intended for a much shorter person than their present owner. His ankles and wrists were left naked for several inches. In his shoes, however, a pair of very brilliant buckles gave the lie to the extreme poverty implied by the other portions of his dress. His head was bare, and entirely bald, with the exception of a hinder part, from which depended a queue of considerable length. A pair of green spectacles, with side glasses, protected his eyes from the influence of the light, and at the same time prevented our hero from ascertaining either their color or their conformation. About the entire person there was no evidence of a shirt, but a white cravat, of filthy appearance, was tied with extreme precision around the throat and the ends hanging down formally side by side gave (although I dare say unintentionally) the idea of an ecclesiastic. Indeed, many other points both in his appearance and demeanor might have very well sustained a conception of that nature. Over his left ear, he carried, after the fashion of a modern clerk, an instrument resembling the stylus of the ancients. In a breast–pocket of his coat appeared conspicuously a small black volume fastened with clasps of steel. This book, whether accidentally or not, was so turned outwardly from the person as to discover the words "Rituel Catholique" in white letters upon the back. His entire physiognomy was interestingly saturnine– even cadaverously pale. The forehead was lofty, and deeply furrowed with the ridges of contemplation. The corners of the mouth were drawn down into an expression of the most submissive humility. There was also a clasping of the hands, as he stepped toward our hero– a deep sigh– and altogether a look of such utter sanctity as could not have failed to be unequivocally preposessing. Every shadow of anger faded from the countenance of the metaphysician, as, having completed a satisfactory survey of his visiter's person, he shook him cordially by the hand, and conducted him to a seat.

There would however be a radical error in attributing this instantaneous transition of feeling in the philosopher, to any one of those causes which might naturally be supposed to have had an influence. Indeed, Pierre Bon–Bon, from what I have been able to understand of his disposition, was of all men the least likely to be imposed upon by any speciousness of exterior deportment. It was impossible that so accurate an observer of men and things should have failed to discover, upon the moment, the real character of the personage who had thus intruded upon his hospitality. To say no more, the conformation of his visiter's feet was sufficiently remarkable– he maintained lightly upon his head an inordinately tall hat– there was a tremulous swelling about the hinder part of his breeches– and the vibration of his coat tail was a palpable fact. Judge, then, with what feelings of satisfaction our hero found himself thrown thus at once into the society of a person for whom he had at all times entertained the most unqualified respect. He was, however, too much of the diplomatist to let escape him any intimation of his suspicions in regard to the true state of affairs. It was not his cue to appear at all conscious of the high honor he thus unexpectedly enjoyed; but, by leading his guest into the conversation, to elicit some important ethical ideas, which might, in obtaining a place in his contemplated publication, enlighten the human race, and at the same time immortalize himself– ideas which, I should have added, his visitor's great age, and well–known proficiency in the science of morals, might very well have enabled him to afford.

Actuated by these enlightened views, our hero bade the gentleman sit down, while he himself took occasion to throw some fagots upon the fire, and place upon the now re–established table some bottles of Mousseux. Having quickly completed these operations, he drew his chair vis–a–vis to his companion's, and waited until the latter should open the conversation. But plans even the most skilfully matured are often thwarted in the outset of their application– and the restaurateur found himself nonplussed by the very first words of his visiter's speech.

"I see you know me, Bon–Bon," said he; "ha! ha! ha!– he! he! he!– hi! hi! hi!– ho! ho! ho!– hu! hu! hu!"– and the devil, dropping at once the sanctity of his demeanor, opened to its fullest extent a mouth from ear to ear, so as to display a set of jagged and fang–like teeth, and, throwing back his head, laughed long, loudly, wickedly, and uproariously, while the black dog, crouching down upon his haunches, joined lustily in the chorus, and the tabby cat, flying off at a tangent, stood up on end, and shrieked in the farthest corner of the apartment.

Not so the philosopher; he was too much a man of the world either to laugh like the dog, or by shrieks to betray the indecorous trepidation of the cat. It must be confessed, he felt a little astonishment to see the white letters which formed the words "Rituel Catholique" on the book in his guest's pocket, momently changing both their color and their import, and in a few seconds, in place of the original title the words Regitre des Condamnes blazed forth in characters of red. This startling circumstance, when Bon–Bon replied to his visiter's remark, imparted to his manner an air of embarrassment which probably might, not otherwise have been observed.

"Why sir," said the philosopher, "why sir, to speak

sincerely– I I imagine– I have some faint– some very
faint idea– of the remarkable honor–"

"Oh!– ah!– yes!– very well!" interrupted his Majesty;
"say no more– I see how it is." And hereupon, taking
off his green spectacles, he wiped the glasses carefully
with the sleeve of his coat, and deposited them in his
pocket.

If Bon–Bon had been astonished at the incident of the
book, his amazement was now much increased by the
spectacle which here presented itself to view. In raising
his eyes, with a strong feeling of curiosity to ascertain
the color of his guest's, he found them by no means
black, as he had anticipated– nor gray, as might have
been imagined– nor yet hazel nor blue– nor indeed
yellow nor red– nor purple– nor white– nor green– nor
any other color in the heavens above, or in the earth
beneath, or in the waters under the earth. In short,
Pierre Bon–Bon not only saw plainly that his Majesty
had no eyes whatsoever, but could discover no
indications of their having existed at any previous
period– for the space where eyes should naturally have
been was, I am constrained to say, simply a dead level
of flesh.

It was not in the nature of the metaphysician to forbear
making some inquiry into the sources of so strange a
phenomenon, and the reply of his Majesty was at once
prompt, dignified, and satisfactory.

"Eyes! my dear Bon–Bon– eyes! did you say?– oh!–
ah!– I perceive! The ridiculous prints, eh, which are in,
circulation, have given you a false idea of my personal
appearance? Eyes!– true. Eyes, Pierre Bon–Bon, are
very well in their proper place– that, you would say, is

the head?– right– the head of a worm. To you, likewise, these optics are indispensable– yet I will convince you that my vision is more penetrating than your own. There is a cat I see in the corner– a pretty cat– look at her– observe her well. Now, Bon–Bon, do you behold the thoughts– the thoughts, I say,– the ideas– the reflections– which are being engendered in her pericranium? There it is, now– you do not! She is thinking we admire the length of her tail and the profundity of her mind. She has just concluded that I am the most distinguished of ecclesiastics, and that you are the most superficial of metaphysicians. Thus you see I am not altogether blind; but to one of my profession, the eyes you speak of would be merely an incumbrance, liable at any time to be put out by a toasting–iron, or a pitchfork. To you, I allow, these optical affairs are indispensable. Endeavor, Bon–Bon, to use them well;– my vision is the soul."

Hereupon the guest helped himself to the wine upon the table, and pouring out a bumper for Bon–Bon, requested him to drink it without scruple, and make himself perfectly at home.

"A clever book that of yours, Pierre," resumed his Majesty, tapping our friend knowingly upon the shoulder, as the latter put down his glass after a thorough compliance with his visiter's injunction. "A clever book that of yours, upon my honor. It's a work after my own heart. Your arrangement of the matter, I think, however, might be improved, and many of your notions remind me of Aristotle. That philosopher was one of my most intimate acquaintances. I liked him as much for his terrible ill temper, as for his happy knack at making a blunder. There is only one solid truth in all that he has written, and for that I gave him the hint out of pure compassion for his absurdity. I suppose, Pierre Bon–Bon, you very well know to what divine moral truth I am alluding?"

"Cannot say that I–"

"Indeed!– why it was I who told Aristotle that by sneezing, men expelled superfluous ideas through the proboscis."

"Which is– hiccup!– undoubtedly the case," said the metaphysician, while he poured out for himself another bumper of Mousseux, and offered his snuff–box to the fingers of his visiter.

"There was Plato, too," continued his Majesty, modestly declining the snuff–box and the compliment it implied– "there was Plato, too, for whom I, at one time, felt all the affection of a friend. You knew Plato, Bon–Bon?– ah, no, I beg a thousand pardons. He met me at Athens, one day, in the Parthenon, and told me he was distressed for an idea. I bade him write, down that o nous estin aulos. He said that he would do so, and went home, while I stepped over to the pyramids. But my conscience smote me for having uttered a truth, even to aid a friend, and hastening back to Athens, I arrived behind the philosopher's chair as he was inditing the 'aulos.'"

"Giving the lambda a fillip with my finger, I turned it upside down. So the sentence now read 'o nous estin augos', and is, you perceive, the fundamental doctrines in his metaphysics."

"Were you ever at Rome?" asked the restaurateur, as he finished his second bottle of Mousseux, and drew from the closet a larger supply of Chambertin.

But once, Monsieur Bon–Bon, but once. There was a time," said the devil, as if reciting some passage from a book– "there was a time when occurred an anarchy of five years, during which the republic, bereft of all its officers, had no magistracy besides the tribunes of the people, and these were not legally vested with any degree of executive power– at that time, Monsieur Bon–Bon– at that time only I was in Rome, and I have no earthly acquaintance, consequently, with any of its philosophy." [2]

---

[2] Ils ecrivaient sur la Philosophie (Cicero, Lucretius, Seneca) mais c'etait la Philosophie Grecque.– Condorcet.

"What do you think of– what do you think of– hiccup! – Epicurus?"

"What do I think of whom?" said the devil, in astonishment, "you cannot surely mean to find any fault with Epicurus! What do I think of Epicurus! Do you mean me, sir?– I am Epicurus! I am the same philosopher who wrote each of the three hundred treatises commemorated by Diogenes Laertes."

"That's a lie!" said the metaphysician, for the wine had gotten a little into his head.

"Very well!– very well, sir!– very well, indeed, sir!" said his Majesty, apparently much flattered.

"That's a lie!" repeated the restaurateur, dogmatically; "that's a– hiccup!– a lie!"

"Well, well, have it your own way!" said the devil, pacifically, and Bon–Bon, having beaten his Majesty at argument, thought it his duty to conclude a second bottle of Chambertin.

"As I was saying," resumed the visiter– "as I was observing a little while ago, there are some very outre notions in that book of yours Monsieur Bon–Bon. What, for instance, do you mean by all that humbug about the soul? Pray, sir, what is the soul?"

"The– hiccup!– soul," replied the metaphysician, referring to his MS., "is undoubtedly–"

"No, sir!"

"Indubitably–"

"No, sir!"

"Indisputably–"

"No, sir!"

"Evidently–"

"No, sir!"

"Incontrovertibly–"

"No, sir!"

"Hiccup!–"

Edgar Allan Poe

"No, sir!"

"And beyond all question, a–"

"No sir, the soul is no such thing!" (Here the philosopher, looking daggers, took occasion to make an end, upon the spot, of his third bottle of Chambertin.)

"Then– hic–cup!– pray, sir– what– what is it?"

"That is neither here nor there, Monsieur Bon–Bon," replied his Majesty, musingly. "I have tasted– that is to say, I have known some very bad souls, and some too– pretty good ones." Here he smacked his lips, and, having unconsciously let fall his hand upon the volume in his pocket, was seized with a violent fit of sneezing.

He continued.

"There was the soul of Cratinus– passable: Aristophanes– racy: Plato– exquisite– not your Plato, but Plato the comic poet; your Plato would have turned the stomach of Cerberus– faugh! Then let me see! there were Naevius, and Andronicus, and Plautus, and Terentius. Then there were Lucilius, and Catullus, and Naso, and Quintus Flaccus,– dear Quinty! as I called him when he sung a seculare for my amusement, while I toasted him, in pure good humor, on a fork. But they want flavor, these Romans. One fat Greek is worth a dozen of them, and besides will keep, which cannot be said of a Quirite.– Let us taste your Sauterne."

Bon–Bon had by this time made up his mind to nil admirari and endeavored to hand down the bottles in question. He was, however, conscious of a strange sound in the room like the wagging of a tail. Of this, although extremely indecent in his Majesty, the philosopher took no notice:– simply kicking the dog, and requesting him to be quiet. The visiter continued:

"I found that Horace tasted very much like Aristotle;– you know I am fond of variety. Terentius I could not have told from Menander. Naso, to my astonishment, was Nicander in disguise. Virgilius had a strong twang of Theocritus. Martial put me much in mind of Archilochus– and Titus Livius was positively Polybius and none other."

"Hic–cup!" here replied Bon–Bon, and his majesty proceeded:

"But if I have a penchant, Monsieur Bon–Bon– if I have a penchant, it is for a philosopher. Yet, let me tell you, sir, it is not every dev– I mean it is not every gentleman who knows how to choose a philosopher. Long ones are not good; and the best, if not carefully shelled, are apt to be a little rancid on account of the gall!"

"Shelled!"

"I mean taken out of the carcass."

"What do you think of a– hic–cup!– physician?"

"Don't mention them!– ugh! ugh! ugh!" (Here his Majesty retched violently.) "I never tasted but one– that rascal Hippocrates!– smelt of asafoetida– ugh! ugh! ugh!– caught a wretched cold washing him in the Styx– and after all he gave me the cholera morbus."

"The– hiccup– wretch!" ejaculated Bon–Bon, "the–hic–cup!– absorption of a pill–box!"– and the philosopher dropped a tear.

"After all," continued the visiter, "after all, if a dev– if a gentleman wishes to live, he must have more talents than one or two; and with us a fat face is an evidence of diplomacy."

"How so?"

"Why, we are sometimes exceedingly pushed for provisions. You must know that, in a climate so sultry as mine, it is frequently impossible to keep a spirit alive for more than two or three hours; and after death, unless pickled immediately (and a pickled spirit is not good), they will– smell– you understand, eh? Putrefaction is always to be apprehended when the souls are consigned to us in the usual way."

"Hiccup!– hiccup!– good God! how do you manage?"

Here the iron lamp commenced swinging with redoubled violence, and the devil half started from his seat;– however, with a slight sigh, he recovered his composure, merely saying to our hero in a low tone: "I tell you what, Pierre Bon–Bon, we must have no more swearing."

The host swallowed another bumper, by way of denoting thorough comprehension and acquiescence, and the visiter continued.

"Why, there are several ways of managing. The most of us starve: some put up with the pickle: for my part I purchase my spirits vivente corpore, in which case

I find they keep very well."

"But the body!– hiccup!– the body!"

"The body, the body– well, what of the body?– oh! ah! I perceive. Why, sir, the body is not at all affected by the transaction. I have made innumerable purchases of the kind in my day, and the parties never experienced any inconvenience. There were Cain and Nimrod, and Nero, and Caligula, and Dionysius, and Pisistratus, and– and a thousand others, who never knew what it was to have a soul during the latter part of their lives; yet, sir, these men adorned society. Why possession of his faculties, mental and corporeal? Who writes a keener epigram? Who reasons more wittily? Who– but stay! I have his agreement in my pocket-book."

Thus saying, he produced a red leather wallet, and took from it a number of papers. Upon some of these Bon–Bon caught a glimpse of the letters Machi– Maza– Robesp– with the words Caligula, George, Elizabeth. His Majesty selected a narrow slip of parchment, and from it read aloud the following words:

"In consideration of certain mental endowments which it is unnecessary to specify, and in further consideration of one thousand louis d'or, I being aged one year and one month, do hereby make over to the bearer of this agreement all my right, title, and appurtenance in the shadow called my soul. (Signed) A...."[3] (Here His Majesty repeated a name which I did not feel justified in indicating more unequivocally.)

[3]Quere–Arouet?

"A clever fellow that," resumed he; "but like you, Monsieur Bon–Bon, he was mistaken about the soul. The soul a shadow, truly! The soul a shadow; Ha! ha! ha!– he! he! he!– hu! hu! hu! Only think of a fricasseed shadow!"

"Only think– hiccup!– of a fricasseed shadow!" exclaimed our hero, whose faculties were becoming much illuminated by the profundity of his Majesty's discourse.

"Only think of a hiccup!– fricasseed shadow!! Now, damme!– hiccup!– humph! If I would have been such a– hiccup!– nincompoop! My soul, Mr.– humph!"

"Your soul, Monsieur Bon–Bon?"

"Yes, sir– hiccup!– my soul is–"

"What, sir?"

"No shadow, damme!"

"Did you mean to say–"

"Yes, sir, my soul is– hiccup!– humph!– yes, sir."
"Did you not intend to assert–"

"My soul is– hiccup!– peculiarly qualified for– hiccup!– a–"

"What, sir?"

"Stew."

"Ha!"

"Soufflee."

"Eh!"

"Fricassee."

"Indeed!"

"Ragout and fricandeau– and see here, my good fellow! I'll let you have it– hiccup!– a bargain." Here the philosopher slapped his Majesty upon the back.

"Couldn't think of such a thing," said the latter calmly, at the same time rising from his seat. The metaphysician stared.

"Am supplied at present," said his Majesty.

"Hiccup– e–h?" said the philosopher.

"Have no funds on hand."

"What?"
"Besides, very unhandsome in me–"

"Sir!"

"To take advantage of–"

"Hiccup!"

"Your present disgusting and ungentlemanly situation."

Here the visiter bowed and withdrew– in what manner could not precisely be ascertained– but in a well–concerted effort to discharge a bottle at "the villain," the slender chain was severed that depended from the ceiling, and the metaphysician prostrated by the downfall of the lamp.

THE MAN THAT WAS USED UP

A Tale of the Late Bugaboo and Kickapoo Campaign

Pleurez, pleurez, mes yeux, et fondez vous en eau! La moitie de ma vie a mis l'autre au tombeau.—

CORNEILLE

I CANNOT just now remember when or where I first made the acquaintance of that truly fine–looking fellow, Brevet Brigadier General John A. B. C. Smith. Some one did introduce me to the gentleman, I am sure– at some public meeting, I know very well– held about something of great importance, no doubt– at some place or other, I feel convinced, whose name I have unaccountably forgotten. The truth is– that the introduction was attended, upon my part, with a degree of anxious embarrassment which operated to prevent any definite impressions of either time or place. I am constitutionally nervous– this, with me, is a family failing, and I can't help it. In especial, the slightest appearance of mystery– of any point I cannot exactly comprehend– puts me at once into a pitiable state of agitation.

There was something, as it were, remarkable– yes, remarkable, although this is but a feeble term to express my full meaning– about the entire individuality of the personage in question. He was, perhaps, six feet in height, and of a presence singularly commanding. There was an air distingue pervading the whole man, which spoke of high breeding, and hinted at high birth. Upon this topic– the topic of Smith's personal appearance– I have a kind of melancholy satisfaction in being minute. His head of hair would have done honor to a Brutus,– nothing could be more richly flowing, or possess a brighter gloss. It was of a jetty black,– which was also the color, or more properly the no–color of his unimaginable whiskers. You perceive I cannot speak of these latter without enthusiasm; it is not too much to say that they were the handsomest pair of whiskers under the sun. At all events, they encircled, and at times partially overshadowed, a mouth utterly unequalled. Here were the most entirely even, and the most brilliantly white of all conceivable teeth. From between them, upon every proper occasion, issued a voice of surpassing clearness, melody, and strength. In the matter of eyes, also, my acquaintance was pre–eminently endowed. Either one of such a pair was worth a couple of the ordinary ocular organs. They were of a deep hazel exceedingly large and lustrous; and there was perceptible about them, ever and anon, just that amount of interesting obliquity which gives pregnancy to expression.

The bust of the General was unquestionably the finest bust I ever saw. For your life you could not have found a fault with its wonderful proportion. This rare peculiarity set off to great advantage a pair of shoulders which would have called up a blush of conscious inferiority into the countenance of the marble Apollo. I have a passion for fine shoulders, and may say that I never beheld them in perfection before. The arms altogether were admirably modelled. Nor were the lower limbs less superb. These were, indeed, the ne plus ultra of good legs. Every connoisseur in such matters admitted the legs to be good. There was neither too much flesh nor too little,– neither rudeness nor fragility. I could not imagine a more graceful curve than that of the os femoris, and there was just that due gentle prominence in the rear of the fibula which goes to the conformation of a properly proportioned calf. I wish to God my young and talented friend Chipon-chipino, the sculptor, had but seen the legs of Brevet Brigadier General John A. B. C. Smith.

But although men so absolutely fine–looking are neither as plenty as reasons or blackberries, still I could not bring myself to believe that the remarkable something to which I alluded just now,– that the odd air of je ne sais quoi which hung about my new acquaintance,– lay altogether, or indeed at all, in the supreme excellence of his bodily endowments. Perhaps it might be traced to the manner,– yet here again I could not pretend to be positive. There was a primness, not to say stiffness, in his carriage– a degree of measured and, if I may so express it, of rectangular precision attending his every movement, which, observed in a more diminutive figure, would have had the least little savor in the world of affectation, pomposity, or constraint, but which, noticed in a gentleman of his undoubted dimensions, was readily placed to the account of reserve, hauteur– of a commendable sense, in short, of what is due to the dignity of colossal proportion.

The kind friend who presented me to General Smith whispered in my ear some few words of comment upon the man. He was a remarkable man– a very remarkable man– indeed one of the most remarkable men of the age. He was an especial favorite, too, with the ladies– chiefly on account of his high reputation for courage.

"In that point he is unrivalled– indeed he is a perfect desperado– a downright fire–eater, and no mistake," said my friend, here dropping his voice excessively low, and thrilling me with the mystery of his tone.

"A downright fire–eater, and no mistake. Showed that, I should say, to some purpose, in the late tremendous swamp–fight, away down South, with the Bugaboo and Kickapoo Indians." [Here my friend opened his eyes to some extent.] "Bless my soul!– blood and thunder, and all that!– prodigies of valor!– heard of him of course?– you know he's the man–"

"Man alive, how do you do? why, how are ye? very glad to see ye, indeed!" here interrupted the General himself, seizing my companion by the hand as he drew near, and bowing stiffly but profoundly, as I was presented. I then thought (and I think so still) that I never heard a clearer nor a stronger voice, nor beheld a finer set of teeth: but I must say that I was sorry for the interruption just at that moment, as, owing to the whispers and insinuations aforesaid, my interest had been greatly excited in the hero of the Bugaboo and Kickapoo campaign.

However, the delightfully luminous conversation of Brevet Brigadier General John A. B. C. Smith soon completely dissipated this chagrin. My friend leaving us immediately, we had quite a long tete–a–tete, and I was not only pleased but really–instructed. I never heard a more fluent talker, or a man of greater general information. With becoming modesty, he forebore, nevertheless, to touch upon the theme I had just then most at heart– I mean the mysterious circumstances attending the Bugaboo war– and, on my own part, what I conceive to be a proper sense of delicacy forbade me to broach the subject; although, in truth, I was exceedingly tempted to do so. I perceived, too, that the gallant soldier preferred topics of philosophical interest, and that he delighted, especially, in commenting upon the rapid march of mechanical invention. Indeed, lead him where I would, this was a point to which he invariably came back.

"There is nothing at all like it," he would say, "we are a wonderful people, and live in a wonderful age. Parachutes and rail–roads–mantraps and spring–guns! Our steam–boats are upon every sea, and the Nassau balloon packet is about to run regular trips (fare either way only twenty pounds sterling) between London and Timbuctoo. And who shall calculate the immense influence upon social life– upon arts– upon commerce– upon literature– which will be the immediate result of the great principles of electro–magnetics! Nor, is this all, let me assure you! There is really no end to the march of invention. The most wonderful– the most ingenious– and let me add, Mr.– Mr.– Thompson, I believe, is your name– let me add, I say the most useful– the most truly useful– mechanical contrivances are daily springing up like mushrooms, if I may so express myself, or, more figuratively, like– ah– grasshoppers– like grasshoppers, Mr. Thompson– about us and ah– ah– ah– around us!"

Thompson, to be sure, is not my name; but it is needless to say that I left General Smith with a heightened interest in the man, with an exalted opinion of his conversational powers, and a deep sense of the valuable privileges we enjoy in living in this age of mechanical invention. My curiosity, however, had not been altogether satisfied, and I resolved to prosecute immediate inquiry among my acquaintances, touching the Brevet Brigadier General himself, and particularly respecting the tremendous events quorum pars magna fuit, during the Bugaboo and Kickapoo campaign.

The first opportunity which presented opportunity which presented itself, and which (horresco referens) I did not in the least scruple to seize, occurred at the Church of the Reverend Doctor Drummummupp, where I found myself established, one Sunday, just at sermon time, not only in the pew, but by the side of that worthy and communicative little friend of mine, Miss Tabitha T. Thus seated, I congratulated myself, and with much reason, upon the very flattering state of affairs. If any person knew any thing about Brevet Brigadier General John A. B. C. Smith, that person it was clear to me, was Miss Tabitha T. We telegraphed a few signals and then commenced, soto voce, a brisk tete–a–tete.

"Smith!" said she in reply to my very earnest inquiry: "Smith!– why, not General John A. B. C.? Bless me, I thought you knew all about him! This is a wonderfully inventive age! Horrid affair that!– a bloody set of wretches, those Kickapoos!– fought like a hero– prodigies of valor– immortal renown. Smith!– Brevet Brigadier General John A. B. C.! Why, you know he's the man–

"Man," here broke in Doctor Drummummupp, at the top of his voice, and with a thump that came near knocking the pulpit about our ears; "man that is born of a woman hath but a short time to live; he cometh up and is cut down like a flower!" I started to the extremity of the pew, and perceived by the animated looks of the divine, that the wrath which had nearly proved fatal to the pulpit had been excited by the whispers of the lady and myself. There was no help for it; so I submitted with a good grace, and listened, in all the martyrdom of dignified silence, to the balance of that very capital discourse.

Next evening found me a somewhat late visitor at the Rantipole Theatre, where I felt sure of satisfying my curiosity at once, by merely stepping into the box of those exquisite specimens of affability and omnis-cience, the Misses Arabella and Miranda Cognoscenti. That fine tragedian, Climax, was doing Iago to a very crowded house, and I experienced some little difficulty in making my wishes understood; especially as our box was next the slips, and completely overlooked the stage.

"Smith!" said Miss Arabella, as she at comprehended the purport of my query; "Smith?– why, not General John A. B. C.?"

"Smith!" inquired Miranda, musingly. "God bless me, did you ever behold a finer figure?"

"Never, madam, but do tell me–"

"Or so inimitable grace?"

"Never, upon my word!– But pray, inform me–"

"Or so just an appreciation of stage effect?"

"Madam!"

"Or a more delicate sense of the true beauties of Shakespeare? Be so good as to look at that leg!"

"The devil!" and I turned again to her sister.

"Smith!" said she, "why, not General John A. B. C.? Horrid affair that, wasn't it?– great wretches, those Bugaboos– savage and so on– but we live in a wonderfully inventive age!– Smith!– O yes! great man!– perfect desperado– immortal renown– prodigies of valor! Never heard!" [This was given in a scream.] "Bless my soul! why, he's the man–"

"-mandragora
Nor all the drowsy syrups of the world
Shall ever medicine thee to that sweet sleep
Which thou ow'dst yesterday!"

here roared our Climax just in my ear, and shaking his fist in my face all the time, in a way that I couldn't stand, and I wouldn't. I left the Misses Cognoscenti immediately, went behind the scenes forthwith, and gave the beggarly scoundrel such a thrashing as I trust he will remember till the day of his death.

At the soiree of the lovely widow, Mrs. Kathleen O'Trump, I was confident that I should meet with no similar disappointment. Accordingly, I was no sooner seated at the card–table, with my pretty hostess for a vis–a–vis, than I propounded those questions the solution of which had become a matter so essential to my peace.

"Smith!" said my partner, "why, not General John A. B. C.? Horrid affair that, wasn't it?– diamonds did you say?– terrible wretches those Kickapoos!– we are playing whist, if you please, Mr. Tattle— however, this is the age of invention, most certainly the age, one may say— the age par excellence— speak French?— oh, quite a hero— perfect desperado!— no hearts, Mr. Tattle? I don't believe it!— Immortal renown and all that!— prodigies of valor! Never heard!!— why, bless me, he's the man—"

"Mann?— Captain Mann!" here screamed some little feminine interloper from the farthest corner of the room. "Are you talking about Captain Mann and the duel?— oh, I must hear— do tell— go on, Mrs. O'Trump!— do now go on!" And go on Mrs. O'Trump did— all about a certain Captain Mann, who was either shot or hung, or should have been both shot and hung. Yes! Mrs. O'Trump, she went on, and I— I went off. There was no chance of hearing any thing farther that evening in regard to Brevet Brigadier General John A. B. C. Smith.

Still I consoled myself with the reflection that the tide of ill–luck would not run against me forever, and so determined to make a bold push for information at the rout of that bewitching little angel, the graceful Mrs. Pirouette.

"Smith!" said Mrs. P., as we twirled about together in a pas de zephyr, "Smith?— why, not General John A. B. C.? Dreadful business that of the Bugaboos, wasn't it?— dreadful creatures, those Indians!— do turn out your toes! I really am ashamed of you— man of great courage, poor fellow!— but this is a wonderful age for invention— O dear me, I'm out of breath— quite a desperado— prodigies of valor— never heard!!— can't believe it— I shall have to sit down and enlighten you— Smith! why, he's the man—"

"Man–Fred, I tell you!" here bawled out Miss Bas–Bleu, as I led Mrs. Pirouette to a seat. "Did ever anybody hear the like? It's Man–Fred, I say, and not at all by any means Man–Friday." Here Miss Bas–Bleu beckoned to me in a very peremptory manner; and I was obliged, will I nill I, to leave Mrs. P. for the purpose of deciding a dispute touching the title of a certain poetical drama of Lord Byron's. Although I pronounced, with great promptness, that the true title was Man–Friday, and not by any means Man–Fred yet when I returned to seek Mrs. Pirouette she was not to be discovered, and I made my retreat from the house in a very bitter spirit of animosity against the whole race of the Bas–Bleus.

Matters had now assumed a really serious aspect, and I resolved to call at once upon my particular friend, Mr. Theodore Sinivate; for I knew that here at least I should get something like definite information.

"Smith!" said he, in his well known peculiar way of drawling out his syllables; "Smith!– why, not General John A. B. C.? Savage affair that with the Kickapo–o–o–os, wasn't it? Say, don't you think so?– perfect despera–a–ado– great pity, 'pon my honor!– wonderfully inventive age!– pro–o–digies of valor! By the by, did you ever hear about Captain Ma–a–a–a–n?"

"Captain Mann be d–d!" said I; "please to go on with your story."

"Hem!– oh well!– quite la meme cho–o–ose, as we say in France. Smith, eh? Brigadier–General John A. B. C.? I say"– [here Mr. S. thought proper to put his finger to the side of his nose]– "I say, you don't mean to insinuate now, really and truly, and conscientiously, that you don't know all about that affair of Smith's, as well as I do, eh? Smith? John A–B–C.? Why, bless me, he's the ma–a–an–"

"Mr. Sinivate," said I, imploringly, "is he the man in the mask?"

"No–o–o!" said he, looking wise, "nor the man in the mo–o–on."

This reply I considered a pointed and positive insult, and so left the house at once in high dudgeon, with a firm resolve to call my friend, Mr. Sinivate, to a speedy account for his ungentlemanly conduct and ill breeding.

In the meantime, however, I had no notion of being thwarted touching the information I desired. There was one resource left me yet. I would go to the fountain head. I would call forthwith upon the General himself, and demand, in explicit terms, a solution of this abominable piece of mystery. Here, at least, there should be no chance for equivocation. I would be plain, positive, peremptory– as short as pie–crust– as concise as Tacitus or Montesquieu.

It was early when I called, and the General was dressing, but I pleaded urgent business, and was shown at once into his bedroom by an old negro valet, who remained in attendance during my visit. As I entered the chamber, I looked about, of course, for the occupant, but did not immediately perceive him. There was a large and exceedingly odd looking bundle of something which lay close by my feet on the floor, and, as I was not in the best humor in the world, I gave it a kick out of the way.

"Hem! ahem! rather civil that, I should say!" said the bundle, in one of the smallest, and altogether the funniest little voices, between a squeak and a whistle, that I ever heard in all the days of my existence.

"Ahem! rather civil that I should observe."

I fairly shouted with terror, and made off, at a tangent, into the farthest extremity of the room.

"God bless me, my dear fellow!" here again whistled the bundle, "what– what– what– why, what is the matter?
I really believe you don't know me at all."

What could I say to all this– what could I? I staggered into an armchair, and, with staring eyes and open mouth, awaited the solution of the wonder.

"Strange you shouldn't know me though, isn't it?" presently resqueaked the nondescript, which I now perceived was performing upon the floor some inexplicable evolution, very analogous to the drawing on of a stocking. There was only a single leg, however, apparent.

"Strange you shouldn't know me though, isn't it? Pompey, bring me that leg!" Here Pompey handed the bundle a very capital cork leg, already dressed, which it screwed on in a trice; and then it stood upright before my eyes.

"And a bloody action it was," continued the thing, as if in a soliloquy; "but then one mustn't fight with the Bugaboos and Kickapoos, and think of coming off with a mere scratch. Pompey, I'll thank you now for that arm. Thomas" [turning to me] "is decidedly the best hand at a cork leg; but if you should ever want an arm, my dear fellow, you must really let me recommend you to Bishop." Here Pompey screwed on an arm.

"We had rather hot work of it, that you may say. Now, you dog, slip on my shoulders and bosom. Pettit makes the best shoulders, but for a bosom you will have to go to Ducrow."

"Bosom!" said I.

"Pompey, will you never be ready with that wig? Scalping is a rough process, after all; but then you can procure such a capital scratch at De L'Orme's."

"Scratch!"

"Now, you nigger, my teeth! For a good set of these you had better go to Parmly's at once; high prices, but excellent work. I swallowed some very capital articles, though, when the big Bugaboo rammed me down with the butt end of his rifle."

"Butt end! ram down!! my eye!!"

"O yes, by the way, my eye– here, Pompey, you scamp, screw it in! Those Kickapoos are not so very slow at a gouge; but he's a belied man, that Dr. Williams, after all; you can't imagine how well I see with the eyes of his make."

I now began very clearly to perceive that the object before me was nothing more nor less than my new acquaintance, Brevet Brigadier General John A. B. C.

Smith. The manipulations of Pompey had made, I must confess, a very striking difference in the appearance of the personal man. The voice, however, still puzzled me no little; but even this apparent mystery was speedily cleared up.

"Pompey, you black rascal," squeaked the General, "I really do believe you would let me go out without my palate."

Hereupon, the negro, grumbling out an apology, went up to his master, opened his mouth with the knowing air of a horse–jockey, and adjusted therein a somewhat singular–looking machine, in a very dexterous manner, that I could not altogether comprehend. The alteration, however, in the entire expression of the General's countenance was instantaneous and surprising. When he again spoke, his voice had resumed all that rich melody and strength which I had noticed upon our original introduction.

"D–n the vagabonds!" said he, in so clear a tone that I positively started at the change, "D–n the vagabonds! they not only knocked in the roof of my mouth, but took the trouble to cut off at least seven–eighths of my tongue. There isn't Bonfanti's equal, however, in America, for really good articles of this description. I can recommend you to him with confidence," [here the General bowed,] "and assure you that I have the greatest pleasure in so doing."

I acknowledged his kindness in my best manner, and took leave of him at once, with a perfect understanding of the true state of affairs– with a full comprehension of the mystery which had troubled me so long. It was evident. It was a clear case. Brevet Brigadier General

John A. B. C. Smith was the man– the man that was used up.

KING PEST

A Tale Containing an Allegory

The gods do bear and will allow in kings
The things which they abhor in rascal routes.
Buckhurst's Tragedy of Ferrex and Porrex.

ABOUT twelve o'clock, one night in the month of October, and

during the chivalrous reign of the third Edward, two seamen belonging to the crew of the "Free and Easy," a trading schooner plying between Sluys and the Thames, and then at anchor in that river, were much astonished to find themselves seated in the tap–room of an ale–house in the parish of St. Andrews, London —which ale–house bore for sign the portraiture of a "Jolly Tar."

The room, although ill-contrived, smoke-blackened, low-pitched,

and in every other respect agreeing with the general character of such places at the period —was, nevertheless, in the opinion of the grotesque groups scattered here and there within it, sufficiently well adapted to its purpose.

Of these groups our two seamen formed, I

think, the most

interesting, if not the most conspicuous.

The one who appeared to be the elder, and whom his companion

addressed by the characteristic appellation of "Legs," was at the same time much the taller of the two. He might have measured six feet and a half, and an habitual stoop in the shoulders seemed to have been the necessary consequence of an altitude so enormous.—Superfluities in height were, however, more than accounted for by deficiencies in other respects. He was exceedingly thin; and might, as his associates asserted, have answered, when drunk, for a pennant at the mast–head, or, when sober, have served for a jib–boom. But these jests, and others of a similar nature, had evidently produced, at no time, any effect upon the cachinnatory muscles of the tar. With high cheek–bones, a large hawk–nose, retreating chin, fallen under–jaw, and huge protruding white eyes, the expression of his countenance, although tinged with a species of dogged indifference to matters and things in general, was not the less utterly solemn and serious beyond all attempts at imitation or description.

The younger seaman was, in all outward appearance, the converse of

his companion. His stature could not have exceeded four feet. A pair of stumpy bow–legs supported his squat, unwieldy figure, while his unusually short and thick arms, with no ordinary fists at their extremities, swung off dangling from his sides like the fins of a sea–turtle. Small eyes, of no particular color, twinkled far back in his head. His nose remained buried in the mass of flesh which enveloped his round, full, and purple face; and his thick upper–lip rested upon the still thicker one beneath with an air of complacent self–satisfaction, much heightened by the owner's habit of licking them at intervals. He evidently regarded his tall shipmate with a feeling half–wondrous, half–quizzical; and stared up occasionally in his face as the red setting sun stares up at the crags of Ben Nevis.

Various and eventful, however, had been the peregrinations of

the worthy couple in and about the different tap–houses of the neighbourhood during the earlier hours of the night. Funds even the most ample, are not always everlasting: and it was with empty pockets our friends had ventured upon the present hostelrie.

At the precise period, then, when this history properly commences,

Legs, and his fellow Hugh Tarpaulin, sat, each with both elbows resting upon the large oaken table in the middle of the floor, and with a hand upon either cheek. They were eyeing, from behind a huge flagon of unpaid–for "humming–stuff," the portentous words, "No Chalk," which to their indignation and astonishment were scored over the doorway by means of that very mineral whose presence they purported to deny. Not that the gift of decyphering written characters —a gift among the commonalty of that day considered little less cabalistical than the art of inditing —could, in strict justice, have been laid to the charge of either disciple of the sea; but there was, to say the truth, a certain twist in the formation of the letters —an indescribable lee–lurch about the whole ——which foreboded, in the opinion of both seamen, a long run of dirty weather; and determined them at once, in the allegorical words of Legs himself, to "pump ship, clew up all sail, and scud before the wind."

Having accordingly disposed of what remained of the ale, and

looped up the points of their short doublets, they finally made a bolt for the street. Although Tarpaulin rolled twice into the fire–place, mistaking it for the door, yet their escape was at length happily effected — and half after twelve o'clock found our heroes ripe for mischief, and running for life down a dark alley in the direction of St. Andrew's Stair, hotly pursued by the landlady of the "Jolly Tar."

At the epoch of this eventful tale, and periodically, for many

years before and after, all England, but more especially the metropolis, resounded with the fearful cry of "Plague!" The city was in a great measure depopulated —and in those horrible regions, in the vicinity of the Thames, where amid the dark, narrow, and filthy lanes and alleys, the Demon of Disease was supposed to have had his nativity, Awe, Terror, and Superstition were alone to be found stalking abroad.

By authority of the king such districts were placed under ban, and

all persons forbidden, under pain of death, to intrude upon their dismal solitude. Yet neither the mandate of the monarch, nor the huge barriers erected at the entrances of the streets, nor the prospect of that loathsome death which, with almost absolute certainty, overwhelmed the wretch whom no peril could deter from the adventure, prevented the unfurnished and untenanted dwellings from being stripped, by the hand of nightly rapine, of every article, such as iron, brass, or lead–work, which could in any manner be turned to a profitable account.

Above all, it was usually found, upon the annual winter opening of

the barriers, that locks, bolts, and secret cellars, had proved but slender protection to those rich stores of wines and liquors which, in consideration of the risk and trouble of removal, many of the numerous dealers having shops in the neighbourhood had consented to trust, during the period of exile, to so insufficient a security.

But there were very few of the terror-stricken people who

attributed these doings to the agency of human hands. Pest–spirits, plague–goblins, and fever–demons, were the popular imps of mischief; and tales so blood–chilling were hourly told, that the whole mass of forbidden buildings was, at length, enveloped in terror as in a shroud, and the plunderer himself was often scared away by the horrors his own depreciations had created; leaving the entire vast circuit of prohibited district to gloom, silence, pestilence, and death.

It was by one of the terrific barriers already mentioned, and which indicated the region beyond to be under the Pest–ban, that, in scrambling down an alley, Legs and the worthy Hugh Tarpaulin found their progress suddenly impeded. To return was out of the question, and no time was to be lost, as their pursuers were close upon their heels. With thorough–bred seamen to clamber up the roughly fashioned plank–work was a trifle; and, maddened with the twofold excitement of exercise and liquor, they leaped unhesitatingly down within the enclosure, and holding on their drunken course with shouts and yellings, were soon bewildered in its noisome and intricate recesses.

Had they not, indeed, been intoxicated beyond moral sense, their

reeling footsteps must have been palsied by the horrors of their situation. The air was cold and misty. The paving–stones, loosened from their beds, lay in wild disorder amid the tall, rank grass, which sprang up around the feet and ankles. Fallen houses choked up the streets. The most fetid and poisonous smells everywhere prevailed; —and by the aid of that ghastly light which, even at midnight, never fails to emanate from a vapory and pestilential at atmosphere, might be discerned lying in the by–paths and alleys, or rotting in the windowless habitations, the carcass of many a nocturnal plunderer arrested by the hand of the plague in the very perpetration of his robbery.

But it lay not in the power of images, or sensations, or

impediments such as these, to stay the course of men who, naturally brave, and at that time especially, brimful of courage and of "humming–stuff!" would have reeled, as straight as their condition might have permitted, undauntedly into the very jaws of Death. Onward —still onward stalked the grim Legs, making the desolate solemnity echo and re–echo with yells like the terrific war–whoop of the Indian: and onward, still onward rolled the dumpy Tarpaulin, hanging on to the doublet of his more active companion, and far surpassing the latter's most strenuous exertions in the way of vocal music, by bull–roarings in basso, from the profundity of his stentorian lungs.

They had now evidently reached the strong hold of the

pestilence. Their way at every step or plunge grew more noisome and more horrible —the paths more narrow and more intricate. Huge stones and beams falling momently from the decaying roofs above them, gave evidence, by their sullen and heavy descent, of the vast height of the surrounding houses; and while actual exertion became necessary to force a passage through frequent heaps of rubbish, it was by no means seldom that the hand fell upon a skeleton or rested upon a more fleshly corpse.

Suddenly, as the seamen stumbled against the entrance of a tall

and ghastly–looking building, a yell more than usually shrill from the throat of the excited Legs, was replied to from within, in a rapid succession of wild, laughter–like, and fiendish shrieks. Nothing daunted at sounds which, of such a nature, at such a time, and in such a place, might have curdled the very blood in hearts less irrevocably on fire, the drunken couple rushed headlong against the door, burst it open, and staggered into the midst of things with a volley of curses.

The room within which they found themselves proved to be the

shop of an undertaker; but an open trap–door, in a corner of the floor near the entrance, looked down upon a long range of wine–cellars, whose depths the occasional sound of bursting bottles proclaimed to be well stored with their appropriate contents. In the middle of the room stood a table —in the centre of which again arose a huge tub of what appeared to be punch. Bottles of various wines and cordials, together with jugs, pitchers, and flagons of every shape and quality, were scattered profusely upon the board. Around it, upon coffin–tressels, was seated a company of six. This company I will endeavor to delineate one by one.

Fronting the entrance, and elevated a little above his companions,

sat a personage who appeared to be the president of the table. His stature was gaunt and tall, and Legs was confounded to behold in him a figure more emaciated than himself. His face was as yellow as saffron —but no feature excepting one alone, was sufficiently marked to merit a particular description. This one consisted in a forehead so unusually and hideously lofty, as to have the appearance of a bonnet or crown of flesh superadded upon the natural head. His mouth was puckered and dimpled into an expression of ghastly affability, and his eyes, as indeed the eyes of all at table, were glazed over with the fumes of intoxication. This gentleman was clothed from head to foot in a richly–embroidered black silk–velvet pall, wrapped negligently around his form after the fashion of a Spanish cloak. —His head was stuck full of sable hearse–plumes, which he nodded to and fro with a jaunty and knowing air; and, in his right hand, he held a huge human thigh–bone, with which he appeared to have been just knocking down some member of the company for a song.

Opposite him, and with her back to the door, was a lady of no whit

the less extraordinary character. Although quite as tall as the person just described, she had no right to complain of his unnatural emaciation. She was evidently in the last stage of a dropsy; and her figure resembled nearly that of the huge puncheon of October beer which stood, with the head driven in, close by her side, in a corner of the chamber. Her face was exceedingly round, red, and full; and the same peculiarity, or rather want of peculiarity, attached itself to her countenance, which I before mentioned in the case of the president —that is to say, only one feature of her face was sufficiently distinguished to need a separate characterization: indeed the acute Tarpaulin immediately observed that the same remark might have applied to each individual person of the party; every one of whom seemed to possess a monopoly of some particular portion of physiognomy. With the lady in question this portion proved to be the mouth. Commencing at the right ear, it swept with a terrific chasm to the left —the short pendants which she wore in either auricle continually bobbing into the aperture. She made, however, every exertion to keep her mouth closed and look dignified, in a dress consisting of a newly starched and ironed shroud coming up close under her chin, with a crimpled ruffle of cambric muslin.

At her right hand sat a diminutive young lady whom she appeared to

patronise. This delicate little creature, in the trembling of her wasted fingers, in the livid hue of her lips, and in the slight hectic spot which tinged her otherwise leaden complexion, gave evident indications of a galloping consumption. An air of gave extreme haut ton, however, pervaded her whole appearance; she wore in a graceful and degage manner, a large and beautiful winding–sheet of the finest India lawn; her hair hung in ringlets over her neck; a soft smile played about her mouth; but her nose, extremely long, thin, sinuous, flexible and pimpled, hung down far below her under lip, and in spite of the delicate manner in which she now and then moved it to one side or the other with her tongue, gave to her countenance a somewhat equivocal expression.

Over against her, and upon the left of the dropsical lady, was

seated a little puffy, wheezing, and gouty old man, whose cheeks reposed upon the shoulders of their owner, like two huge bladders of Oporto wine. With his arms folded, and with one bandaged leg deposited upon the table, he seemed to think himself entitled to some consideration. He evidently prided himself much upon every inch of his personal appearance, but took more especial delight in calling attention to his gaudy–colored surtout. This, to say the truth, must have cost him no little money, and was made to fit him exceedingly well —being fashioned from one of the curiously embroidered silken covers appertaining to those glorious escutcheons which, in England and elsewhere, are customarily hung up, in some conspicuous place, upon the dwellings of departed aristocracy.

Next to him, and at the right hand of the president, was a

gentleman in long white hose and cotton drawers. His frame shook, in a ridiculous manner, with a fit of what Tarpaulin called "the horrors." His jaws, which had been newly shaved, were tightly tied up by a bandage of muslin; and his arms being fastened in a similar way at the wrists, I I prevented him from helping himself too freely to the liquors upon the table; a precaution rendered necessary, in the opinion of Legs, by the peculiarly sottish and wine–bibbing cast of his visage. A pair of prodigious ears, nevertheless, which it was no doubt found impossible to confine, towered away into the atmosphere of the apartment, and were occasionally pricked up in a spasm, at the sound of the drawing of a cork.

Fronting him, sixthly and lastly, was situated a singularly

stiff–looking personage, who, being afflicted with paralysis, must, to speak seriously, have felt very ill at ease in his unaccommodating habiliments. He was habited, somewhat uniquely, in a new and handsome mahogany coffin. Its top or head–piece pressed upon the skull of the wearer, and extended over it in the fashion of a hood, giving to the entire face an air of indescribable interest. Arm–holes had been cut in the sides, for the sake not more of elegance than of convenience; but the dress, nevertheless, prevented its proprietor from sitting as erect as his associates; and as he lay reclining against his tressel, at an angle of forty–five degrees, a pair of huge goggle eyes rolled up their awful whites towards the celling in absolute amazement at their own enormity.

Before each of the party lay a portion of a skull, which was

used as a drinking cup. Overhead was suspended a human skeleton, by means of a rope tied round one of the legs and fastened to a ring in the ceiling. The other limb, confined by no such fetter, stuck off from the body at right angles, causing the whole loose and rattling frame to dangle and twirl about at the caprice of every occasional puff of wind which found its way into the apartment. In the cranium of this hideous thing lay quantity of ignited charcoal, which threw a fitful but vivid light over the entire scene; while coffins, and other wares appertaining to the shop of an undertaker, were piled high up around the room, and against the windows, preventing any ray from escaping into the street.

At sight of this extraordinary assembly, and of their still more

extraordinary paraphernalia, our two seamen did not conduct themselves with that degree of decorum which might have been expected. Legs, leaning against the wall near which he happened to be standing, dropped his lower jaw still lower than usual, and spread open his eyes to their fullest extent: while Hugh Tarpaulin, stooping down so as to bring his nose upon a level with the table, and spreading out a palm upon either knee, burst into a long, loud, and obstreperous roar of very ill–timed and immoderate laughter.

Without, however, taking offence at behaviour so excessively rude,

the tall president smiled very graciously upon the intruders —nodded to them in a dignified manner with his head of sable plumes —and, arising, took each by an arm, and led him to a seat which some others of the company had placed in the meantime for his accommodation. Legs to all this offered not the slightest resistance, but sat down as he was directed; while tile gallant Hugh, removing his coffin tressel from its station near the head of the table, to the vicinity of the little consumptive lady in the winding sheet, plumped down by her side in high glee, and pouring out a skull of red wine, quaffed it to their better acquaintance. But at this presumption the stiff gentleman in the coffin seemed exceedingly nettled; and serious consequences might have ensued, had not the president, rapping upon the table with his truncheon, diverted the attention of all present to the following speech:

"It becomes our duty upon the present happy occasion"-

"Avast there!" interrupted Legs, looking very serious, "avast

there a bit, I say, and tell us who the devil ye all are, and what business ye have here, rigged off like the foul fiends, and swilling the snug blue ruin stowed away for the winter by my honest shipmate, Will Wimble the undertaker!"

At this unpardonable piece of ill-breeding, all the original company half started to their feet, and uttered the same rapid succession of wild fiendish shrieks which had before caught the attention of the seamen. The president, however, was the first to recover his composure, and at length, turning to Legs with great dignity, recommenced:

"Most willingly will we gratify any reasonable curiosity on the

part of guests so illustrious, unbidden though they be. Know then that in these dominions I am monarch, and here rule with undivided empire under the title of 'King Pest the First.'

"This apartment, which you no doubt profanely suppose to be the

shop of Will Wimble the undertaker —a man whom we know not, and whose plebeian appellation has never before this night thwarted our royal ears —this apartment, I say, is the Dais–Chamber of our Palace, devoted to the councils of our kingdom, and to other sacred and lofty purposes.

"The noble lady who sits opposite is Queen Pest, our Serene

Consort. The other exalted personages whom you behold are all of our family, and wear the insignia of the blood royal under the respective titles of 'His Grace the Arch Duke Pest–Iferous' —'His Grace the Duke Pest–Ilential' —'His Grace the Duke Tem–Pest' —and 'Her Serene Highness the Arch Duchess Ana–Pest.'

"As regards," continued he, "your demand of the business upon

which we sit here in council, we might be pardoned for replying that it concerns, and concerns alone, our own private and regal interest, and is in no manner important to any other than ourself. But in consideration of those rights to which as guests and strangers you may feel yourselves entitled, we will furthermore explain that we are here this night, prepared by deep research and accurate investigation, to examine, analyze, and thoroughly determine the indefinable spirit —the incomprehensible qualities and nature —of those inestimable treasures of the palate, the wines, ales, and liqueurs of this goodly metropolis: by so doing to advance not more our own designs than the true welfare of that unearthly sovereign whose reign is over us all, whose dominions are unlimited, and whose name is 'Death.'

"Whose name is Davy Jones!" ejaculated Tarpaulin, helping the lady

by his side to a skull of liqueur, and pouring out a second for himself.

"Profane varlet!" said the president, now turning his attention to

the worthy Hugh, "profane and execrable wretch! — we have said, that in consideration of those rights which, even in thy filthy person, we feel no inclination to violate, we have condescended to make reply to thy rude and unseasonable inquiries. We nevertheless, for your unhallowed intrusion upon our councils, believe it our duty to mulct thee and thy companion in each a gallon of Black Strap —having imbibed which to the prosperity of our kingdom —at a single draught —and upon your bended knees —ye shall be forthwith free either to proceed upon your way, or remain and be admitted to the privileges of our table, according to your respective and individual pleasures."

"It would be a matter of utter impossibility," replied Legs,

whom the assumptions and dignity of King Pest the First had evidently inspired some feelings of respect, and who arose and steadied himself by the table as he spoke —"It would, please your majesty, be a matter of utter impossibility to stow away in my hold even one–fourth part of the same liquor which your majesty has just mentioned. To say nothing of the stuffs placed on board in the forenoon by way of ballast, and not to mention the various ales and liqueurs shipped this evening at different sea–ports, I have, at present, a full cargo of 'humming stuff' taken in and duly paid for at the sign of the 'Jolly Tar.' You will, therefore, please your majesty, be so good as to take the will for the deed —for by no manner of means either can I or will I swallow another drop —least of all a drop of that villainous bilge–water that answers to the hall of 'Black Strap.'"

"Belay that!" interrupted Tarpaulin, astonished not more at the

length of his companion's speech than at the nature of his refusal —"Belay that you tubber! —and I say, Legs, none of your palaver! My hull is still light, although I confess you yourself seem to be a little top–heavy; and as for the matter of your share of the cargo, why rather than raise a squall I would find stowageroom for it myself, but" —

"This proceeding," interposed the president, "is by no means in

accordance with the terms of the mulct or sentence, which is in its nature Median, and not to be altered or recalled. The conditions we have imposed must be fulfilled to the letter, and that without a moment's hesitation —in failure of which fulfilment we decree that you do here be tied neck and heels together, and duly drowned as rebels in yon hogshead of October beer!"

"A sentence! -a sentence! -a righteous and just sentence! -a

glorious decree! —a most worthy and upright, and holy condemnation!" shouted the Pest family altogether. The king elevated his forehead into innumerable wrinkles; the gouty little old man puffed like a pair of bellows; the lady of the winding sheet waved her nose to and fro; the gentleman in the cotton drawers pricked up his ears; she of the shroud gasped like a dying fish; and he of the coffin looked stiff and rolled up his eyes.

"Ugh! ugh! ugh!" chuckled Tarpaulin without heeding the general

excitation, "ugh! ugh! ugh! —ugh! ugh! ugh! —ugh! ugh! ugh! —I was saying," said he, "I was saying when Mr. King Pest poked in his marlin–spike, that as for the matter of two or three gallons more or less of Black Strap, it was a trifle to a tight sea–boat like myself not overstowed —but when it comes to drinking the health of the Devil (whom God assoilzie) and going down upon my marrow bones to his ill–favored majesty there, whom I know, as well as I know myself to be a sinner, to be nobody in the whole world, but Tim Hurlygurly the stage–player —why! it's quite another guess sort of a thing, and utterly and altogether past my comprehension."

He was not allowed to finish this speech in tranquillity. At the

name Tim Hurlygurly the whole assembly leaped from their name seats.

"Treason!" shouted his Majesty King Pest the First.
"Treason!" said the little man with the gout.
"Treason!" screamed the Arch Duchess Ana-Pest.
"Treason!" muttered the gentleman with his jaws tied up.
"Treason!" growled he of the coffin.
"Treason! treason!" shrieked her majesty of the mouth; and,

seizing by the hinder part of his breeches the unfortunate Tarpaulin, who had just commenced pouring out for himself a skull of liqueur, she lifted him high into the air, and let him fall without ceremony into the huge open puncheon of his beloved ale. Bobbing up and down, for a few seconds, like an apple in a bowl of toddy, he, at length, finally disappeared amid the whirlpool of foam which, in the already effervescent liquor, is struggles easily succeeded in creating.

Not tamely, however, did the tall seaman

behold the discomfiture

of his companion. Jostling King Pest through the open trap, the valiant Legs slammed the door down upon him with an oath, and strode towards the centre of the room. Here tearing down the skeleton which swung over the table, he laid it about him with so much energy and good will, that, as the last glimpses of light died away within the apartment, he succeeded in knocking out the brains of the little gentleman with the gout. Rushing then with all his force against the fatal hogshead full of October ale and Hugh Tarpaulin, he rolled it over and over in an instant. Out burst a deluge of liquor so fierce —so impetuous —so overwhelming —that the room was flooded from wall to wall —the loaded table was overturned —the tressels were thrown upon their backs —the tub of punch into the fire–place —and the ladies into hysterics. Piles of death–furniture floundered about. Jugs, pitchers, and carboys mingled promiscuously in the melee, and wicker flagons encountered desperately with bottles of junk. The man with the horrors was drowned upon the spot–the little stiff gentleman floated off in his coffin —and the victorious Legs, seizing by the waist the fat lady in the shroud, rushed out with her into the street, and made a bee–line for the "Free and Easy," followed under easy sail by the redoubtable Hugh Tarpaulin, who, having sneezed three or four times, panted and puffed after him with the Arch Duchess Ana–Pest.

LOSS OF BREATH

A Tale Neither In nor Out of "Blackwood"

O Breathe not, etc.
> Moore's Melodies

THE MOST notorious ill-fortune must in the end yield to the untiring courage of philosophy— as the most stubborn city to the ceaseless vigilance of an enemy. Shalmanezer, as we have it in holy writings, lay three years before Samaria; yet it fell. Sardanapalus— see Diodorus— maintained himself seven in Nineveh; but to no purpose. Troy expired at the close of the second lustrum; and Azoth, as Aristaeus declares upon his honour as a gentleman, opened at last her gates to Psammetichus, after having barred them for the fifth part of a century....

"Thou wretch!— thou vixen!— thou shrew!" said I to my wife on the morning after our wedding; "thou witch!— thou hag!— thou whippersnapper— thou sink of iniquity! thou fiery-faced quintessence of all that is abominable!— thou— thou—" here standing upon tiptoe, seizing her by the throat, and placing my mouth close to her ear, I was preparing to launch forth a new and more decided epithet of opprobrium, which should not fail, if ejaculated, to convince her of her insignificance, when to my extreme horror and astonishment I discovered that I had lost my breath.

The phrases "I am out of breath," "I have lost my breath," etc., are often enough repeated in common conversation; but it had never occurred to me that the terrible accident of which I speak could bona fide and actually happen! Imagine– that is if you have a fanciful turn– imagine, I say, my wonder– my consternation– my despair!

There is a good genius, however, which has never entirely deserted me. In my most ungovernable moods I still retain a sense of propriety, et le chemin des passions me conduit– as Lord Edouard in the "Julie" says it did him– a la philosophie veritable.

Although I could not at first precisely ascertain to what degree the occurence had affected me, I determined at all events to conceal the matter from my wife, until further experience should discover to me the extent of this my unheard of calamity. Altering my countenance, therefore, in a moment, from its bepuffed and distorted appearance, to an expression of arch and coquettish benignity, I gave my lady a pat on the one cheek, and a kiss on the other, and without saying one syllable (Furies! I could not), left her astonished at my drollery, as I pirouetted out of the room in a Pas de Zephyr.

Behold me then safely ensconced in my private boudoir, a fearful instance of the ill consequences attending upon irascibility– alive, with the qualifications of the dead– dead, with the propensities of the living– an anomaly on the face of the earth– being very calm, yet breathless.

Yes! breathless. I am serious in asserting that my

breath was entirely gone. I could not have stirred with it a feather if my life had been at issue, or sullied even the delicacy of a mirror. Hard fate!– yet there was some alleviation to the first overwhelming paroxysm of my sorrow. I found, upon trial, that the powers of utterance which, upon my inability to proceed in the conversation with my wife, I then concluded to be totally destroyed, were in fact only partially impeded, and I discovered that had I, at that interesting crisis, dropped my voice to a singularly deep guttural, I might still have continued to her the communication of my sentiments; this pitch of voice (the guttural) depending, I find, not upon the current of the breath, but upon a certain spasmodic action of the muscles of the throat.

Throwing myself upon a chair, I remained for some time absorbed in meditation. My reflections, be sure, were of no consolatory kind. A thousand vague and lachrymatory fancies took possesion of my soul– and even the idea of suicide flitted across my brain; but it is a trait in the perversity of human nature to reject the obvious and the ready, for the far–distant and equivocal. Thus I shuddered at self–murder as the most decided of atrocities while the tabby cat purred strenuously upon the rug, and the very water dog wheezed assiduously under the table, each taking to itself much merit for the strength of its lungs, and all obviously done in derision of my own pulmonary incapacity.

Oppressed with a tumult of vague hopes and fears, I at length heard the footsteps of my wife descending the staircase. Being now assured of her absence, I returned with a palpitating heart to the scene of my disaster.

Carefully locking the door on the inside, I commenced

a vigorous search. It was possible, I thought, that, concealed in some obscure corner, or lurking in some closet or drawer, might be found the lost object of my inquiry. It might have a vapory– it might even have a tangible form. Most philosophers, upon many points of philosophy, are still very unphilosophical. William Godwin, however, says in his "Mandeville," that "invisible things are the only realities," and this, all will allow, is a case in point. I would have the judicious reader pause before accusing such asseverations of an undue quantum of absurdity. Anaxagoras, it will be remembered, maintained that snow is black, and this I have since found to be the case.

Long and earnestly did I continue the investigation: but the contemptible reward of my industry and perseverance proved to be only a set of false teeth, two pair of hips, an eye, and a bundle of billets–doux from Mr. Windenough to my wife. I might as well here observe that this confirmation of my lady's partiality for Mr W. occasioned me little uneasiness. That Mrs. Lackobreath should admire anything so dissimilar to myself was a natural and necessary evil. I am, it is well known, of a robust and corpulent appearance, and at the same time somewhat diminutive in stature. What wonder, then, that the lath–like tenuity of my acquaintance, and his altitude, which has grown into a proverb, should have met with all due estimation in the eyes of Mrs. Lackobreath. But to return.

My exertions, as I have before said, proved fruitless. Closet after closet– drawer after drawer– corner after corner– were scrutinized to no purpose. At one time, however, I thought myself sure of my prize, having, in rummaging a dressing–case, accidentally demolished a bottle of Grandjean's Oil of Archangels– which, as an agreeable perfume, I here take the liberty of recommending.

With a heavy heart I returned to my boudoir– there to ponder upon some method of eluding my wife's penetration, until I could make arrangements prior to my leaving the country, for to this I had already made up my mind. In a foreign climate, being unknown, I might, with some probability of success, endeavor to conceal my unhappy calamity– a calamity calculated, even more than beggary, to estrange the affections of the multitude, and to draw down upon the wretch the well–merited indignation of the virtuous and the happy. I was not long in hesitation. Being naturally quick, I committed to memory the entire tragedy of "Metamora." I had the good fortune to recollect that in the accentuation of this drama, or at least of such portion of it as is allotted to the hero, the tones of voice in which I found myself deficient were altogether unnecessary, and the deep guttural was expected to reign monotonously throughout.

I practised for some time by the borders of a well frequented marsh;– herein, however, having no reference to a similar proceeding of Demosthenes, but from a design peculiarly and conscientiously my own. Thus armed at all points, I determined to make my wife believe that I was suddenly smitten with a passion for the stage. In this, I succeeded to a miracle; and to every question or suggestion found myself at liberty to reply in my most frog–like and sepulchral tones with some passage from the tragedy– any portion of which, as I soon took great pleasure in observing, would apply equally well to any particular subject. It is not to be supposed, however, that in the delivery of such passages I was found at all deficient in the looking asquint– the showing my teeth– the working my knees– the shuffling my feet– or in any of those unmentionable graces which are now justly considered the characteristics of a popular performer. To be sure they spoke of confining me in a strait–jacket– but, good God! they never suspected me of having lost my breath.

Having at length put my affairs in order, I took my seat very early one morning in the mail stage for —, giving it to be understood, among my acquaintances, that business of the last importance required my immediate personal attendance in that city.

The coach was crammed to repletion; but in the uncertain twilight the features of my companions could not be distinguished. Without making any effectual resistance, I suffered myself to be placed between two gentlemen of colossal dimensions; while a third, of a size larger, requesting pardon for the liberty he was about to take, threw himself upon my body at full length, and falling asleep in an instant, drowned all my guttural ejaculations for relief, in a snore which would have put to blush the roarings of the bull of Phalaris. Happily the state of my respiratory faculties rendered suffocation an accident entirely out of the question.

As, however, the day broke more distinctly in our approach to the outskirts of the city, my tormentor, arising and adjusting his shirt–collar, thanked me in a very friendly manner for my civility. Seeing that I remained motionless (all my limbs were dislocated and my head twisted on one side), his apprehensions began to be excited; and arousing the rest of the passengers, he communicated, in a very decided manner, his opinion that a dead man had been palmed upon them during the night for a living and responsible fellow–traveller; here giving me a thump on the right eye, by way of demonstrating the truth of his suggestion.

Hereupon all, one after another (there were nine in company), believed it their duty to pull me by the ear. A young practising physician, too, having applied a pocket–mirror to my mouth, and found me without breath, the assertion of my persecutor was pronounced a true bill; and the whole party expressed a determination to endure tamely no such impositions for the future, and to proceed no farther with any such carcasses for the present.

I was here, accordingly, thrown out at the sign of the "Crow" (by which tavern the coach happened to be passing), without meeting with any farther accident than the breaking of both my arms, under the left hind wheel of the vehicle. I must besides do the driver the justice to state that he did not forget to throw after me the largest of my trunks, which, unfortunately falling on my head, fractured my skull in a manner at once interesting and extraordinary.

The landlord of the "Crow," who is a hospitable man, finding that my trunk contained sufficient to indemnify him for any little trouble he might take in my behalf, sent forthwith for a surgeon of his acquaintance, and delivered me to his care with a bill and receipt for ten dollars.

The purchaser took me to his apartments and comm-enced operations immediately. Having cut off my ears, however, he discovered signs of animation. He now rang the bell, and sent for a neighboring apothecary with whom to consult in the emergency. In case of his suspicions with regard to my existence proving ultimately correct, he, in the meantime, made an incision in my stomach, and removed several of my viscera for private dissection.

The apothecary had an idea that I was actually dead. This idea I endeavored to confute, kicking and plunging with all my might, and making the most furious contortions– for the operations of the surgeon had, in a measure, restored me to the possession of my faculties. All, however, was attributed to the effects of a new galvanic battery, wherewith the apothecary, who is really a man of information, performed several curious experiments, in which, from my personal share in their fulfillment, I could not help feeling deeply interested. It was a course of mortification to me, nevertheless, that although I made several attempts at conversation, my powers of speech were so entirely in abeyance, that I could not even open my mouth; much less, then, make reply to some ingenious but fanciful theories of which, under other circumstances, my minute acquaintance with the Hippocratian pathology would have afforded me a ready confutation.

Not being able to arrive at a conclusion, the practitioners remanded me for farther examination. I was taken up into a garret; and the surgeon's lady having accommodated me with drawers and stockings, the surgeon himself fastened my hands, and tied up my jaws with a pocket–handkerchief– then bolted the door on the outside as he hurried to his dinner, leaving me alone to silence and to meditation.

I now discovered to my extreme delight that I could have spoken had not my mouth been tied up with the pocket–handkerchief. Consoling myself with this reflection, I was mentally repeating some passages of the "Omnipresence of the Deity," as is my custom before resigning myself to sleep, when two cats, of a greedy and vituperative turn, entering at a hole in the wall, leaped up with a flourish a la Catalani, and alighting opposite one another on my visage, betook themselves to indecorous contention for the paltry consideration of my nose.

But, as the loss of his ears proved the means of elevating to the throne of Cyrus, the Magian or Mige–Gush of Persia, and as the cutting off his nose gave Zopyrus possession of Babylon, so the loss of a few ounces of my countenance proved the salvation of my body. Aroused by the pain, and burning with indignation, I burst, at a single effort, the fastenings and the bandage. Stalking across the room I cast a glance of contempt at the belligerents, and throwing open the sash to their extreme horror and disappointment, precipitated myself, very dexterously, from the window. this moment passing from the city jail to the scaffold erected for his execution in the suburbs. His extreme infirmity and long continued ill health had obtained him the privilege of remaining unmanacled; and habited in his gallows costume– one very similar to my own,– he lay at full length in the bottom of the hangman's cart (which happened to be under the windows of the surgeon at the moment of my precipitation) without any other guard than the driver, who was asleep, and two recruits of the sixth infantry, who were drunk.

As ill–luck would have it, I alit upon my feet within the vehicle. immediately, he bolted out behind, and turning down an alley, was out of sight in the twinkling of an eye. The recruits, aroused by the bustle, could not exactly comprehend the merits of the transaction. Seeing, however, a man, the precise counterpart of the felon, standing upright in the cart before their eyes, they were of (so they expressed themselves,) and, having communicated this opinion to one another, they took each a dram, and then knocked me down with the butt–ends of their muskets.

It was not long ere we arrived at the place of destination. Of course nothing could be said in my defence. Hanging was my inevitable fate. I resigned myself thereto with a feeling half stupid, half acrimonious. Being little of a cynic, I had all the sentiments of a dog. The hangman, however, adjusted the noose about my neck. The drop fell.

I forbear to depict my sensations upon the gallows; although here, undoubtedly, I could speak to the point, and it is a topic upon which nothing has been well said. In fact, to write upon such a theme it is necessary to have been hanged. Every author should confine himself to matters of experience. Thus Mark Antony composed a treatise upon getting drunk.

I may just mention, however, that die I did not. My body was, but I had no breath to be, suspended; and but for the knot under my left ear (which had the feel of a military stock) I dare say that I should have experienced very little inconvenience. As for the jerk given to my neck upon the falling of the drop, it merely proved a corrective to the twist afforded me by the fat gentleman in the coach.

For good reasons, however, I did my best to give the crowd the worth of their trouble. My convulsions were said to be extraordinary. My spasms it would have been difficult to beat. The populace encored. Several gentlemen swooned; and a multitude of ladies were carried home in hysterics. Pinxit availed himself of the opportunity to retouch, from a sketch taken upon the spot, his admirable painting of the "Marsyas flayed alive."

When I had afforded sufficient amusement, it was thought proper to remove my body from the gallows;– this the more especially as the real culprit had in the meantime been retaken and recognized, a fact which I was so unlucky as not to know.

Much sympathy was, of course, exercised in my behalf, and as no one made claim to my corpse, it was ordered that I should be interred in a public vault.

Here, after due interval, I was deposited. The sexton departed, and I was left alone. A line of Marston's "Malcontent"–

Death's a good fellow and keeps open house–

struck me at that moment as a palpable lie.

I knocked off, however, the lid of my coffin, and stepped out. The place was dreadfully dreary and damp, and I became troubled with ennui. By way of amusement, I felt my way among the numerous coffins ranged in order around. I lifted them down, one by one, and breaking open their lids, busied myself in speculations about the mortality within.

"This," I soliloquized, tumbling over a carcass, puffy, bloated, and rotund– "this has been, no doubt, in every sense of the word, an unhappy– an unfortunate man. It has been his terrible lot not to walk but to waddle– to pass through life not like a human being, but like an elephant– not like a man, but like a rhinoceros.

"His attempts at getting on have been mere abortions, and his circumgyratory proceedings a palpable failure. Taking a step forward, it has been his misfortune to take two toward the right, and three toward the left. His studies have been confined to the poetry of Crabbe. He can have no idea of the wonder of a pirouette. To him a pas de papillon has been an abstract conception. He has never ascended the summit of a hill. He has never viewed from any steeple the glories of a metropolis. Heat has been his mortal enemy. In the dog–days his days have been the days of a dog. Therein, he has dreamed of flames and suffocation– of mountains upon mountains– of Pelion upon Ossa. He was short of breath– to say all in a word, he was short of breath. He thought it extravagant to play upon wind instruments. He was the inventor of self–moving fans, wind–sails, and ventilators. He patronized Du Pont the bellows–maker, and he died miserably in attempting to smoke a cigar. His was a case in which I feel a deep interest– a lot in which I sincerely sympathize.

"But here,"– said I– "here"– and I dragged spitefully from its receptacle a gaunt, tall and peculiar–looking form, whose remarkable appearance struck me with a sense of unwelcome familiarity– "here is a wretch entitled to no earthly commiseration." Thus saying, in order to obtain a more distinct view of my subject, I applied my thumb and forefinger to its nose, and causing it to assume a sitting position upon the ground, held it thus, at the length of my arm, while I continued my soliloquy.

–"Entitled," I repeated, "to no earthly commiseration. Who indeed would think of compassioning a shadow? Besides, has he not had his full share of the blessings of mortality? He was the originator of tall monuments– shot–towers– lightning–rods– Lombardy poplars. His treatise upon "Shades and Shadows" has immortalized him. He edited with distinguished ability the last edition of "South on the Bones." He went early to college and studied pneumatics. He then came home, talked eternally, and played upon the French–horn. He patronized the bagpipes. Captain Barclay, who walked against Time, would not walk against him. Windham and Allbreath were his favorite writers,– his favorite artist, Phiz. He died gloriously while inhaling gas– levique flatu corrupitur, like the fama pudicitae in Hieronymus. [4] He was indubitably a"–

[4] Tenera res in feminis fama pudicitiae, et quasi flos pulcherrimus, cito ad levem marcessit auram, levique flatu corrumpitur,

maxime, &c.– Hieronymus ad Salvinam.

"How can you?– how– can– you?"– interrupted the object of my animadversions, gasping for breath, and tearing off, with a desperate exertion, the bandage around its jaws– "how can you, Mr. Lackobreath, be so infernally cruel as to pinch me in that manner by the nose? Did you not see how they had fastened up my mouth– and you must know– if you know any thing– how vast a superfluity of breath I have to dispose of! If you do not know, however, sit down and you shall see. In my situation it is really a great relief to be able to open ones mouth– to be able to expatiate– to be able to communicate with a person like yourself, who do not think yourself called upon at every period to interrupt the thread of a gentleman's discourse. Interruptions are annoying and should undoubtedly be abolished– don't you think so?– no reply, I beg you,– one person is enough to be speaking at a time.– I shall be done by and by, and then you may begin.– How the devil sir, did you get into this place?– not a word I beseech you– been here some time myself– terrible accident!– heard of it, I suppose?– awful calamity!– walking under your windows– some short while ago– about the time you were stage–struck– horrible occurrence!– heard of "catching one's breath," eh?– hold your tongue I tell you!– I caught somebody elses!– had always too much of my own– met Blab at the corner of the street– wouldn't give me a chance for a word– couldn't get in a syllable edgeways– attacked, consequently, with epilepsis– Blab made his escape– damn all fools!– they took me up for dead, and put me in this place– pretty doings all of them!– heard all you said about me– every word a lie– horrible!– wonderful– outrageous!– hideous!– incompre-hensible!– et cetera– et cetera– et cetera– et cetera–"

It is impossible to conceive my astonishment at so unexpected a discourse, or the joy with which I became gradually convinced that the breath so fortunately caught by the gentleman (whom I soon recognized as my neighbor Windenough) was, in fact, the identical expiration mislaid by myself in the conversation with my wife. Time, place, and circum-stances rendered it a matter beyond question. I did not at least during the long period in which the inventor of Lombardy poplars continued to favor me with his explanations.

In this respect I was actuated by that habitual prudence which has ever been my predominating trait. I reflected that many difficulties might still lie in the path of my preservation which only extreme exertion on my part would be able to surmount. Many persons, I considered, are prone to estimate commodities in their possession– however valueless to the then proprietor– however troublesome, or distressing– in direct ratio with the advantages to be derived by others from their attainment, or by themselves from their abandonment. Might not this be the case with Mr. Windenough? In displaying anxiety for the breath of which he was at present so willing to get rid, might I not lay myself open to the exactions of his avarice? There are scoundrels in this world, I remembered with a sigh, who will not scruple to take unfair opportunities with even a next door neighbor, and (this remark is from Epictetus) it is precisely at that time when men are most anxious to throw off the burden of their own calamities that they feel the least desirous of relieving them in others.

Upon considerations similar to these, and still retaining my grasp upon the nose of Mr. W., I accordingly thought proper to model my reply.

"Monster!" I began in a tone of the deepest indignation– "monster and double–winded idiot!– dost thou, whom for thine iniquities it has pleased heaven to accurse with a two–fold respimtion– dost thou, I say, presume to address me in the familiar language of an old acquaintance?– 'I lie,' forsooth! and 'hold my tongue,' to be sure!– pretty conversation indeed, to a gentleman with a single breath!– all this, too, when I have it in my power to relieve the calamity under which thou dost so justly suffer– to curtail the superfluities of thine unhappy respiration."

Like Brutus, I paused for a reply– with which, like a tornado, Mr. Windenough immediately overwhelmed me. Protestation followed upon protestation, and apology upon apology. There were no terms with which he was unwilling to comply, and there were none of which I failed to take the fullest advantage.

Preliminaries being at length arranged, my acquaintance delivered me the respiration; for which (having carefully examined it) I gave him afterward a receipt.

I am aware that by many I shall be held to blame for speaking in a manner so cursory, of a transaction so impalpable. It will be thought that I should have entered more minutely, into the details of an occurrence by which– and this is very true– much new light might be thrown upon a highly interesting branch of physical philosophy.

To all this I am sorry that I cannot reply. A hint is the only answer which I am permitted to make. There were circumstances– but I think it much safer upon consideration to say as little as possible about an affair so delicate– so delicate, I repeat, and at the time involving the interests of a third party whose sulphurous resentment I have not the least desire, at this moment, of incurring.

We were not long after this necessary arrangement in effecting an escape from the dungeons of the sepulchre. The united strength of our resuscitated voices was soon sufficiently apparent. Scissors, the Whig editor, republished a treatise upon "the nature and origin of subterranean noises." A reply– rejoinder– confutation– and justification– followed in the columns of a Democratic Gazette. It was not until the opening of the vault to decide the controversy, that the appearance of Mr. Windenough and myself proved both parties to have been decidedly in the wrong.

I cannot conclude these details of some very singular passages in a life at all times sufficiently eventful, without again recalling to the attention of the reader the merits of that indiscriminate philosophy which is a sure and ready shield against those shafts of calamity which can neither be seen, felt nor fully understood. It was in the spirit of this wisdom that, among the ancient Hebrews, it was believed the gates of Heaven would be inevitably opened to that sinner, or saint, who, with good lungs and implicit confidence, should vociferate the word "Amen!" It was in the spirit of this wisdom that, when a great plague raged at Athens, and every means had been in vain attempted for its removal, Epimenides, as Laertius relates, in his second book, of that philosopher, advised the erection of a shrine and temple "to the proper God."

LYTTLETON BARRY.

FOUR BEASTS IN ONE –
THE HOMO – CAMELEOPARD

Chacun a ses vertus.

CREBILLON'S Xerxes.

ANTIOCHUS EPIPHANES is very generally looked upon as the Gog of the prophet Ezekiel. This honor is, however, more properly attributable to Cambyses, the son of Cyrus. And, indeed, the character of the Syrian monarch does by no means stand in need of any adventitious embellishment. His accession to the throne, or rather his usurpation of the sovereignty, a hundred and seventy–one years before the coming of Christ; his attempt to plunder the temple of Diana at Ephesus; his implacable hostility to the Jews; his pollution of the Holy of Holies; and his miserable death at Taba, after a tumultuous reign of eleven years, are circumstances of a prominent kind, and therefore more generally noticed by the historians of his time than the impious, dastardly, cruel, silly, and whimsical achievements which make up the sum total of his private life and reputation.

Let us suppose, gentle reader, that it is now the year of the world three thousand eight hundred and thirty, and let us, for a few minutes, imagine ourselves at that most grotesque habitation of man, the remarkable city of Antioch. To be sure there were, in Syria and other countries, sixteen cities of that appellation, besides the one to which I more particularly allude. But ours is that which went by the name of Antiochia Epidaphne, from its vicinity to the little village of Daphne, where stood a temple to that divinity. It was built (although about this matter there is some dispute) by Seleucus Nicanor, the first king of the country after Alexander the Great, in memory of his father Antiochus, and became immediately the residence of the Syrian monarchy. In the flourishing times of the Roman Empire, it was the ordinary station of the prefect of the eastern provinces; and many of the emperors of the queen city (among whom may be mentioned, especially, Verus and Valens) spent here the greater part of their time. But I perceive we have arrived at the city itself. Let us ascend this battlement, and throw our eyes upon the town and neighboring country.

"What broad and rapid river is that which forces its way, with innumerable falls, through the mountainous wilderness, and finally through the wilderness of buildings?"

That is the Orontes, and it is the only water in sight, with the exception of the Mediterranean, which stretches, like a broad mirror, about twelve miles off to the southward. Every one has seen the Mediterranean; but let me tell you, there are few who have had a peep at Antioch. By few, I mean, few who, like you and me, have had, at the same time, the advantages of a modern education. Therefore cease to regard that sea, and give your whole attention to the mass of houses that lie beneath us. You will remember that it is now the year of the world three thousand eight hundred and thirty. Were it later– for example, were it the year of our Lord eighteen hundred and forty–five, we should be deprived of this extraordinary spectacle. In the nineteenth century Antioch is– that is to say, Antioch will be– in a lamentable state of decay. It will have been, by that time, totally destroyed, at three different periods, by three successive earthquakes. Indeed, to say the truth, what little of its former self may then remain, will be found in so desolate and ruinous a state that the patriarch shall have removed his residence to Damascus. This is well. I see you profit by my advice, and are making the most of your time in inspecting the premises– in

> -satisfying your eyes
>   With the memorials and the things of fame
>   That most renown this city.-

I beg pardon; I had forgotten that Shakespeare will not flourish for seventeen hundred and fifty years to come. But does not the appearance of Epidaphne justify me in calling it grotesque?

"It is well fortified; and in this respect is as much indebted to nature as to art."

Very true.

"There are a prodigious number of stately palaces."

There are.

"And the numerous temples, sumptuous and magnificent, may bear comparison with the most lauded of antiquity."

All this I must acknowledge. Still there is an infinity of

mud huts, and abominable hovels. We cannot help perceiving abundance of filth in every kennel, and, were it not for the over–powering fumes of idolatrous incense, I have no doubt we should find a most intolerable stench. Did you ever behold streets so insufferably narrow, or houses so miraculously tall? What gloom their shadows cast upon the ground! It is well the swinging lamps in those endless colonnades are kept burning throughout the day; we should otherwise have the darkness of Egypt in the time of her desolation.

"It is certainly a strange place! What is the meaning of yonder singular building? See! it towers above all others, and lies to the eastward of what I take to be the royal palace."

That is the new Temple of the Sun, who is adored in Syria under the title of Elah Gabalah. Hereafter a very notorious Roman Emperor will institute this worship in Rome, and thence derive a cognomen, Heliogabalus. I dare say you would like to take a peep at the divinity of the temple. You need not look up at the heavens; his Sunship is not there– at least not the Sunship adored by the Syrians. That deity will be found in the interior of yonder building. He is worshipped under the figure of a large stone pillar terminating at the summit in a cone or pyramid, whereby is denoted Fire.

"Hark– behold!– who can those ridiculous beings be, half naked, with their faces painted, shouting and gesticulating to the rabble?"

Some few are mountebanks. Others more particularly belong to the race of philosophers. The greatest portion, however– those especially who belabor the populace with clubs– are the principal courtiers of the palace, executing as in duty bound, some laudable comicality of the king's.

"But what have we here? Heavens! the town is swarming with wild beasts! How terrible a spectacle!– how dangerous a peculiarity!"

Terrible, if you please; but not in the least degree dangerous. Each animal if you will take the pains to observe, is following, very quietly, in the wake of its master. Some few, to be sure, are led with a rope about the neck, but these are chiefly the lesser or timid species. The lion, the tiger, and the leopard are entirely without restraint. They have been trained without difficulty to their present profession, and attend upon their respective owners in the capacity of valets–de–chambre. It is true, there are occasions when Nature asserts her violated dominions;– but then the devouring of a man–at–arms, or the throttling of a consecrated bull, is a circumstance of too little moment to be more than hinted at in Epidaphne.

"But what extraordinary tumult do I hear? Surely this is a loud noise even for Antioch! It argues some commotion of unusual interest."

Yes– undoubtedly. The king has ordered some novel spectacle– some gladiatorial exhibition at the hippodrome– or perhaps the massacre of the Scythian prisoners– or the conflagration of his new palace– or the tearing down of a handsome temple– or, indeed, a bonfire of a few Jews. The uproar increases. Shouts of laughter ascend the skies. The air becomes dissonant with wind instruments, and horrible with clamor of a million throats. Let us descend, for the love of fun, and see what is going on! This way– be careful! Here we are in the principal street, which is called the street of Timarchus. The sea of people is coming this way, and we shall find a difficulty in stemming the tide. They are pouring through the alley of Heraclides, which leads directly from the palace;– therefore the king is most probably among the rioters. Yes;– I hear the shouts of the herald proclaiming his approach in the pompous phraseology of the East. We shall have a glimpse of his person as he passes by the temple of Ashimah. Let us ensconce ourselves in the vestibule of the sanctuary; he will be here anon. In the meantime let us survey this image. What is it? Oh! it is the god Ashimah in proper person. You perceive, however, that he is neither a lamb, nor a goat, nor a satyr, neither has he much resemblance to the Pan of the Arcadians. Yet all these appearances have been given– I beg pardon– will be given– by the learned of future ages, to the Ashimah of the Syrians. Put on your spectacles, and tell me what it is. What is it?

"Bless me! it is an ape!"

True– a baboon; but by no means the less a deity. His name is a derivation of the Greek Simia– what great fools are antiquarians! But see!– see!– yonder scampers a ragged little urchin. Where is he going? What is he bawling about? What does he say? Oh! he says the king is coming in triumph; that he is dressed in state; that he has just finished putting to death, with his own hand, a thousand chained Israelitish prisoners! For this exploit the ragamuffin is lauding him to the skies. Hark! here comes a troop of a similar description. They have made a Latin hymn upon the valor of the king, and are singing it as they go:

Mille, mille, mille,
Mille, mille, mille,
Decollavimus, unus homo!
Mille, mille, mille, mille, decollavimus!
Mille, mille, mille,
Vivat qui mille mille occidit!
Tantum vini habet nemo
Quantum sanguinis effudit![5]

Which may be thus paraphrased:

A thousand, a thousand, a thousand,
A thousand, a thousand, a thousand,
We, with one warrior, have slain!

A thousand, a thousand, a thousand, a thousand.

Sing a thousand over again!
Soho!- let us sing
Long life to our king,
Who knocked over a thousand so fine!
Soho!- let us roar,
He has given us more
Red gallons of gore
Than all Syria can furnish of wine!

[5] Flavius Vospicus says, that the hymn here introduced was sung by the rabble upon the occasion of Aurelian, in the Sarmatic war, having slain, with his own hand, nine hundred and fifty of the enemy.

"Do you hear that flourish of trumpets?"

Yes: the king is coming! See! the people are aghast with admiration, and lift up their eyes to the heavens in reverence. He comes;– he is coming;– there he is!

"Who?– where?– the king?– do not behold him– cannot say that I perceive him."

Then you must be blind.

"Very possible. Still I see nothing but a tumultuous mob of idiots and madmen, who are busy in prostrating themselves before a gigantic cameleopard, and endeavoring to obtain a kiss of the animal's hoofs. See! the beast has very justly kicked one of the rabble over– and another– and another– and another. Indeed, I cannot help admiring the animal for the excellent use he is making of his feet."

Rabble, indeed!– why these are the noble and free citizens of Epidaphne! Beasts, did you say?– take care that you are not overheard. Do you not perceive that the animal has the visage of a man? Why, my dear sir, that cameleopard is no other than Antiochus Epiphanes, Antiochus the Illustrious, King of Syria, and the most potent of all the autocrats of the East! It is true, that he is entitled, at times, Antiochus Epimanes– Antiochus the madman– but that is because all people have not the capacity to appreciate his merits. It is also certain that he is at present ensconced in the hide of a beast, and is doing his best to play the part of a cameleopard; but this is done for the better sustaining his dignity as king. Besides, the monarch is of gigantic stature, and the dress is therefore neither unbecoming nor over large. We may, however, presume he would not have adopted it but for some occasion of especial state. Such, you will allow, is the massacre of a thousand Jews. With how superior a dignity the monarch perambulates on all fours! His tail, you perceive, is held aloft by his two principal concubines, Elline and Argelais; and his whole appearance would be infinitely prepossessing, were it not for the protuberance of his eyes, which will certainly start out of his head, and the queer color of his face, which has become nondescript from the quantity of wine he has swallowed. Let us follow him to the hippodrome, whither he is proceeding, and listen to the song of triumph which he is commencing:

> Who is king but Epiphanes?
>   Say- do you know?
> Who is king but Epiphanes?
>   Bravo!- bravo!
> There is none but Epiphanes,
>   No- there is none:
> So tear down the temples,
>   And put out the sun!

Well and strenuously sung! The populace are hailing him 'Prince of Poets,' as well as 'Glory of the East,' 'Delight of the Universe,' and 'Most Remarkable of Cameleopards.' They have encored his effusion, and do you hear?– he is singing it over again. When he arrives at the hippodrome, he will be crowned with the poetic wreath, in anticipation of his victory at the approaching Olympics.

"But, good Jupiter! what is the matter in the crowd behind us?"

Behind us, did you say?– oh! ah!– I perceive. My friend, it is well that you spoke in time. Let us get into a place of safety as soon as possible. Here!– let us conceal ourselves in the arch of this aqueduct, and I will inform you presently of the origin of the commotion. It has turned out as I have been anticipating. The singular appearance of the cameleopard and the head of a man, has, it seems, given offence to the notions of propriety entertained, in general, by the wild animals domesticated in the city. A mutiny has been the result; and, as is usual upon such occasions, all human efforts will be of no avail in quelling the mob. Several of the Syrians have already been devoured; but the general voice of the four–footed patriots seems to be for eating up the cameleopard. 'The Prince of Poets,' therefore, is upon his hinder legs, running for his life. His courtiers have left him in the lurch, and his concubines have followed so excellent an example. 'Delight of the Universe,' thou art in a sad predicament! 'Glory of the East,' thou art in danger of mastication! Therefore never regard so piteously thy tail; it will undoubtedly be draggled in the mud, and for this there is no help. Look not behind thee, then, at its unavoidable degradation; but take courage, ply thy legs with vigor, and scud for the hippodrome! Remember that thou art Antiochus Epiphanes. Antiochus the Illustrious!– also 'Prince of Poets,' 'Glory of the East,' 'Delight of the Universe,' and 'Most Remarkable of Cameleopards!' Heavens! what a power of speed thou art displaying! What a capacity for leg–bail thou art developing! Run, Prince!– Bravo, Epiphanes! Well done, Cameleopard!– Glorious Antiochus!– He runs!– he leaps!– he flies! Like an arrow from a catapult he approaches the hippodrome! He leaps!– he shrieks!– he is there! This is well; for hadst thou, 'Glory of the East,' been half a second longer in reaching the gates of the Amphitheatre, there is not a bear's cub in Epidaphne that would not have had a nibble at thy carcase. Let us be off– let us take

Edgar Allan Poe

our departure!– for we shall find our delicate modern ears unable to endure the vast uproar which is about to commence in celebration of the king's escape! Listen! it has already commenced. See!– the whole town is topsy–turvy.

"Surely this is the most populous city of the East! What a wilderness of people! what a jumble of all ranks and ages! what a multiplicity of sects and nations! what a variety of costumes! what a Babel of languages! what a screaming of beasts! what a tinkling of instruments! what a parcel of philosophers!"

Come let us be off.

"Stay a moment! I see a vast hubbub in the hippodrome; what is the meaning of it, I beseech you?" That?– oh, nothing! The noble and free citizens of Epidaphne being, as they declare, well satisfied of the faith, valor, wisdom, and divinity of their king, and having, moreover, been eye–witnesses of his late superhuman agility, do think it no more than their duty to invest his brows (in addition to the poetic crown) with the wreath of victory in the footrace– a wreath which it is evident he must obtain at the celebration of the next Olympiad, and which, therefore, they now give him in advance.

THE DEVIL IN THE BELFRY

What o'clock is it?

Old Saying.

EVERYBODY knows, in a general way, that the finest place in the world is– or, alas, was– the Dutch borough of Vondervotteimittiss. Yet as it lies some distance from any of the main roads, being in a somewhat out–of–the–way situation, there are perhaps very few of my readers who have ever paid it a visit. For the benefit of those who have not, therefore, it will be only proper that I should enter into some account of it. And this is indeed the more necessary, as with the hope of enlisting public sympathy in behalf of the inhabitants, I design here to give a history of the calamitous events which have so lately occurred within its limits. No one who knows me will doubt that the duty thus self–imposed will be executed to the best of my ability, with all that rigid impartiality, all that cautious examination into facts, and diligent collation of authorities, which should ever distinguish him who aspires to the title of historian.

By the united aid of medals, manuscripts, and inscriptions, I am enabled to say, positively, that the borough of Vondervotteimittiss has existed, from its origin, in precisely the same condition which it at present preserves. Of the date of this origin, however, I grieve that I can only speak with that species of indefinite definiteness which mathematicians are, at times, forced to put up with in certain algebraic formulae. The date, I may thus say, in regard to the remoteness of its antiquity, cannot be less than any assignable quantity whatsoever.

Touching the derivation of the name Vondervotteimittiss, I confess myself, with sorrow, equally at fault. Among a multitude of opinions upon this delicate point– some acute, some learned, some sufficiently the reverse– I am able to select nothing which ought to be considered satisfactory. Perhaps the idea of Grogs-wigg– nearly coincident with that of Kroutaplenttey– is to be cautiously preferred.– It runs:– Vondervo-tteimittis– Vonder, lege Donder– Votteimittis, quasi und Bleitziz– Bleitziz obsol:– pro Blitzen." This derivative, to say the truth, is still countenanced by some traces of the electric fluid evident on the summit of the steeple of the House of the Town–Council. I do not choose, however, to commit myself on a theme of such importance, and must refer the reader desirous of information to the "Oratiunculae de Rebus Praeter–Veteris," of Dundergutz. See, also, Blunderbuzzard "De Derivationibus," pp. 27 to 5010, Folio, Gothic edit., Red and Black character, Catch–word and No Cypher; wherein consult, also, marginal notes in the autograph of Stuffundpuff, with the Sub–Commen-taries of Gruntundguzzell.

Notwithstanding the obscurity which thus envelops the date of the foundation of Vondervotteimittis, and the derivation of its name, there can be no doubt, as I said before, that it has always existed as we find it at this epoch. The oldest man in the borough can remember not the slightest difference in the appearance of any portion of it; and, indeed, the very suggestion of such a possibility is considered an insult. The site of the village is in a perfectly circular valley, about a quarter of a mile in circumference, and entirely surrounded by gentle hills, over whose summit the people have never yet ventured to pass. For this they assign the very good reason that they do not believe there is anything at all on the other side.

Round the skirts of the valley (which is quite level, and paved throughout with flat tiles), extends a continuous row of sixty little houses. These, having their backs on the hills, must look, of course, to the centre of the plain, which is just sixty yards from the front door of each dwelling. Every house has a small garden before it, with a circular path, a sun–dial, and twenty–four cabbages. The buildings themselves are so precisely alike, that one can in no manner be distinguished from the other. Owing to the vast antiquity, the style of architecture is somewhat odd, but it is not for that reason the less strikingly picturesque. They are fashioned of hard–burned little bricks, red, with black ends, so that the walls look like a chess–board upon a great scale. The gables are turned to the front, and there are cornices, as big as all the rest of the house, over the eaves and over the main doors. The windows are narrow and deep, with very tiny panes and a great deal of sash. On the roof is a vast quantity of tiles with long curly ears. The woodwork, throughout, is of a dark hue and there is much carving about it, with but a trifling variety of pattern for, time out of mind, the carvers of Vondervotteimittiss have never been able to carve more than two objects– a time–piece and a cabbage. But these they do exceedingly well, and intersperse them, with singular ingenuity, wherever they find room for the chisel.

The dwellings are as much alike inside as out, and the furniture is all upon one plan. The floors are of square tiles, the chairs and tables of black–looking wood with thin crooked legs and puppy feet. The mantelpieces are wide and high, and have not only time–pieces and cabbages sculptured over the front, but a real time–piece, which makes a prodigious ticking, on the top in the middle, with a flower–pot containing a cabbage standing on each extremity by way of outrider. Between each cabbage and the time–piece, again, is a little China man having a large stomach with a great round hole in it, through which is seen the dial–plate of a watch.

The fireplaces are large and deep, with fierce crooked–looking fire–dogs. There is constantly a rousing fire, and a huge pot over it, full of sauer–kraut and pork, to which the good woman of the house is always busy in attending. She is a little fat old lady, with blue eyes and a red face, and wears a huge cap like a sugar–loaf, ornamented with purple and yellow ribbons. Her dress is of orange–colored linsey–woolsey, made very full behind and very short in the waist– and indeed very short in other respects, not reaching below the middle of her leg. This is somewhat thick, and so are her ankles, but she has a fine pair of green stockings to cover them. Her shoes– of pink leather– are fastened each with a bunch of yellow ribbons puckered up in the shape of a cabbage. In her left hand she has a little heavy Dutch watch; in her right she wields a ladle for the sauerkraut and pork. By her side there stands a fat tabby cat, with a gilt toy–repeater tied to its tail, which "the boys" have there fastened by way of a quiz.

The boys themselves are, all three of them, in the garden attending the pig. They are each two feet in height. They have three–cornered cocked hats, purple waistcoats reaching down to their thighs, buckskin knee–breeches, red stockings, heavy shoes with big silver buckles, long surtout coats with large buttons of mother–of–pearl. Each, too, has a pipe in his mouth, and a little dumpy watch in his right hand. He takes a puff and a look, and then a look and a puff. The pig– which is corpulent and lazy– is occupied now in picking up the stray leaves that fall from the cabbages, and now in giving a kick behind at the gilt repeater, which the urchins have also tied to his tail in order to make him look as handsome as the cat.

Right at the front door, in a high–backed leather–bottomed armed chair, with crooked legs and puppy feet like the tables, is seated the old man of the house himself. He is an exceedingly puffy little old gentleman, with big circular eyes and a huge double chin. His dress resembles that of the boys– and I need say nothing farther about it. All the difference is, that his pipe is somewhat bigger than theirs and he can make a greater smoke. Like them, he has a watch, but he carries his watch in his pocket. To say the truth, he has something of more importance than a watch to attend to– and what that is, I shall presently explain. He sits with his right leg upon his left knee, wears a grave countenance, and always keeps one of his eyes, at least, resolutely bent upon a certain remarkable object in the centre of the plain.

This object is situated in the steeple of the House of the Town Council. The Town Council are all very little, round, oily, intelligent men, with big saucer eyes and fat double chins, and have their coats much longer and their shoe–buckles much bigger than the ordinary inhabitants of Vondervotteimittiss. Since my sojourn in the borough, they have had several special meetings, and have adopted these three important resolutions:

"That it is wrong to alter the good old course of things:"

"That there is nothing tolerable out of Vonder-votteimittiss:" and–

"That we will stick by our clocks and our cabbages."

Above the session–room of the Council is the steeple, and in the steeple is the belfry, where exists, and has existed time out of mind, the pride and wonder of the village– the great clock of the borough of Vonder-votteimittiss. And this is the object to which the eyes of the old gentlemen are turned who sit in the leather–bottomed arm–chairs.

The great clock has seven faces– one in each of the seven sides of the steeple– so that it can be readily seen from all quarters. Its faces are large and white, and its hands heavy and black. There is a belfry–man whose sole duty is to attend to it; but this duty is the most perfect of sinecures– for the clock of Vondervotteimittis was never yet known to have anything the matter with it. Until lately, the bare supposition of such a thing was considered heretical. From the remotest period of antiquity to which the archives have reference, the hours have been regularly struck by the big bell. And, indeed the case was just the same with all the other clocks and watches in the borough. Never was such a place for keeping the true time. When the large clapper thought proper to say

"Twelve o'clock!" all its obedient followers opened their throats simultaneously, and responded like a very echo. In short, the good burghers were fond of their sauer–kraut, but then they were proud of their clocks.

All people who hold sinecure offices are held in more or less respect, and as the belfry– man of Vondervotteimittiss has the most perfect of sinecures, he is the most perfectly respected of any man in the world. He is the chief dignitary of the borough, and the very pigs look up to him with a sentiment of reverence. His coat–tail is very far longer– his pipe, his shoe–buckles, his eyes, and his stomach, very far bigger– than those of any other old gentleman in the village; and as to his chin, it is not only double, but triple.

I have thus painted the happy estate of Vonder-votteimittiss: alas, that so fair a picture should ever experience a reverse!

There has been long a saying among the wisest inhabitants, that "no good can come from over the hills"; and it really seemed that the words had in them something of the spirit of prophecy. It wanted five minutes of noon, on the day before yesterday, when there appeared a very odd–looking object on the summit of the ridge of the eastward. Such an occurrence, of course, attracted universal attention, and every little old gentleman who sat in a leather–ottomed arm–chair turned onc of his eyes with a stare of dismay upon the phenomenon, still keeping the other upon the clock in the steeple.

By the time that it wanted only three minutes to noon, the droll object in question was perceived to be a very diminutive foreign–looking young man. He descended the hills at a great rate, so that every body had soon a good look at him. He was really the most finicky little personage that had ever been seen in Vonder-votteimittiss. His countenance was of a dark snuff–color, and he had a long hooked nose, pea eyes, a wide mouth, and an excellent set of teeth, which latter he seemed anxious of displaying, as he was grinning from ear to ear. What with mustachios and whiskers, there was none of the rest of his face to be seen. His head was uncovered, and his hair neatly done up in papillotes. His dress was a tight–fitting swallow–tailed black coat (from one of whose pockets dangled a vast length of white handkerchief), black kerseymere knee–breeches, black stockings, and stumpy–looking pumps, with huge bunches of black satin ribbon for bows. Under one arm he carried a huge chapeau–de–bras, and under the other a fiddle nearly five times as big as himself. In his left hand was a gold snuff–box, from which, as he capered down the hill, cutting all manner of fantastic steps, he took snuff incessantly with an air of the greatest possible self–satisfaction. God bless me!– here was a sight for the honest burghers of Vondervotteimittiss!

To speak plainly, the fellow had, in spite of his grinning, an audacious and sinister kind of face; and as he curvetted right into the village, the old stumpy appearance of his pumps excited no little suspicion; and many a burgher who beheld him that day would have given a trifle for a peep beneath the white cambric handkerchief which hung so obtrusively from the pocket of his swallow–tailed coat. But what mainly occasioned a righteous indignation was, that the scoundrelly popinjay, while he cut a fandango here, and a whirligig there, did not seem to have the remotest idea in the world of such a thing as keeping time in his steps.

The good people of the borough had scarcely a chance, however, to get their eyes thoroughly open, when, just as it wanted half a minute of noon, the rascal bounced, as I say, right into the midst of them; gave a chassez here, and a balancez there; and then, after a pirouette and a pas–de–zephyr, pigeon–winged himself right up into the belfry of the House of the Town Council, where the wonder–stricken belfry–man sat smoking in a state of dignity and dismay. But the little chap seized him at once by the nose; gave it a swing and a pull; clapped the big chapeau de–bras upon his head; knocked it down over his eyes and mouth; and then, lifting up the big fiddle, beat him with it so long and so soundly, that what with the belfry–man being so fat, and the fiddle being so hollow, you would have sworn that there was a regiment of double–bass drummers all beating the devil's tattoo up in the belfry of the steeple of Vondervotteimittiss.

There is no knowing to what desperate act of vengeance this unprincipled attack might have aroused the inhabitants, but for the important fact that it now wanted only half a second of noon. The bell was about to strike, and it was a matter of absolute and pre–eminent necessity that every body should look well at his watch. It was evident, however, that just at this moment the fellow in the steeple was doing something that he had no business to do with the clock. But as it now began to strike, nobody had any time to attend to his manoeuvres, for they had all to count the strokes of the bell as it sounded.

"One!" said the clock.

Edgar Allan Poe

"Von!" echoed every little old gentleman in every leather–bottomed arm–chair in Vondervotteimittiss. "Von!" said his watch also; "von!" said the watch of his vrow; and "von!" said the watches of the boys, and the little gilt repeaters on the tails of the cat and pig.

"Two!" continued the big bell; and

"Doo!" repeated all the repeaters.

"Three! Four! Five! Six! Seven! Eight! Nine! Ten!" said the bell.

"Dree! Vour! Fibe! Sax! Seben! Aight! Noin! Den!" answered the others.

"Eleven!" said the big one.

"Eleben!" assented the little ones.
"Twelve!" said the bell.

"Dvelf!" they replied perfectly satisfied, and dropping their voices.

"Und dvelf it is!" said all the little old gentlemen, putting up their watches. But the big bell had not done with them yet.

"Thirteen!" said he.

"Der Teufel!" gasped the little old gentlemen, turning pale, dropping their pipes, and putting down all their right legs from over their left knees.

"Der Teufel!" groaned they, "Dirteen! Dirteen!!– Mein Gott, it is Dirteen o'clock!!"

Why attempt to describe the terrible scene which ensued? All Vondervotteimittiss flew at once into a lamentable state of uproar.

"Vot is cum'd to mein pelly?" roared all the boys– "I've been ongry for dis hour!"

"Vot is com'd to mein kraut?" screamed all the vrows, "It has been done to rags for this hour!"

"Vot is cum'd to mein pipe?" swore all the little old gentlemen, "Donder and Blitzen; it has been smoked out for dis hour!"– and they filled them up again in a great rage, and sinking back in their arm–chairs, puffed away so fast and so fiercely that the whole valley was immediately filled with impenetrable smoke.

Meantime the cabbages all turned very red in the face, and it seemed as if old Nick himself had taken possession of every thing in the shape of a timepiece. The clocks carved upon the furniture took to dancing as if bewitched, while those upon the mantel–pieces could scarcely contain themselves for fury, and kept such a continual striking of thirteen, and such a frisking and wriggling of their pendulums as was really horrible to see. But, worse than all, neither the cats nor the pigs could put up any longer with the behavior of the little repeaters tied to their tails, and resented it by scampering all over the place, scratching and poking, and squeaking and screeching, and caterwauling and squalling, and flying into the faces, and running under the petticoats of the people, and creating altogether the most abominable din and confusion which it is possible for a reasonable person to conceive. And to make matters still more distressing, the rascally little scape–grace in the steeple was evidently exerting himself to the utmost. Every now and then one might catch a glimpse of the scoundrel through the smoke. There he sat in the belfry upon the belfry–man, who was lying flat upon his back. In his teeth the villain held the bell–rope, which he kept jerking about with his head, raising such a clatter that my ears ring again even to think of it. On his lap lay the big fiddle, at which he was scraping, out of all time and tune, with both hands, making a great show, the nincompoop! of playing "Judy O'Flannagan and Paddy O'Rafferty."

Affairs being thus miserably situated, I left the place in disgust, and now appeal for aid to all lovers of correct time and fine kraut. Let us proceed in a body to the borough, and restore the ancient order of things in Vondervotteimittiss by ejecting that little fellow from the steeple.

THREE SUNDAYS IN A WEEK

YOU hard–headed, dunder–headed, obstinate, rusty, crusty, musty, fusty, old savage!" said I, in fancy, one afternoon, to my grand uncle Rumgudgeon– shaking my fist at him in imagination.

Only in imagination. The fact is, some trivial discrepancy did exist, just then, between what I said and what I had not the courage to say– between what I did and what I had half a mind to do.

The old porpoise, as I opened the drawing–room door, was sitting with his feet upon the mantel–piece, and a bumper of port in his paw, making strenuous efforts to accomplish the ditty.

> Remplis ton verre vide!
> Vide ton verre plein!

"My dear uncle," said I, closing the door gently, and approaching him with the blandest of smiles, "you are always so very kind and considerate, and have evinced your benevolence in so many– so very many ways– that– that I feel I have only to suggest this little point to you once more to make sure of your full acquiescence."

"Hem!" said he, "good boy! go on!"

"I am sure, my dearest uncle [you confounded old rascal!], that you have no design really, seriously, to oppose my union with Kate. This is merely a joke of yours, I know– ha! ha! ha!– how very pleasant you are at times."

"Ha! ha! ha!" said he, "curse you! yes!"

"To be sure– of course! I knew you were jesting. Now, uncle, all that Kate and myself wish at present, is that you would oblige us with your advice as– as regards the time– you know, uncle– in short, when will it be most convenient for yourself, that the wedding shall– shall come off, you know?"

"Come off, you scoundrel!– what do you mean by that?– Better wait till it goes on."

"Ha! ha! ha!– he! he! he!– hi! hi! hi!– ho! ho! ho!– hu! hu! hu!– that's good!– oh that's capital– such a wit! But all we want just now, you know, uncle, is that you would indicate the time precisely."

"Ah!– precisely?"

"Yes, uncle– that is, if it would be quite agreeable to yourself."

"Wouldn't it answer, Bobby, if I were to leave it at random– some time within a year or so, for example?– must I say precisely?"

"If you please, uncle– precisely."

"Well, then, Bobby, my boy– you're a fine fellow, aren't you?– since you will have the exact time

I'll– why I'll oblige you for once:"

"Dear uncle!"

"Hush, sir!" [drowning my voice]– I'll oblige you for once. You shall have my consent– and the plum, we mus'n't forget the plum– let me see! when shall it be? To–day's Sunday– isn't it? Well, then, you shall be married precisely– precisely, now mind!– when three Sundays come together in a week! Do you hear me, sir! What are you gaping at? I say, you shall have Kate and her plum when three Sundays come together in a week– but not till then– you young scapegrace– not till then, if I die for it. You know me– I'm a man of my word– now be off!" Here he swallowed his bumper of port, while I rushed from the room in despair.

A very "fine old English gentleman," was my grand–uncle Rumgudgeon, but unlike him of the song, he had his weak points. He was a little, pursy, pompous, passionate semicircular somebody, with a red nose, a thick scull, [sic] a long purse, and a strong sense of his own consequence. With the best heart in the world, he contrived, through a predominant whim of contra–diction, to earn for himself, among those who only knew him superficially, the character of a curmudgeon. Like many excellent people, he seemed possessed with a spirit of tantalization, which might easily, at a casual glance, have been mistaken for malevolence. To every request, a positive "No!" was his immediate answer, but in the end– in the long, long end– there were exceedingly few requests which he refused. Against all attacks upon his purse he made the most sturdy defence; but the amount extorted from him, at last, was generally in direct ratio with the length of the siege and the stubbornness of the resistance. In charity no one gave more liberally or with a worse grace.

For the fine arts, and especially for the belles–lettres, he entertained a profound contempt. With this he had been inspired by Casimir Perier, whose pert little query "A quoi un poete est il bon?" he was in the habit of quoting, with a very droll pronunciation, as the ne plus ultra of logical wit. Thus my own inkling for the Muses had excited his entire displeasure. He assured me one day, when I asked him for a new copy of Horace, that the translation of "Poeta nascitur non fit" was "a nasty poet for nothing fit"– a remark which I took in high dudgeon. His repugnance to "the humanities" had, also, much increased of late, by an accidental bias in favor of what he supposed to be natural science. Somebody had accosted him in the street, mistaking him for no less a personage than Doctor Dubble L. Dee, the lecturer upon quack physics. This set him off at a tangent; and just at the epoch of this story– for story it is getting to be after all– my grand–uncle Rumgudgeon was accessible and pacific only upon points which happened to chime in with the caprioles of the hobby he was riding. For the rest, he laughed with his arms and legs, and his politics were stubborn and easily understood. He thought, with Horsley, that "the people have nothing to do with the laws but to obey them."

I had lived with the old gentleman all my life. My parents, in dying, had bequeathed me to him as a rich legacy. I believe the old villain loved me as his own child– nearly if not quite as well as he loved Kate– but it was a dog's existence that he led me, after all. From my first year until my fifth, he obliged me with very regular floggings. From five to fifteen, he threatened me, hourly, with the House of Correction. From fifteen to twenty, not a day passed in which he did not promise to cut me off with a shilling. I was a sad dog, it is true– but then it was a part of my nature– a point of my faith. In Kate, however, I had a firm friend, and I knew it. She was a good girl, and told me very sweetly that I might have her (plum and all) whenever I could badger my grand–uncle Rumgudgeon, into the necessary consent. Poor girl!– she was barely fifteen, and without this consent, her little amount in the funds was not come–at–able until five immeasurable summers had "dragged their slow length along." What, then, to do? At fifteen, or even at twenty–one [for I had now passed my fifth olympiad] five years in prospect are very much the same as five hundred. In vain we besieged the old gentleman with importunities. Here was a piece de resistance (as Messieurs Ude and Careme would say) which suited his perverse fancy to a T. It would have stiffed the indignation of Job himself, to see how much like an old mouser he behaved to us two poor wretched little mice. In his heart he wished for nothing more ardently than our union. He had made up his mind to this all along. In fact, he would have given ten thousand pounds from his own pocket (Kate's plum was her own) if he could have invented any thing like an excuse for complying with our very natural wishes. But then we had been so imprudent as to broach the subject ourselves. Not to oppose it under such circumstances, I sincerely believe, was not in his power.

I have said already that he had his weak points; but in speaking of these, I must not be understood as referring to his obstinacy: which was one of his strong points– "assurement ce n' etait pas sa foible." When I mention his weakness I have allusion to a bizarre old–womanish superstition which beset him. He was great in dreams, portents, et id genus omne of rigmarole. He was excessively punctilious, too, upon small points of honor, and, after his own fashion, was a man of his word, beyond doubt. This was, in fact, one of his hobbies. The spirit of his vows he made no scruple of setting at naught, but the letter was a bond inviolable. Now it was this latter peculiarity in his disposition, of which Kates ingenuity enabled us one fine day, not long after our interview in the dining–room, to take a very unexpected advantage, and, having thus, in the fashion of all modern bards and orators, exhausted in prolegomena, all the time at my command, and nearly all the room at my disposal, I will sum up in a few words what constitutes the whole pith of the story.

It happened then– so the Fates ordered it– that among the naval acquaintances of my betrothed, were two gentlemen who had just set foot upon the shores of England, after a year's absence, each, in foreign travel. In company with these gentlemen, my cousin and I, preconcertedly paid uncle Rumgudgeon a visit on the afternoon of Sunday, October the tenth,– just three weeks after the memorable decision which had so cruelly defeated our hopes. For about half an hour the conversation ran upon ordinary topics, but at last, we contrived, quite naturally, to give it the following turn: CAPT. PRATT. "Well I have been absent just one year.– Just one year to–day, as I live– let me see! yes!– this is October the tenth. You remember, Mr. Rumgudgeon, I called, this day year to bid you good–bye. And by the way, it does seem something like a coincidence, does it not– that our friend, Captain Smitherton, here, has been absent exactly a year also– a year to–day!"

SMITHERTON. "Yes! Just one year to a fraction.

You will remember, Mr. Rumgudgeon, that I called with Capt. Pratol on this very day, last year, to pay my parting respects."

UNCLE. "Yes, yes, yes– I remember it very well– very queer indeed! Both of you gone just one year. A very strange coincidence, indeed! Just what Doctor Dubble L. Dee would denominate an extraordinary concurrence of events. Doctor Dub–"

KATE. [Interrupting.] "To be sure, papa, it is something strange; but then Captain Pratt and Captain Smitherton didn't go altogether the same route, and that makes a difference, you know."

UNCLE. "I don't know any such thing, you huzzy! How should I? I think it only makes the matter more remarkable, Doctor Dubble L. Dee–

KATE. Why, papa, Captain Pratt went round Cape Horn, and Captain Smitherton doubled the Cape of Good Hope."

UNCLE. "Precisely!– the one went east and the other went west, you jade, and they both have gone quite round the world. By the by, Doctor Dubble L. Dee–

MYSELF. [Hurriedly.] "Captain Pratt, you must come and spend the evening with us to–morrow– you and Smitherton– you can tell us all about your voyage, and well have a game of whist and–

PRATT. "Wist, my dear fellow– you forget. To–morrow will be Sunday. Some other evening–

KATE. "Oh, no. fie!– Robert's not quite so bad as that.

To–day's Sunday."

PRATT. "I beg both your pardons– but I can't be so much mistaken. I know to–morrow's Sunday, be-cause–"

SMITHERTON. [Much surprised.] "What are you all thinking about? Wasn't yesterday, Sunday, I should like to know?"

ALL. "Yesterday indeed! you are out!"

UNCLE. "To–days Sunday, I say– don't I know?"

PRATT. "Oh no!– to–morrow's Sunday."

SMITHERTON. "You are all mad– every one of you. I am as positive that yesterday was Sunday as I am that I sit upon this chair."

KATE. [jumping up eagerly.] "I see it– I see it all. Papa, this is a judgment upon you, about– about you know what. Let me alone, and I'll explain it all in a minute. It's a very simple thing, indeed. Captain Smitherton says that yesterday was Sunday: so it was; he is right. Cousin Bobby, and uncle and I say that to–day is Sunday: so it is; we are right. Captain Pratt maintains that to–morrow will be Sunday: so it will; he is right, too. The fact is, we are all right, and thus three Sundays have come together in a week."

SMITHERTON. [After a pause.] "By the by, Pratt, Kate has us completely. What fools we two are! Mr. Rumgudgeon, the matter stands thus: the earth, you know, is twenty–four thousand miles in circumference. Now this globe of the earth turns upon its own axis– revolves– spins round– these twenty–four thousand miles of extent, going from west to east, in precisely twenty–four hours. Do you understand Mr. Rumgudgeon?–"

UNCLE. "To be sure– to be sure– Doctor Dub–"

SMITHERTON. [Drowning his voice.] "Well, sir; that is at the rate of one thousand miles per hour. Now, suppose that I sail from this position a thousand miles east. Of course I anticipate the rising of the sun here at London by just one hour. I see the sun rise one hour before you do. Proceeding, in the same direction, yet another thousand miles, I anticipate the rising by two hours– another thousand, and I anticipate it by three hours, and so on, until I go entirely round the globe, and back to this spot, when, having gone twenty–four thousand miles east, I anticipate the rising of the London sun by no less than twenty–four hours; that is to say, I am a day in advance of your time. Understand, eh?"

UNCLE. "But Double L. Dee–"

SMITHERTON. [Speaking very loud.] "Captain Pratt, on the contrary, when he had sailed a thousand miles west of this position, was an hour, and when he had sailed twenty–four thousand miles west, was twenty–four hours, or one day, behind the time at London. Thus, with me, yesterday was Sunday– thus, with you, to–day is Sunday– and thus, with Pratt, to–morrow will be Sunday. And what is more, Mr. Rumgudgeon, it is positively clear that we are all right; for there can be no philosophical reason assigned why the idea of one of us should have preference over that of the other."

UNCLE. "My eyes!– well, Kate– well, Bobby!– this is a judgment upon me, as you say. But I am a man of my word– mark that! you shall have her, boy, (plum and all), when you please. Done up, by Jove! Three Sundays all in a row! I'll go, and take Dubble L. Dee's opinion upon that."

NEVER BET THE DEVIL YOUR HEAD

A Tale With a Moral

CON tal que las costumbres de un autor," says Don
Thomas de las Torres, in the preface to his "Amatory
Poems" "sean puras y castas, importo muy poco que no
sean igualmente severas sus obras"– meaning, in plain
English, that, provided the morals of an author are pure
personally, it signifies nothing what are the morals of
his books. We presume that Don Thomas is now in
Purgatory for the assertion. It would be a clever thing,
too, in the way of poetical justice, to keep him there
until his "Amatory Poems" get out of print, or are laid
definitely upon the shelf through lack of readers. Every
fiction should have a moral; and, what is more to the
purpose, the critics have discovered that every fiction
has. Philip Melanchthon, some time ago, wrote a
commentary upon the "Batrachomyomachia," and
proved that the poet's object was to excite a distaste for
sedition. Pierre la Seine, going a step farther, shows
that the intention was to recommend to young men
temperance in eating and drinking. Just so, too,
Jacobus Hugo has satisfied himself that, by Euenis,
Homer meant to insinuate John Calvin; by Antinous,
Martin Luther; by the Lotophagi, Protestants in
general; and, by the Harpies, the Dutch. Our more
modern Scholiasts are equally acute. These fellows
demonstrate a hidden meaning in "The Antediluvians,"
a parable in Powhatan," new views in "Cock Robin,"

and transcendentalism in "Hop O' My Thumb." In short, it has been shown that no man can sit down to write without a very profound design. Thus to authors in general much trouble is spared. A novelist, for example, need have no care of his moral. It is there– that is to say, it is somewhere– and the moral and the critics can take care of themselves. When the proper time arrives, all that the gentleman intended, and all that he did not intend, will be brought to light, in the "Dial," or the "Down–Easter," together with all that he ought to have intended, and the rest that he clearly meant to intend:– so that it will all come very straight in the end.

There is no just ground, therefore, for the charge brought against me by certain ignoramuses– that I have never written a moral tale, or, in more precise words, a tale with a moral. They are not the critics predestined to bring me out, and develop my morals:– that is the secret. By and by the "North American Quarterly Humdrum" will make them ashamed of their stupidity. In the meantime, by way of staying execution– by way of mitigating the accusations against me– I offer the sad history appended,– a history about whose obvious moral there can be no question whatever, since he who runs may read it in the large capitals which form the title of the tale. I should have credit for this arrangement– a far wiser one than that of La Fontaine and others, who reserve the impression to be conveyed until the last moment, and thus sneak it in at the fag end of their fables.

Defuncti injuria ne afficiantur was a law of the twelve tables, and De mortuis nil nisi bonum is an excellent injunction– even if the dead in question be nothing but dead small beer. It is not my design, therefore, to vituperate my deceased friend, Toby Dammit. He was a sad dog, it is true, and a dog's death it was that he died; but he himself was not to blame for his vices. They grew out of a personal defect in his mother. She did her best in the way of flogging him while an infant– for duties to her well– regulated mind were always pleasures, and babies, like tough steaks, or the modern Greek olive trees, are invariably the better for beating– but, poor woman! she had the misfortune to be left–handed, and a child flogged left–handedly had better be left unflogged. The world revolves from right to left. It will not do to whip a baby from left to right. If each blow in the proper direction drives an evil propensity out, it follows that every thump in an opposite one knocks its quota of wickedness in. I was often present at Toby's chastisements, and, even by the way in which he kicked, I could perceive that he was getting worse and worse every day. At last I saw, through the tears in my eyes, that there was no hope of the villain at all, and one day when he had been cuffed until he grew so black in the face that one might have mistaken him for a little African, and no effect had been produced beyond that of making him wriggle himself into a fit, I could stand it no longer, but went down upon my knees forthwith, and, uplifting my voice, made prophecy of his ruin.

The fact is that his precocity in vice was awful. At five months of age he used to get into such passions that he was unable to articulate. At six months, I caught him gnawing a pack of cards. At seven months he was in the constant habit of catching and kissing the female babies. At eight months he peremptorily refused to put his signature to the Temperance pledge. Thus he went on increasing in iniquity, month after month, until, at the close of the first year, he not only insisted upon wearing moustaches, but had contracted a propensity for cursing and swearing, and for backing his assertions by bets.

Through this latter most ungentlemanly practice, the ruin which I had predicted to Toby Dammit overtook him at last. The fashion had "grown with his growth and strengthened with his strength," so that, when he came to be a man, he could scarcely utter a sentence without interlarding it with a proposition to gamble. Not that he actually laid wagers– no. I will do my friend the justice to say that he would as soon have laid eggs. With him the thing was a mere formula– nothing more. His expressions on this head had no meaning attached to them whatever. They were simple if not altogether innocent expletives– imaginative phrases wherewith to round off a sentence. When he said "I'll bet you so and so," nobody ever thought of taking him up; but still I could not help thinking it my duty to put him down. The habit was an immoral one, and so I told him. It was a vulgar one– this I begged him to believe. It was discountenanced by society– here I said nothing but the truth. It was forbidden by act of Congress– here I had not the slightest intention of telling a lie. I remonstrated– but to no purpose. I demonstrated– in vain. I entreated– he smiled. I implored– he laughed. I preached– he sneered. I threatened– he swore. I kicked him– he called for the police. I pulled his nose– he blew it, and offered to bet the Devil his head that I would not venture to try that experiment again.

 Poverty was another vice which the peculiar physical deficiency of Dammit's mother had entailed upon her son. He was detestably poor, and this was the reason, no doubt, that his expletive expressions about betting, seldom took a pecuniary turn. I will not be bound to say that I ever heard him make use of such a figure of speech as "I'll bet you a dollar." It was usually "I'll bet you what you please," or "I'll bet you what you dare," or "I'll bet you a trifle," or else, more significantly still, "I'll bet the Devil my head."

This latter form seemed to please him best;– perhaps because it involved the least risk; for Dammit had become excessively parsimonious. Had any one taken him up, his head was small, and thus his loss would have been small too. But these are my own reflections and I am by no means sure that I am right in attributing them to him. At all events the phrase in question grew daily in favor, notwithstanding the gross impropriety of a man betting his brains like bank–notes:– but this was a point which my friend's perversity of disposition would not permit him to comprehend. In the end, he abandoned all other forms of wager, and gave himself up to "I'll bet the Devil my head," with a pertinacity and exclusiveness of devotion that displeased not less than it surprised me. I am always displeased by circumstances for which I cannot account. Mysteries force a man to think, and so injure his health. The truth is, there was something in the air with which Mr. Dammit was wont to give utterance to his offensive expression– something in his manner of enunciation– which at first interested, and afterwards made me very uneasy– something which, for want of a more definite term at present, I must be permitted to call queer; but which Mr. Coleridge would have called mystical, Mr. Kant pantheistical, Mr. Carlyle twistical, and Mr. Emerson hyperquizzitistical. I began not to like it at all. Mr. Dammits soul was in a perilous state. I resolved to bring all my eloquence into play to save it. I vowed to serve him as St. Patrick, in the Irish chronicle, is said to have served the toad,– that is to say, "awaken him to a sense of his situation." I addressed myself to the task forthwith. Once more I betook myself to remonstrance. Again I collected my energies for a final attempt at expostulation.

When I had made an end of my lecture, Mr. Dammit indulged himself in some very equivocal behavior. For some moments he remained silent, merely looking me inquisitively in the face. But presently he threw his head to one side, and elevated his eyebrows to a great extent. Then he spread out the palms of his hands and shrugged up his shoulders. Then he winked with the right eye. Then he repeated the operation with the left. Then he shut them both up very tight. Then he opened them both so very wide that I became seriously alarmed for the consequences. Then, applying his thumb to his nose, he thought proper to make an indescribable movement with the rest of his fingers. Finally, setting his arms a–kimbo, he condescended to reply.

I can call to mind only the beads of his discourse. He would be obliged to me if I would hold my tongue. He wished none of my advice. He despised all my insinuations. He was old enough to take care of himself. Did I still think him baby Dammit? Did I mean to say any thing against his character? Did I intend to insult him? Was I a fool? Was my maternal parent aware, in a word, of my absence from the domiciliary residence? He would put this latter question to me as to a man of veracity, and he would bind himself to abide by my reply. Once more he would demand explicitly if my mother knew that I was out. My confusion, he said, betrayed me, and he would be willing to bet the Devil his head that she did not.

Mr. Dammit did not pause for my rejoinder. Turning upon his heel, he left my presence with undignified precipitation. It was well for him that he did so. My feelings had been wounded. Even my anger had been aroused. For once I would have taken him up upon his insulting wager. I would have won for the Arch–Enemy Mr. Dammit's little head– for the fact is, my mamma was very well aware of my merely temporary absence from home.

But Khoda shefa midehed– Heaven gives relief– as the Mussulmans say when you tread upon their toes. It was in pursuance of my duty that I had been insulted, and I bore the insult like a man. It now seemed to me, however, that I had done all that could be required of me, in the case of this miserable individual, and I resolved to trouble him no longer with my counsel, but to leave him to his conscience and himself. But although I forebore to intrude with my advice, I could not bring myself to give up his society altogether. I even went so far as to humor some of his less reprehensible propensities; and there were times when I found myself lauding his wicked jokes, as epicures do mustard, with tears in my eyes:– so profoundly did it grieve me to hear his evil talk.

One fine day, having strolled out together, arm in arm, our route led us in the direction of a river. There was a bridge, and we resolved to cross it. It was roofed over, by way of protection from the weather, and the archway, having but few windows, was thus very uncomfortably dark. As we entered the passage, the contrast between the external glare and the interior gloom struck heavily upon my spirits. Not so upon those of the unhappy Dammit, who offered to bet the Devil his head that I was hipped. He seemed to be in an unusual good humor. He was excessively lively– so much so that I entertained I know not what of uneasy suspicion. It is not impossible that he was affected with the transcendentals. I am not well enough versed, however, in the diagnosis of this disease to speak with decision upon the point; and unhappily there were none of my friends of the "Dial" present. I suggest the idea, nevertheless, because of a certain species of austere Merry–Andrewism which seemed to beset my poor friend, and caused him to make quite a Tom–Fool of himself. Nothing would serve him but wriggling and skipping about under and over every thing that came in his way; now shouting out, and now lisping out, all manner of odd little and big words, yet preserving the gravest face in the world all the time. I really could not make up my mind whether to kick or to pity him. At length, having passed nearly across the bridge, we approached the termination of the footway, when our progress was impeded by a turnstile of some height. Through this I made my way quietly, pushing it around as usual. But this turn would not serve the turn of Mr. Dammit. He insisted upon leaping the stile, and said he could cut a pigeon–wing over it in the air. Now this, conscientiously speaking, I did not think he could do. The best pigeon–winger over all kinds of style was my friend Mr. Carlyle, and as I knew he could not do it, I would not believe that it could be done by Toby Dammit. I therefore told him, in so many words, that he was a braggadocio, and could not do what he said. For this I had reason to be sorry afterward;– for he straightway offered to bet the Devil his head that he could.

I was about to reply, notwithstanding my previous resolutions, with some remonstrance against his impiety, when I heard, close at my elbow, a slight cough, which sounded very much like the ejaculation "ahem!" I started, and looked about me in surprise. My glance at length fell into a nook of the frame– work of the bridge, and upon the figure of a little lame old gentleman of venerable aspect. Nothing could be more reverend than his whole appearance; for he not only had on a full suit of black, but his shirt was perfectly clean and the collar turned very neatly down over a white cravat, while his hair was parted in front like a girl's. His hands were clasped pensively together over his stomach, and his two eyes were carefully rolled up into the top of his head.

Upon observing him more closely, I perceived that he wore a black silk apron over his small–clothes; and this was a thing which I thought very odd. Before I had time to make any remark, however, upon so singular a circumstance, he interrupted me with a second "ahem!"

To this observation I was not immediately prepared to reply. The fact is, remarks of this laconic nature are nearly unanswerable. I have known a Quarterly Review non–plussed by the word "Fudge!" I am not ashamed to say, therefore, that I turned to Mr. Dammit for assistance.

"Dammit," said I, "what are you about? don't you hear?– the gentleman says 'ahem!'" I looked sternly at my friend while I thus addressed him; for, to say the truth, I felt particularly puzzled, and when a man is particularly puzzled he must knit his brows and look savage, or else he is pretty sure to look like a fool.

"Dammit," observed I– although this sounded very much like an oath, than which nothing was further from my thoughts – "Dammit," I suggested – "the

Edgar Allan Poe

gentleman says 'ahem!'"

I do not attempt to defend my remark on the score of profundity; I did not think it profound myself; but I have noticed that the effect of our speeches is not always proportionate with their importance in our own eyes; and if I had shot Mr. D. through and through with a Paixhan bomb, or knocked him in the head with the "Poets and Poetry of America," he could hardly have been more discomfited than when I addressed him with those simple words: "Dammit, what are you about?– don't you hear?– the gentleman says 'ahem!'"

"You don't say so?" gasped he at length, after turning more colors than a pirate runs up, one after the other, when chased by a man–of–war. "Are you quite sure he said that? Well, at all events I am in for it now, and may as well put a bold face upon the matter. Here goes, then– ahem!"

At this the little old gentleman seemed pleased– God only knows why. He left his station at the nook of the bridge, limped forward with a gracious air, took Dammit by the hand and shook it cordially, looking all the while straight up in his face with an air of the most unadulterated benignity which it is possible for the mind of man to imagine.

"I am quite sure you will win it, Dammit," said he, with the frankest of all smiles, "but we are obliged to have a trial, you know, for the sake of mere form."

"Ahem!" replied my friend, taking off his coat, with a deep sigh, tying a pocket–handkerchief around his waist, and producing an unaccountable alteration in his countenance by twisting up his eyes and bringing down the corners of his mouth– "ahem!" And "ahem!" said he again, after a pause; and not another word more than "ahem!" did I ever know him to say after that. "Aha!" thought I, without expressing myself aloud– "this is quite a remarkable silence on the part of Toby Dammit, and is no doubt a consequence of his verbosity upon a previous occasion. One extreme induces another. I wonder if he has forgotten the many unanswerable questions which he propounded to me so fluently on the day when I gave him my last lecture? At all events, he is cured of the transcendentals."

"Ahem!" here replied Toby, just as if he had been reading my thoughts, and looking like a very old sheep in a revery.

The old gentleman now took him by the arm, and led him more into the shade of the bridge– a few paces back from the turnstile. "My good fellow," said he, "I make it a point of conscience to allow you this much run. Wait here, till I take my place by the stile, so that I may see whether you go over it handsomely, and transcendentally, and don't omit any flourishes of the pigeon–wing. A mere form, you know. I will say 'one, two, three, and away.' Mind you, start at the word 'away'" Here he took his position by the stile, paused a moment as if in profound reflection, then looked up and, I thought, smiled very slightly, then tightened the strings of his apron, then took a long look at Dammit, and finally gave the word as agreed upon–

One- two- three- and- away!

Punctually at the word "away," my poor friend set off in a strong gallop. The stile was not very high, like Mr. Lord's– nor yet very low, like that of Mr. Lord's reviewers, but upon the whole I made sure that he would clear it. And then what if he did not?– ah, that was the question– what if he did not? "What right," said I, "had the old gentleman to make any other gentleman jump? The little old dot–and–carry–one! who is he? If he asks me to jump, I won't do it, that's flat, and I don't care who the devil he is." The bridge, as I say, was arched and covered in, in a very ridiculous manner, and there was a most uncomfortable echo about it at all times– an echo which I never before so particularly observed as when I uttered the four last words of my remark.

But what I said, or what I thought, or what I heard, occupied only an instant. In less than five seconds from his starting, my poor Toby had taken the leap. I saw him run nimbly, and spring grandly from the floor of the bridge, cutting the most awful flourishes with his legs as he went up. I saw him high in the air, pigeon–winging it to admiration just over the top of the stile; and of course I thought it an unusually singular thing that he did not continue to go over. But the whole leap was the affair of a moment, and, before I had a chance to make any profound reflections, down came Mr. Dammit on the flat of his back, on the same side of the stile from which he had started. At the same instant I saw the old gentleman limping off at the top of his speed, having caught and wrapt up in his apron something that fell heavily into it from the darkness of the arch just over the turnstile. At all this I was much astonished; but I had no leisure to think, for Dammit lay particularly still, and I concluded that his feelings had been hurt, and that he stood in need of my assistance. I hurried up to him and found that he had received what might be termed a serious injury. The truth is, he had been deprived of his head, which after a close search I could not find anywhere; so I determined to take him home and send for the homoeopathists. In the meantime a thought struck me, and I threw open an adjacent window of the bridge, when the sad truth flashed upon me at once. About five feet just above the top of the turnstile, and crossing the arch of the foot–path so as to constitute a brace, there extended a flat iron bar, lying with its breadth horizontally, and forming one of a series that served to strengthen the structure throughout its extent. With the edge of this brace it appeared evident that the neck of my unfortunate friend had come precisely in contact.

He did not long survive his terrible loss. The homeopathists did not give him little enough physic, and what little they did give him he hesitated to take. So in the end he grew worse, and at length died, a lesson to all riotous livers. I bedewed his grave with my tears, worked a bar sinister on his family escutcheon, and, for the general expenses of his funeral, sent in my very moderate bill to the transcendentalists. The scoundrels refused to pay it, so I had Mr. Dammit dug up at once, and sold him for dog's meat.

WHY THE LITTLE FRENCHMAN WEARS HIS HAND IN A SLING

IT'S on my visiting cards sure enough (and it's them that's all o' pink satin paper) that inny gintleman that plases may behould the intheristhin words, "Sir Pathrick O'Grandison, Barronitt, 39 Southampton Row, Russell Square, Parrish o' Bloomsbury." And shud ye be wantin' to diskiver who is the pink of purliteness quite, and the laider of the hot tun in the houl city o' Lonon– why it's jist mesilf. And fait that same is no wonder at all at all (so be plased to stop curlin your nose), for every inch o' the six wakes that I've been a gintleman, and left aff wid the bogthrothing to take up wid the Barronissy, it's Pathrick that's been living like a houly imperor, and gitting the iddication and the graces. Och! and wouldn't it be a blessed thing for your spirrits if ye cud lay your two peepers jist, upon Sir Pathrick O'Grandison, Barronitt, when he is all riddy drissed for the hopperer, or stipping into the Brisky for the drive into the Hyde Park. But it's the illigant big figgur that I ave, for the rason o' which all the ladies fall in love wid me. Isn't it my own swate silf now that'll missure the six fut, and the three inches more nor that, in me stockins, and that am excadingly will proportioned all over to match? And it is ralelly more than three fut and a bit that there is, inny how, of the little ould furrener Frinchman that lives jist over the way, and that's a oggling and a goggling the houl day, (and bad luck to him,) at the purty widdy

Misthress Tracle that's my own nixt–door neighbor, (God bliss her!) and a most particuller frind and acquaintance? You percave the little spalpeen is summat down in the mouth, and wears his lift hand in a sling, and it's for that same thing, by yur lave, that I'm going to give you the good rason.

The truth of the houl matter is jist simple enough; for the very first day that I com'd from Connaught, and showd my swate little silf in the strait to the widdy, who was looking through the windy, it was a gone case althegither with the heart o' the purty Misthress Tracle. I percaved it, ye see, all at once, and no mistake, and that's God's truth. First of all it was up wid the windy in a jiffy, and thin she threw open her two peepers to the itmost, and thin it was a little gould spy–glass that she clapped tight to one o' them and divil may burn me if it didn't spake to me as plain as a peeper cud spake, and says it, through the spy–glass: "Och! the tip o' the mornin' to ye, Sir Pathrick O'Grandison, Barronitt, mavourneen; and it's a nate gintleman that ye are, sure enough, and it's mesilf and me forten jist that'll be at yur sarvice, dear, inny time o' day at all at all for the asking." And it's not mesilf ye wud have to be bate in the purliteness; so I made her a bow that wud ha' broken yur heart altegither to behould, and thin I pulled aff me hat with a flourish, and thin I winked at her hard wid both eyes, as much as to say, "True for you, yer a swate little crature, Mrs. Tracle, me darlint, and I wish I may be drownthed dead in a bog, if it's not mesilf, Sir Pathrick O'Grandison, Barronitt, that'll make a houl bushel o' love to yur leddyship, in the twinkling o' the eye of a Londonderry purraty."

And it was the nixt mornin', sure, jist as I was making up me mind whither it wouldn't be the purlite thing to

sind a bit o' writin' to the widdy by way of a love–
litter, when up com'd the delivery servant wid an
illigant card, and he tould me that the name on it (for I
niver could rade the copperplate printin on account of
being lift handed) was all about Mounseer, the Count,
A Goose, Look– aisy, Maiter–di–dauns, and that the
houl of the divilish lingo was the spalpeeny long name
of the little ould furrener Frinchman as lived over the
way.

And jist wid that in cum'd the little willian himself, and
then he made me a broth of a bow, and thin he said he
had ounly taken the liberty of doing me the honor of
the giving me a call, and thin he went on to palaver at a
great rate, and divil the bit did I comprehind what he
wud be afther the tilling me at all at all, excipting and
saving that he said "pully wou, woolly wou," and tould
me, among a bushel o' lies, bad luck to him, that he
was mad for the love o' my widdy Misthress Tracle,
and that my widdy Mrs. Tracle had a puncheon for
him.

At the hearin' of this, ye may swear, though, I was as
mad as a grasshopper, but I remimbered that I was Sir
Pathrick O'Grandison, Barronitt, and that it wasn't
althegither gentaal to lit the anger git the upper hand o'
the purliteness, so I made light o' the matter and kipt
dark, and got quite sociable wid the little chap, and
afther a while what did he do but ask me to go wid him
to the widdy's, saying he wud give me the feshionable
inthroduction to her leddyship.

"Is it there ye are?" said I thin to mesilf, "and it's thrue
for you, Pathrick, that ye're the fortunittest mortal in
life. We'll soon see now whither it's your swate silf, or
whither it's little Mounseer Maiter–di–dauns, that

Misthress Tracle is head and ears in the love wid."

Wid that we wint aff to the widdy's, next door, and ye may well say it was an illigant place; so it was. There was a carpet all over the floor, and in one corner there was a forty–pinny and a Jew's harp and the divil knows what ilse, and in another corner was a sofy, the beautifullest thing in all natur, and sitting on the sofy, sure enough, there was the swate little angel, Misthress Tracle.

"The tip o' the mornin' to ye," says I, "Mrs. Tracle," and thin I made sich an illigant obaysance that it wud ha quite althegither bewildered the brain o' ye. "Wully woo, pully woo, plump in the mud," says the little furrenner Frinchman, "and sure Mrs. Tracle," says he, that he did, "isn't this gintleman here jist his reverence Sir Pathrick O'Grandison, Barronitt, and isn't he althegither and entirely the most particular frind and acquaintance that I have in the houl world?"

And wid that the widdy, she gits up from the sofy, and makes the swatest curthchy nor iver was seen; and thin down she sits like an angel; and thin, by the powers, it was that little spalpeen Mounseer Maiter–di–dauns that plumped his silf right down by the right side of her. Och hon! I ixpicted the two eyes o' me wud ha cum'd out of my head on the spot, I was so dispirate mad! Howiver, "Bait who!" says I, after awhile. "Is it there ye are, Mounseer Maiter–di–dauns?" and so down I plumped on the lift side of her leddyship, to be aven with the willain. Botheration! it wud ha done your heart good to percave the illigant double wink that I gived her jist thin right in the face with both eyes.

But the little ould Frinchman he niver beginned to

suspict me at all at all, and disperate hard it was he made the love to her leddyship. "Woully wou," says he, Pully wou," says he, "Plump in the mud," says he.

"That's all to no use, Mounseer Frog, mavourneen," thinks I; and I talked as hard and as fast as I could all the while, and throth it was mesilf jist that divarted her leddyship complately and intirely, by rason of the illigant conversation that I kipt up wid her all about the dear bogs of Connaught. And by and by she gived me such a swate smile, from one ind of her mouth to the ither, that it made me as bould as a pig, and I jist took hould of the ind of her little finger in the most dillikitest manner in natur, looking at her all the while out o' the whites of my eyes.

And then ounly percave the cuteness of the swate angel, for no sooner did she obsarve that I was afther the squazing of her flipper, than she up wid it in a jiffy, and put it away behind her back, jist as much as to say, "Now thin, Sir Pathrick O'Grandison, there's a bitther chance for ye, mavourneen, for it's not altogether the gentaal thing to be afther the squazing of my flipper right full in the sight of that little furrenner Frinchman, Mounseer Maiter–di–dauns."

Wid that I giv'd her a big wink jist to say, "lit Sir Pathrick alone for the likes o' them thricks," and thin I wint aisy to work, and you'd have died wid the divarsion to behould how cliverly I slipped my right arm betwane the back o' the sofy, and the back of her leddyship, and there, sure enough, I found a swate little flipper all a waiting to say, "the tip o' the mornin' to ye, Sir Pathrick O'Grandison, Barronitt." And wasn't it mesilf, sure, that jist giv'd it the laste little bit of a squaze in the world, all in the way of a commincement, and not to be too rough wid her leddyship? and och, botheration, wasn't it the gentaalest and dilikittest of all the little squazes that I got in return? "Blood and thunder, Sir Pathrick, mavourneen," thinks I to mesilf, "fait it's jist the mother's son of you, and nobody else at all at all, that's the handsomest and the fortunittest young bog–throtter that ever cum'd out of Connaught!" And with that I givd the flipper a big squaze, and a big squaze it was, by the powers, that her leddyship giv'd to me back. But it would ha split the seven sides of you wid the laffin' to behould, jist then all at once, the consated behavior of Mounseer Maiter–di–dauns. The likes o' sich a jabbering, and a smirking, and a parley–wouing as he begin'd wid her leddyship, niver was known before upon arth; and divil may burn me if it wasn't me own very two peepers that cotch'd him tipping her the wink out of one eye. Och, hon! if it wasn't mesilf thin that was mad as a Kilkenny cat I shud like to be tould who it was!

"Let me infarm you, Mounseer Maiter–di–dauns," said I, as purlite as iver ye seed, "that it's not the gintaal thing at all at all, and not for the likes o' you inny how, to be afther the oggling and a goggling at her leddyship in that fashion," and jist wid that such another squaze as it was I giv'd her flipper, all as much as to say, "isn't it Sir Pathrick now, my jewel, that'll be able to the proticting o' you, my darlint?" and then there cum'd another squaze back, all by way of the answer. "Thrue for you, Sir Pathrick," it said as plain as iver a squaze said in the world, "Thrue for you, Sir Pathrick, mavourneen, and it's a proper nate gintleman ye are–that's God's truth," and with that she opened her two beautiful peepers till I belaved they wud ha' cum'd out of her hid althegither and intirely, and she looked first as mad as a cat at Mounseer Frog, and thin as smiling as all out o' doors at mesilf.

"Thin," says he, the willian, "Och hon! and a wolly–
wou, pully–wou," and then wid that he shoved up his
two shoulders till the divil the bit of his hid was to be
diskivered, and then he let down the two corners of his
purraty–trap, and thin not a haporth more of the
satisfaction could I git out o' the spalpeen.

Belave me, my jewel, it was Sir Pathrick that was
unreasonable mad thin, and the more by token that the
Frinchman kipt an wid his winking at the widdy; and
the widdy she kept an wid the squazing of my flipper,
as much as to say, "At him again, Sir Pathrick
O'Grandison, mavourneen:" so I just ripped out wid a
big oath, and says I;

"Ye little spalpeeny frog of a bog–throtting son of a
bloody noun!"– and jist thin what d'ye think it was that
her leddyship did? Troth she jumped up from the sofy
as if she was bit, and made off through the door, while
I turned my head round afther her, in a complate
bewilderment and botheration, and followed her wid
me two peepers. You percave I had a reason of my
own for knowing that she couldn't git down the stares
althegither and intirely; for I knew very well that I had
hould of her hand, for the divil the bit had I iver lit it
go. And says I; "Isn't it the laste little bit of a mistake
in the world that ye've been afther the making, yer
leddyship? Come back now, that's a darlint, and I'll
give ye yur flipper." But aff she wint down the stairs
like a shot, and thin I turned round to the little Frinch
furrenner. Och hon! if it wasn't his spalpeeny little paw
that I had hould of in my own– why thin– thin it
wasn't– that's all.

And maybe it wasn't mesilf that jist died then outright wid the laffin', to behold the little chap when he found out that it wasn't the widdy at all at all that he had had hould of all the time, but only Sir Pathrick O'Grandison. The ould divil himself niver behild sich a long face as he pet an! As for Sir Pathrick O'Grandison, Barronitt, it wasn't for the likes of his riverence to be afther the minding of a thrifle of a mistake. Ye may jist say, though (for it's God's thruth), that afore I left hould of the flipper of the spalpeen (which was not till afther her leddyship's futman had kicked us both down the stairs, I giv'd it such a nate little broth of a squaze as made it all up into raspberry jam.

"Woully wou," says he, "pully wou," says he– "Cot tam!"

And that's jist the thruth of the rason why he wears his lift hand in a sling.

LITTLETON BARRY.

THE ANGEL OF THE ODD –
AN EXTRAVAGANZA

IT WAS a chilly November afternoon. I had just consummated an unusually hearty dinner, of which the dyspeptic truffe formed not the least important item, and was sitting alone in the dining–room, with my feet upon the fender, and at my elbow a small table which I had rolled up to the fire, and upon which were some apologies for dessert, with some miscellaneous bottles of wine, spirit, and liqueur. In the morning I had been reading Glover's "Leonidas," Wilkies "Epigoniad," Lamartine's "Pilgrimage," Barlow's "Columbiad," Tuckermann's "Sicily," and Griswold's "Curiosities"; I am willing to confess, therefore, that I now felt a little stupid. I made effort to arouse myself by aid of frequent Lafitte, and, all failing, I betook myself to a stray newspaper in despair. Having carefully perused the column of "houses to let," and the column of "dogs lost," and then the two columns of "wives and apprentices runaway," I attacked with great resolution the editorial matter, and, reading it from beginning to end without understanding a syllable, conceived the possibility of its being Chinese, and so re–read it from the end to the beginning, but with no more satisfactory result. I was about throwing away, in disgust,

> This folio of four pages, happy work
> Which not even poets criticise,

when I felt my attention somewhat aroused by the paragraph which follows:

"The avenues to death are numerous and strange. A London paper mentions the decease of a person from a singular cause. He was playing at 'puff the dart,' which is played with a long needle inserted in some worsted, and blown at a target through a tin tube. He placed the needle at the wrong end of the tube, and drawing his breath strongly to puff the dart forward with force, drew the needle into his throat. It entered the lungs, and in a few days killed him."

Upon seeing this I fell into a great rage, without exactly knowing why. "This thing," I exclaimed, "is a contemptible falsehood– a poor hoax– the lees of the invention of some pitiable penny–a–liner– of some wretched concoctor of accidents in Cocaigne. These fellows, knowing the extravagant gullibility of the age, set their wits to work in the imagination of improbable possibilities– of odd accidents, as they term them; but to a reflecting intellect (like mine," I added, in parenthesis, putting my forefinger unconsciously to the side of my nose), "to a contemplative understanding such as I myself possess, it seems evident at once that the marvelous increase of late in these 'odd accidents' is by far the oddest accident of all. For my own part, I intend to believe nothing henceforward that has anything of the 'singular' about it.

"Mein Gott, den, vat a vool you bees for dat!" replied one of the most remarkable voices I ever heard. At first I took it for a rumbling in my ears– such as man sometimes experiences when getting very drunk– but, upon second thought, I considered the sound as more nearly resembling that which proceeds from an empty barrel beaten with a big stick; and, in fact, this I should have concluded it to be, but for the articulation of the syllables and words. I am by no means naturally nervous, and the very few glasses of Lafitte which I had sipped served to embolden me a little, so that I felt nothing of trepidation, but merely uplifted my eyes with a leisurely movement, and looked carefully around the room for the intruder. I could not, however, perceive any one at all.

"Humph!" resumed the voice, as I continued my survey, "you mus pe so dronk as de pig, den, for not zee me as I zit here at your zide."

Hereupon I bethought me of looking immediately before my nose, and there, sure enough, confronting me at the table sat a personage nondescript, although not altogether indescribable. His body was a wine–pipe, or a rum–puncheon, or something of that character, and had a truly Falstaffian air. In its nether extremity were inserted two kegs, which seemed to answer all the purposes of legs. For arms there dangled from the upper portion of the carcass two tolerably long bottles, with the necks outward for hands. All the head that I saw the monster possessed of was one of those Hessian canteens which resemble a large snuff–box with a hole in the middle of the lid. This canteen (with a funnel on its top, like a cavalier cap slouched over the eyes) was set on edge upon the puncheon, with the hole toward myself; and through this hole, which seemed puckered up like the mouth of a very precise old maid, the creature was emitting certain rumbling and grumbling noises which he evidently intended for intelligible talk.

"I zay," said he, "you mos pe dronk as de pig, vor zit

dare and not zee me zit ere; and I zay, doo, you most pe pigger vool as de goose, vor to dispelief vat iz print in de print. 'Tiz de troof–dat it iz– eberry vord ob it."

"Who are you, pray?" said I, with much dignity, although somewhat puzzled; "how did you get here? and what is it you are talking about?"

"Az vor ow I com'd ere," replied the figure, "dat iz none of your pizzness; and as vor vat I be talking apout, I be talk apout vot I tink proper; and as vor who I be, vy dat is de very ting I com'd here for to let you zee for yourzelf."

"You are a drunken vagabond," said I, "and I shall ring the bell and order my footman to kick you into the street."

"He! he! he!" said the fellow, "hu! hu! hu! dat you can't do."

"Can't do!" said I, "what do you mean?– can't do what?"

"Ring de pell," he replied, attempting a grin with his little villainous mouth.

Upon this I made an effort to get up, in order to put my threat into execution; but the ruffian just reached across the table very deliberately, and hitting me a tap on the forehead with the neck of one of the long bottles, knocked me back into the arm–chair from which I had half arisen. I was utterly astounded; and, for a moment, was quite at a loss what to do. In the meantime, he continued his talk.

Edgar Allan Poe

"You zee," said he, "it iz te bess vor zit still; and now you shall know who I pe. Look at me! zee! I am te Angel ov te Odd!"

"And odd enough, too," I ventured to reply; "but I was always under the impression that an angel had wings."

"Te wing!" he cried, highly incensed, "vat I pe do mit te wing? Mein Gott! do you take me vor a shicken?"

"No– oh, no!" I replied, much alarmed, "you are no chicken– certainly not."

"Well, den, zit still and pehabe yourself, or I'll rap you again mid me vist. It iz te shicken ab te wing, und te owl ab te wing, und te imp ab te wing, und te headteuffel ab te wing. Te angel ab not te wing, and I am te Angel ov te Odd."

"And your business with me at present is– is–"

"My pizzness!" ejaculated the thing, "vy vot a low bred puppy you mos pe vor to ask a gentleman und an angel apout his pizzness!"

This language was rather more than I could bear, even from an angel; so, plucking up courage, I seized a salt-cellar which lay within reach, and hurled it at the head of the intruder. Either he dodged, however, or my aim was inaccurate; for all I accomplished was the demolition of the crystal which protected the dial of the clock upon the mantelpiece. As for the Angel, he evinced his sense of my assault by giving me two or three hard consecutive raps upon the forehead as before. These reduced me at once to submission, and I am almost ashamed to confess that, either through pain or vexation, there came a few tears into my eyes.

"Mein Gott!" said the Angel of the Odd, apparently much softened at my distress; "mein Gott, te man is eder ferry dronck or ferry sorry. You mos not trink it so strong– you mos put de water in te wine. Here, trink dis, like a goot veller, und don't gry now– don't!"

Hereupon the Angel of the Odd replenished my goblet (which was about a third full of Port) with a colorless fluid that he poured from one of his hand bottles. I observed that these bottles had labels about their necks, and that these labels were inscribed "Kirschenwasser."

The considerate kindness of the Angel mollified me in no little measure; and, aided by the water with which he diluted my Port more than once, I at length regained sufficient temper to listen to his very extraordinary discourse. I cannot pretend to recount all that he told me, but I gleaned from what he said that he was the genius who presided over the contre temps of mankind, and whose business it was to bring about the odd accidents which are continually astonishing the skeptic. Once or twice, upon my venturing to express my total incredulity in respect to his pretensions, he grew very angry indeed, so that at length I considered it the wiser policy to say nothing at all, and let him have his own way. He talked on, therefore, at great length, while I merely leaned back in my chair with my eyes shut, and amused myself with munching raisins and flipping the stems about the room. But, by and bye, the Angel suddenly construed this behavior of mine into contempt. He arose in a terrible passion, slouched his funnel down over his eyes, swore a vast oath, uttered a threat of some character which I did not precisely comprehend, and finally made me a low bow and departed, wishing me, in the language of the archbishop in Gil–Blas, "beaucoup de bonheur et un peu plus de bon sens."

His departure afforded me relief. The very few glasses of Lafitte that I had sipped had the effect of rendering me drowsy, and I felt inclined to take a nap of some fifteen or twenty minutes, as is my custom after dinner. At six I had an appointment of consequence, which it was quite indispensable that I should keep. The policy of insurance for my dwelling house had expired the day before; and, some dispute having arisen, it was agreed that, at six, I should meet the board of directors of the company and settle the terms of a renewal. Glancing upward at the clock on the mantel–piece (for I felt too drowsy to take out my watch), I had the pleasure to find that I had still twenty–five minutes to spare. It was half past five; I could easily walk to the insurance office in five minutes; and my usual post prandian siestas had never been known to exceed five and twenty. I felt sufficiently safe, therefore, and composed myself to my slumbers forthwith.

Having completed them to my satisfaction, I again looked toward the time–piece, and was half inclined to believe in the possibility of odd accidents when I found that, instead of my ordinary fifteen or twenty minutes, I had been dozing only three; for it still wanted seven and twenty of the appointed hour. I betook myself again to my nap, and at length a second time awoke, when, to my utter amazement, it still wanted twenty–seven minutes of six. I jumped up to examine the clock, and found that it had ceased running. My watch informed me that it was half past seven; and, of course, having slept two hours, I was too late for my appointment "It will make no difference," I said; "I can call at the office in the morning and apologize; in the meantime what can be the matter with the clock?" Upon examining it I discovered that one of the raisin–stems which I had been flipping about the room during the discourse of the Angel of the Odd had flown through the fractured crystal, and lodging, singularly enough, in the key–hole, with an end projecting outward, had thus arrested the revolution of the minute–hand.

"Ah!" said I; "I see how it is. This thing speaks for itself. A natural accident, such as will happen now and then!"

I gave the matter no further consideration, and at my usual hour retired to bed. Here, having placed a candle upon a reading–stand at the bed–head, and having made an attempt to peruse some pages of the "Omni - presence of the Deity," I unfortunately fell asleep in less than twenty seconds, leaving the light burning as it was.

My dreams were terrifically disturbed by visions of the Angel of the Odd. Methought he stood at the foot of the couch, drew aside the curtains, and, in the hollow, detestable tones of a rum–puncheon, menaced me with the bitterest vengeance for the contempt with which I had treated him. He concluded a long harrangue by taking off his funnelcap, inserting the tube into my gullet, and thus deluging me with an ocean of Kirsch–enwasser, which he poured, in a continuous flood, from one of the long–necked bottles that stood him instead of an arm. My agony was at length insufferable, and I awoke just in time to perceive that a rat had ran off with the lighted candle from the stand, but not in season to prevent his making his escape with it through the hole. Very soon, a strong suffocating odor assailed my nostrils; the house, I clearly perceived, was on fire. In a few minutes the blaze broke forth with violence, and in an incredibly brief period the entire building was wrapped in flames. All egress from my chamber, except through a window, was cut off. The crowd, however, quickly procured and raised a long ladder. By means of this I was descending rapidly, and in apparent safety, when a huge hog, about whose rotund stomach, and indeed about whose whole air and physiognomy, there was something which reminded me of the Angel of the Odd,– when this hog, I say, which hitherto had been quietly slumbering in the mud, took it suddenly into his head that his left shoulder needed scratching, and could find no more convenient rubbing post than that afforded by the foot of the ladder. In an instant I was precipitated, and had the misfortune to fracture my arm.

This accident, with the loss of my insurance, and with the more serious loss of my hair, the whole of which had been singed off by the fire, predisposed me to serious impressions, so that, finally, I made up my mind to take a wife. There was a rich widow disconsolate for the loss of her seventh husband, and to her wounded spirit I offered the balm of my vows. She yielded a reluctant consent to my prayers. I knelt at her feet in gratitude and adoration. She blushed, and bowed her luxuriant tresse into close contact with those supplied me, temporarily, by Grandjean. I know not how the entanglement took place, but so it was. I arose with a shining pate, wigless, she in disdain and wrath, half buried in alien hair. Thus ended my hopes of the widow by an accident which could not have been anticipated, to be sure, but which the natural sequence of events had brought about.

Without despairing, however, I undertook the siege of a less implacable heart. The fates were again propitious for a brief period; but again a trivial incident interfered. Meeting my betrothed in an avenue thronged with the elite of the city, I was hastening to greet her with one of my best considered bows, when a small particle of some foreign matter lodging in the corner of my eye, rendered me, for the moment, completely blind. Before I could recover my sight, the lady of my love had disappeared– irreparably affronted at what she chose to consider my premeditated rudeness in passing her by ungreeted. While I stood bewildered at the suddenness of this accident (which might have happened, nevertheless, to any one under the sun), and while I still continued incapable of sight, I was accosted by the Angel of the Odd, who proffered me his aid with a civility which I had no reason to expect. He examined my disordered eye with much gentleness and skill, informed me that I had a drop in it, and (whatever a "drop" was) took it out, and afforded me relief.

I now considered it time to die, (since fortune had so determined to persecute me,) and accordingly made my way to the nearest river. Here, divesting myself of my clothes, (for there is no reason why we cannot die as we were born,) I threw myself headlong into the current; the sole witness of my fate being a solitary crow that had been seduced into the eating of brandy– saturated corn, and so had staggered away from his fellows. No sooner had I entered the water than this bird took it into its head to fly away with the most indispensable portion of my apparel. Postponing, therefore, for the present, my suicidal design, I just slipped my nether extremities into the sleeves of my coat, and betook myself to a pursuit of the felon with all the nimbleness which the case required and its circumstances would admit. But my evil destiny attended me still. As I ran at full speed, with my nose up in the atmosphere, and intent only upon the purloiner of my property, I suddenly perceived that my feet rested no longer upon terre firma; the fact is, I had thrown myself over a precipice, and should inevitably have been dashed to pieces, but for my good fortune in grasping the end of a long guide–rope, which descended from a passing balloon.

As soon as I sufficiently recovered my senses to comprehend the terrific predicament in which I stood or rather hung, I exerted all the power of my lungs to make that predicament known to the aeronaut overhead. But for a long time I exerted myself in vain. Either the fool could not, or the villain would not perceive me. Meantime the machine rapidly soared, while my strength even more rapidly failed. I was soon upon the point of resigning myself to my fate, and dropping quietly into the sea, when my spirits were suddenly revived by hearing a hollow voice from above, which seemed to be lazily humming an opera air. Looking up, I perceived the Angel of the Odd. He was leaning with his arms folded, over the rim of the car, and with a pipe in his mouth, at which he puffed leisurely, seemed to be upon excellent terms with himself and the universe. I was too much exhausted to speak, so I merely regarded him with an imploring air.

For several minutes, although he looked me full in the face, he said nothing. At length removing carefully his meerschaum from the right to the left corner of his mouth, he condescended to speak.

"Who pe you?" he asked, "und what der teuffel you pe do dare?"

To this piece of impudence, cruelty, and affectation, I could reply only by ejaculating the monosyllable "Help!"

"Elp!" echoed the ruffian– "not I. Dare iz te pottle– elp yourself, und pe tam'd!"

With these words he let fall a heavy bottle of Kirschenwasser which, dropping precisely upon the crown of my head, caused me to imagine that my brains were entirely knocked out. Impressed with this idea, I was about to relinquish my hold and give up the ghost with a good grace, when I was arrested by the cry of the Angel, who bade me hold on.

"Old on!" he said; "don't pe in te urry– don't. Will you pe take de odder pottle, or ave you pe got zober yet and come to your zenzes?"

I made haste, hereupon, to nod my head twice– once in the negative, meaning thereby that I would prefer not taking the other bottle at present– and once in the affirmative, intending thus to imply that I was sober and had positively come to my senses. By these means I somewhat softened the Angel.

"Und you pelief, ten," he inquired, "at te last? You pelief, ten, in te possibilty of te odd?"

I again nodded my head in assent.

"Und you ave pelief in me, te Angel of te Odd?"

I nodded again.

"Und you acknowledge tat you pe te blind dronk and te vool?"

I nodded once more.

"Put your right hand into your left hand preeches pocket, ten, in token oy your vull zubmission unto te Angel ov te Odd."

This thing, for very obvious reasons, I found it quite impossible to do. In the first place, my left arm had been broken in my fall from the ladder, and, therefore, had I let go my hold with the right hand, I must have let go altogether. In the second place, I could have no breeches until I came across the crow. I was therefore obliged, much to my regret, to shake my head in the negative– intending thus to give the Angel to understand that I found it inconvenient, just at that moment, to comply with his very reasonable demand! No sooner, however, had I ceased shaking my head than–

"Go to der teuffel ten!" roared the Angel of the Odd.

In pronouncing these words, he drew a sharp knife across the guide. rope by which I was suspended, and as we then happened to be precisely over my own house, (which, during my peregrinations, had been handsomely rebuilt,) it so occurred that I tumbled headlong down the ample chimney and alit upon the dining–room hearth.

Upon coming to my senses, (for the fall had very thoroughly stunned me,) I found it about four o'clock in the morning. I lay outstretched where I had fallen from the balloon. My head grovelled in the ashes of an extinguished fire, while my feet reposed upon the wreck of a small table, overthrown, and amid the fragments of a miscellaneous dessert, intermingled with a newspaper, some broken glass and shattered bottles, and an empty jug of the Schiedam Kirschenwasser. Thus revenged himself the Angel of the Odd.

THE BUSINESS MAN

Method is the soul of business.

OLD SAYING.

I AM a business man. I am a methodical man. Method is the thing, after all. But there are no people I more heartily despise than your eccentric fools who prate about method without understanding it; attending strictly to its letter, and violating its spirit. These fellows are always doing the most out–of–the–way things in what they call an orderly manner. Now here, I conceive, is a positive paradox. True method appertains to the ordinary and the obvious alone, and cannot be applied to the outre. What definite idea can a body attach to such expressions as "methodical Jack o' Dandy," or "a systematical Will o' the Wisp"?

My notions upon this head might not have been so clear as they are, but for a fortunate accident which happened to me when I was a very little boy. A good–hearted old Irish nurse (whom I shall not forget in my will) took me up one day by the heels, when I was making more noise than was necessary, and swinging me round two or knocked my head into a cocked hat against the bedpost. This, I say, decided my fate, and made my fortune. A bump arose at once on my sinciput, and turned out to be as pretty an organ of order as one shall see on a summer's day. Hence that positive appetite for system and regularity which has made me the distinguished man of business that I am.

If there is any thing on earth I hate, it is a genius. Your geniuses are all arrant asses– the greater the genius the greater the ass– and to this rule there is no exception whatever. Especially, you cannot make a man of business out of a genius, any more than money out of a Jew, or the best nutmegs out of pine–knots. The creatures are always going off at a tangent into some fantastic employment, or ridiculous speculation, entirely at variance with the "fitness of things," and having no business whatever to be considered as a business at all. Thus you may tell these characters immediately by the nature of their occupations. If you ever perceive a man setting up as a merchant or a manufacturer, or going into the cotton or tobacco trade, or any of those eccentric pursuits; or getting to be a drygoods dealer, or soap–boiler, or something of that kind; or pretending to be a lawyer, or a blacksmith, or a physician– any thing out of the usual way– you may set him down at once as a genius, and then, according to the rule–of–three, he's an ass.

Now I am not in any respect a genius, but a regular business man. My Day–book and Ledger will evince this in a minute. They are well kept, though I say it myself; and, in my general habits of accuracy and punctuality, I am not to be beat by a clock. Moreover, my occupations have been always made to chime in with the ordinary habitudes of my fellowmen. Not that I feel the least indebted, upon this score, to my exceedingly weak–minded parents, who, beyond doubt, would have made an arrant genius of me at last, if my guardian angel had not come, in good time, to the rescue. In biography the truth is every thing, and in autobiography it is especially so– yet I scarcely hope to be believed when I state, however solemnly, that my poor father put me, when I was about fifteen years of age, into the counting–house of what be termed "a respectable hardware and commission merchant doing a capital bit of business!" A capital bit of fiddlestick! However, the consequence of this folly was, that in two or three days, I had to be sent home to my button–headed family in a high state of fever, and with a most violent and dangerous pain in the sinciput, all around about my organ of order. It was nearly a gone case with me then– just touch–and–go for six weeks– the physicians giving me up and all that sort of thing. But, although I suffered much, I was a thankful boy in the main. I was saved from being a "respectable hardware and commission merchant, doing a capital bit of business," and I felt grateful to the protuberance which had been the means of my salvation, as well as to the kindhearted female who had originally put these means within my reach.

The most of boys run away from home at ten or twelve years of age, but I waited till I was sixteen. I don't know that I should have gone even then, if I had not happened to hear my old mother talk about setting me up on my own hook in the grocery way. The grocery way!– only think of that! I resolved to be off forthwith, and try and establish myself in some decent occupation, without dancing attendance any longer upon the caprices of these eccentric old people, and running the risk of being made a genius of in the end. In this project I succeeded perfectly well at the first effort, and by the time I was fairly eighteen, found myself doing an extensive and profitable business in the Tailor's Walking–Advertisement line.

I was enabled to discharge the onerous duties of this profession, only by that rigid adherence to system which formed the leading feature of my mind. A scrupulous method characterized my actions as well as my accounts. In my case it was method– not money– which made the man: at least all of him that was not made by the tailor whom I served. At nine, every morning, I called upon that individual for the clothes of the day. Ten o'clock found me in some fashionable promenade or other place of public amusement. The precise regularity with which I turned my handsome person about, so as to bring successively into view every portion of the suit upon my back, was the admiration of all the knowing men in the trade. Noon never passed without my bringing home a customer to the house of my employers, Messrs. Cut & Comeagain. I say this proudly, but with tears in my eyes– for the firm proved themselves the basest of ingrates. The little account, about which we quarreled and finally parted, cannot, in any item, be thought overcharged, by gentlemen really conversant with the nature of the business. Upon this point, however, I feel a degree of proud satisfaction in permitting the reader to judge for himself. My bill ran thus:

Messrs. Cut & Comeagain,

Merchant Tailors.

To Peter Proffit, Walking Advertiser,

Drs.

JULY 10.- to promenade, as usual and customer brought home.... $00 25

JULY 11.- To   do   do   do   25

JULY 12.- To one lie, second class; damaged black cloth sold for invisible green................................………………………………….. 25

JULY 13.- To one lie, first class, extra quality and size; recommended milled satinet as broadcloth...........................……......... . 75

JULY 20.- To purchasing bran new paper shirt collar or dickey, to set off gray Petersham.................................……..................…… 02

AUG. 15.- To wearing double-padded bobtail frock, (thermometer 106 in the shade)..…………………….. …….. 25

AUG. 16.- Standing on one leg three hours, to show off new-style strapped pants at 12 1/2 cents per leg per hour............…................… 37 1/2

AUG. 17.- To promenade, as usual, and large customer brought (fat man)...……………………… …….. 50

AUG. 18.- To   do   do   (medium size)...............….................… 25

AUG. 19.- To   do   do   (small man and bad pay)....... ……….. 06

TOTAL...…………………… [sic] $2 96 1/2

The item chiefly disputed in this bill was the very moderate charge of two pennies for the dickey. Upon my word of honor, this was not an unreasonable price for that dickey. It was one of the cleanest and prettiest little dickeys I ever saw; and I have good reason to believe that it effected the sale of three Petershams. The elder partner of the firm, however, would allow me only one penny of the charge, and took it upon himself to show in what manner four of the same sized conveniences could be got out of a sheet of foolscap. But it is needless to say that I stood upon the principle of the thing. Business is business, and should be done in a business way. There was no system whatever in swindling me out of a penny– a clear fraud of fifty per cent– no method in any respect. I left at once the employment of Messrs. Cut & Comeagain, and set up in the Eye–Sore line by myself– one of the most lucrative, respectable, and independent of the ordinary occupations.

My strict integrity, economy, and rigorous business habits, here again came into play. I found myself driving a flourishing trade, and soon became a marked man upon 'Change. The truth is, I never dabbled in flashy matters, but jogged on in the good old sober routine of the calling– a calling in which I should, no doubt, have remained to the present hour, but for a little accident which happened to me in the prosecution of one of the usual business operations of the profession. Whenever a rich old hunks or prodigal heir or bankrupt corporation gets into the notion of putting up a palace, there is no such thing in the world as stopping either of them, and this every intelligent person knows. The fact in question is indeed the basis of the Eye–Sore trade. As soon, therefore, as a building–project is fairly afoot by one of these parties, we merchants secure a nice corner of the lot in contemplation, or a prime little situation just adjoining, or tight in front. This done, we wait until the palace is half–way up, and then we pay some tasty architect to run us up an ornamental mud hovel, right against it; or a Down–East or Dutch Pagoda, or a pig–sty, or an ingenious little bit of fancy work, either Esquimau, Kickapoo, or Hottentot. Of course we can't afford to take these structures down under a bonus of five hundred per cent upon the prime cost of our lot and plaster. Can we? I ask the question. I ask it of business men. It would be irrational to suppose that we can. And yet there was a rascally corporation which asked me to do this very thing– this very thing! I did not reply to their absurd proposition, of course; but I felt it a duty to go that same night, and lamp–black the whole of their palace. For this the unreasonable villains clapped me into jail; and the gentlemen of the Eye–Sore trade could not well avoid cutting my connection when I came out.

The Assault–and–Battery business, into which I was now forced to adventure for a livelihood, was somewhat ill–adapted to the delicate nature of my constitution; but I went to work in it with a good heart, and found my account here, as heretofore, in those stern habits of methodical accuracy which had been thumped into me by that delightful old nurse– I would indeed be the basest of men not to remember her well in my will. By observing, as I say, the strictest system in all my dealings, and keeping a well–regulated set of books, I was enabled to get over many serious difficulties, and, in the end, to establish myself very decently in the profession. The truth is, that few individuals, in any line, did a snugger little business than I. I will just copy a page or so out of my Day–Book; and this will save me the necessity of blowing my own trumpet– a contemptible practice of which no high–minded man will be guilty. Now, the Day–Book is a thing that don't lie.

"Jan. 1.– New Year's Day. Met Snap in the street, groggy. Mem– he'll do. Met Gruff shortly afterward, blind drunk. Mem– he'll answer, too. Entered both gentlemen in my Ledger, and opened a running account with each.

"Jan. 2.– Saw Snap at the Exchange, and went up and trod on his toe. Doubled his fist and knocked me down. Good!– got up again. Some trifling difficulty with Bag, my attorney. I want the damages at a thousand, but he says that for so simple a knock down we can't lay them at more than five hundred. Mem– must get rid of Bag– no system at all.

"Jan. 3– Went to the theatre, to look for Gruff. Saw him sitting in a side box, in the second tier, between a fat lady and a lean one. Quizzed the whole party through an opera–glass, till I saw the fat lady blush and whisper to G. Went round, then, into the box, and put my nose within reach of his hand. Wouldn't pull it– no go. Blew it, and tried again– no go. Sat down then, and winked at the lean lady, when I had the high satisfaction of finding him lift me up by the nape of the neck, and fling me over into the pit. Neck dislocated, and right leg capitally splintered. Went home in high glee, drank a bottle of champagne, and booked the young man for five thousand. Bag says it'll do.

"Feb. 15– Compromised the case of Mr. Snap. Amount entered in Journal– fifty cents– which see.

"Feb. 16.– Cast by that ruffian, Gruff, who made me a present of five dollars. Costs of suit, four dollars and twenty–five cents. Nett profit,– see Journal,– seventy–five cents."

Now, here is a clear gain, in a very brief period, of no less than one dollar and twenty–five cents– this is in the mere cases of Snap and Gruff; and I solemnly assure the reader that these extracts are taken at random from my Day–Book.

It's an old saying, and a true one, however, that money is nothing in comparison with health. I found the exactions of the profession somewhat too much for my delicate state of body; and, discovering, at last, that I was knocked all out of shape, so that I didn't know very well what to make of the matter, and so that my friends, when they met me in the street, couldn't tell that I was Peter Proffit at all, it occurred to me that the best expedient I could adopt was to alter my line of business. I turned my attention, therefore, to Mud–Dabbling, and continued it for some years.

The worst of this occupation is, that too many people take a fancy to it, and the competition is in consequence excessive. Every ignoramus of a fellow who finds that he hasn't brains in sufficient quantity to make his way as a walking advertiser, or an eye–sore prig, or a salt–and–batter man, thinks, of course, that he'll answer very well as a dabbler of mud. But there never was entertained a more erroneous idea than that it requires no brains to mud–dabble. Especially, there is nothing to be made in this way without method. I did only a retail business myself, but my old habits of system carried me swimmingly along. I selected my street–crossing, in the first place, with great delibe-ration, and I never put down a broom in any part of the town but that. I took care, too, to have a nice little puddle at hand, which I could get at in a minute. By these means I got to be well known as a man to be trusted; and this is one–half the battle, let me tell you, in trade. Nobody ever failed to pitch me a copper, and got over my crossing with a clean pair of pantaloons. And, as my business habits, in this respect, were sufficiently understood, I never met with any attempt at imposition. I wouldn't have put up with it, if I had. Never imposing upon any one myself, I suffered no one to play the possum with me. The frauds of the banks of course I couldn't help. Their suspension put me to ruinous inconvenience. These, however, are not individuals, but corporations; and corporations, it is very well known, have neither bodies to be kicked nor souls to be damned.

I was making money at this business when, in an evil moment, I was induced to merge it in the Cur–Spattering– a somewhat analogous, but, by no means, so respectable a profession. My location, to be sure, was an excellent one, being central, and I had capital blacking and brushes. My little dog, too, was quite fat and up to all varieties of snuff. He had been in the trade a long time, and, I may say, understood it. Our general routine was this:– Pompey, having rolled himself well in the mud, sat upon end at the shop door, until he observed a dandy approaching in bright boots. He then proceeded to meet him, and gave the Wellingtons a rub or two with his wool. Then the dandy swore very much, and looked about for a boot-black. There I was, full in his view, with blacking and brushes. It was only a minute's work, and then came a sixpence. This did moderately well for a time;– in fact, I was not avaricious, but my dog was. I allowed him a third of the profit, but he was advised to insist upon half. This I couldn't stand– so we quarrelled and parted.

I next tried my hand at the Organ–Grinding for a while, and may say that I made out pretty well. It is a plain, straightforward business, and requires no particular abilities. You can get a music–mill for a mere song, and to put it in order, you have but to open the works, and give them three or four smart raps with a hammer. In improves the tone of the thing, for business purposes, more than you can imagine. This done, you have only to stroll along, with the mill on your back, until you see tanbark in the street, and a knocker wrapped up in buckskin. Then you stop and grind; looking as if you meant to stop and grind till doomsday. Presently a window opens, and somebody pitches you a sixpence, with a request to "Hush up and go on," etc. I am aware that some grinders have actually afforded to "go on" for this sum; but for my part, I found the necessary outlay of capital too great to permit of my "going on" under a shilling.

At this occupation I did a good deal; but, somehow, I was not quite satisfied, and so finally abandoned it. The truth is, I labored under the disadvantage of having no monkey– and American streets are so muddy, and a Democratic rabble is so obstrusive, and so full of demnition mischievous little boys.

I was now out of employment for some months, but at length succeeded, by dint of great interest, in procuring a situation in the Sham–Post. The duties, here, are simple, and not altogether unprofitable. For example:– very early in the morning I had to make up my packet of sham letters. Upon the inside of each of these I had to scrawl a few lines on any subject which occurred to me as sufficiently mysterious– signing all the epistles Tom Dobson, or Bobby Tompkins, or anything in that way. Having folded and sealed all, and stamped them with sham postmarks– New Orleans, Bengal, Botany Bay, or any other place a great way off– I set out, forthwith, upon my daily route, as if in a very great hurry. I always called at the big houses to deliver the letters, and receive the postage. Nobody hesitates at paying for a letter– especially for a double one– people are such fools– and it was no trouble to get round a corner before there was time to open the epistles. The worst of this profession was, that I had to walk so much and so fast; and so frequently to vary my route. Besides, I had serious scruples of conscience. I can't bear to hear innocent individuals abused– and the way the whole town took to cursing Tom Dobson and Bobby Tompkins was really awful to hear. I washed my hands of the matter in disgust.

My eighth and last speculation has been in the Cat–Growing way. I have found that a most pleasant and lucrative business, and, really, no trouble at all. The country, it is well known, has become infested with cats– so much so of late, that a petition for relief, most numerously and respectably signed, was brought before the Legislature at its late memorable session. The Assembly, at this epoch, was unusually well–informed, and, having passed many other wise and wholesome enactments, it crowned all with the Cat-Act. In its original form, this law offered a premium for cat–heads (fourpence a–piece), but the Senate succeeded in amending the main clause, so as to substitute the word "tails" for "heads." This amendment was so obviously proper, that the House concurred in it nem. con.

As soon as the governor had signed the bill, I invested my whole estate in the purchase of Toms and Tabbies. At first I could only afford to feed them upon mice (which are cheap), but they fulfilled the scriptural injunction at so marvellous a rate, that I at length considered it my best policy to be liberal, and so indulged them in oysters and turtle. Their tails, at a legislative price, now bring me in a good income; for I have discovered a way, in which, by means of Macassar oil, I can force three crops in a year. It delights me to find, too, that the animals soon get accustomed to the thing, and would rather have the appendages cut off than otherwise. I consider myself, therefore, a made man, and am bargaining for a country seat on the Hudson.

LITERARY LIFE OF THINGUM BOB, ESQ.
LATE EDITOR OF THE
"GOOSETHERUMFOODLE"
BY HIMSELF

I AM now growing in years, and– since I understand that Shakespeare and Mr. Emmons are deceased– it is not impossible that I may even die. It has occurred to me, therefore, that I may as well retire from the field of Letters and repose upon my laurels. But I am ambitious of signalizing my abdication of the literary sceptre by some important bequest to posterity; and, perhaps, I cannot do a better thing than just pen for it an account of my earlier career. My name, indeed, has been so long and so constantly before the public eye, that I am not only willing to admit the naturalness of the interest which it has everywhere excited, but ready to satisfy the extreme curiosity which it has inspired. In fact, it is no more than the duty of him who achieves greatness to leave behind him, in his ascent, such landmarks as may guide others to be great. I propose, therefore, in the present paper (which I had some idea of calling "Memoranda to Serve for the Literary History of America") to give a detail of those important, yet feeble and tottering, first steps, by which, at length, I attained the high road to the pinnacle of human renown.

Of one's very remote ancestors it is superfluous to say much. My father, Thomas Bob, Esq., stood for many years at the summit of his profession, which was that of a merchant–barber, in the city of Smug. His warehouse was the resort of all the principal people of the place, and especially of the editorial corps– a body which inspires all about it with profound veneration and awe. For my own part, I regarded them as gods, and drank in with avidity the rich wit and wisdom which continuously flowed from their august mouths during the process of what is styled "lather." My first moment of positive inspiration must be dated from that ever–memorable epoch, when the brilliant conductor of the "Gad–Fly," in the intervals of the important process just mentioned, recited aloud, before a conclave of our apprentices, an inimitable poem in honor of the "Only Genuine Oil–of–Bob" (so called from its talented inventor, my father), and for which effusion the editor of the "Fly" was remunerated with a regal liberality by the firm of Thomas Bob & Company, merchant–barbers.

The genius of the stanzas to the "Oil–of–Bob" first breathed into me, I say, the divine afflatus. I resolved at once to become a great man, and to commence by becoming a great poet. That very evening I fell upon my knees at the feet of my father.

"Father," I said, "pardon me!– but I have a soul above lather. It is my firm intention to cut the shop. I would be an editor– I would be a poet– I would pen stanzas to the 'Oil–of–Bob.' Pardon me and aid me to be great!"

"My dear Thingum," replied father, (I had been christened Thingum after a wealthy relative so surnamed,) "My dear Thingum," he said, raising me from my knees by the ears– "Thingum, my boy, you're a trump, and take after your father in having a soul.

You have an immense head, too, and it must hold a great many brains. This I have long seen, and therefore had thoughts of making you a lawyer. The business, however, has grown ungenteel and that of a politician don't pay. Upon the whole you judge wisely;– the trade of editor is best:– and if you can be a poet at the same time,– as most of the editors are, by the by, why, you will kill two birds with the one stone. To encourage you in the beginning of things, I will allow you a garret, pen, ink, and paper, a rhyming dictionary; and a copy of the 'Gad–Fly.' I suppose you would scarcely demand any more."

"I would be an ungrateful villain if I did" I replied with enthusiasm. "Your generosity is boundless. I will repay it by making you the father of a genius."

Thus ended my conference with the best of men, and immediately upon its termination, I betook myself with zeal to my poetical labors; as upon these, chiefly, I founded my hopes of ultimate elevation to the editorial chair.

In my first attempts at composition I found the stanzas to "The Oil–of–Bob" rather a drawback than otherwise. Their splendor more dazzled than enlightened me. The contemplation of their excellence tended, naturally, to discourage me by comparison with my own abortions; so that for a long time I labored in vain. At length there came into my head one of those exquisitely original ideas which now and then will permeate the brain of a man of genius. It was this:– or, rather, thus was it carried into execution. From the rubbish of an old book–stall, in a very remote corner of the town, I got together several antique and altogether unknown or forgotten volumes. The bookseller sold them to me for a song. From one of these, which purported to be a translation of one Dantes "Inferno," I copied with remarkable neatness a long passage about a man named Ugolino, who had a parcel of brats. From another, which contained a good many old plays by some person whose name I forget, I enacted in the same manner, and with the same care, a great number of lines about "angels" and "ministers saying grace," and "goblins damned," and more besides of that sort. From a third, which was the composition of some blind man or other, either a Greek or a Choctaw– I cannot be at the pains of remembering every trifle exactly,– I took about fifty verses beginning with "Achilles' wrath," and "grease," and something else. From a fourth, which I recollect was also the work of a blind man, I selected a page or two all about "hail" and "holy light"; and, although a blind man has no business to write about light, still the verses were sufficiently good in their way.

Having made fair copies of these poems, I signed every one of them "Oppodeldoc" (a fine sonorous name), and, doing each up nicely in a separate envelope, I dispatched one to each of the four principal Magazines, with a request for speedy insertion and prompt pay. The result of this well–conceived plan, however, (the success of which would have saved me much trouble in after–life,) served to convince me that some editors are not to be bamboozled, and gave the coup–de–grace (as they say in France) to my nascent hopes (as they say in the city of the transcendentals).

The fact is, that each and every one of the Magazines in question gave Mr. "Oppodeldoc" a complete using–up, in the "Monthly Notices to Correspondents." The "Hum–Drum" gave him a dressing after this fashion:

"'Oppodeldoc' (whoever he is) has sent us a long tirade concerning a bedlamite whom he styles 'Ugolino,' had a great many children that should have been all whipped and sent to bed without their suppers. The whole affair is exceedingly tame– not to say flat. 'Oppodeldoc' (whoever he is) is entirely devoid of imagination– and imagination, in our humble opinion, is not only the soul of Poesy, but also its very heart. 'Oppodeldoc' (whoever he is) has the audacity to demand of us, for his twattle, a 'speedy insertion and prompt pay.' We neither insert nor purchase any stuff of the sort. There can be no doubt, however, that he would meet with a ready sale for all the balderdash he can scribble, at the office of either the 'Rowdy–Dow,' the 'Lollipop,' or the 'Goosetherumfoodle.'

All this, it must be acknowledged, was very severe upon "Oppodeldoc,"– but the unkindest cut was putting the word Poesy in small caps. In those five pre–eminent letters what a world of bitterness is there not involved!

But "Oppodeldoc" was punished with equal severity in the "Rowdy Dow," which spoke thus:

"We have received a most singular and insolent communication from a person (whoever he is) signing himself 'Oppodeldoc,'– thus desecrating the greatness of the illustrious Roman emperor so named. Accompanying the letter of 'Oppodeldoc' (whoever he is) we find sundry lines of most disgusting and unmeaning rant about 'angels and ministers of grace,'– rant such as no madman short of a Nat Lee, or an 'Oppodeldoc,' could possibly perpetrate. And for this trash of trash, we are modestly requested to 'pay promptly.' No, sir– no! We pay for nothing of that sort. Apply to the

'Hum–Drum,' the 'Lollipop,' or the 'Goosethe -
rumfoodle.' These periodicals will undoubtedly accept
any literary offal you may send them– and as
undoubtedly promise to pay for it."

This was bitter indeed upon poor "Oppodeldoc"; but,
in this instance, the weight of the satire falls upon the
"Hum–Drum," the "Lollipop," and the "Goosetherumfoodle," who are pungently styled "periodicals"– in
Italics, too– a thing that must have cut them to the
heart.

Scarcely less savage was the "Lollipop," which thus
discoursed:

"Some individual, who rejoices in the appellation
'Oppodeldoc,' (to what low uses are the names of the
illustrious dead too often applied!) has enclosed us
some fifty or sixty verses commencing after this
fashion:

> 'Achilles' wrath, to Greece the direful spring
> Of woes unnumbered, &c., &c., &c, &c.'

"'Oppodeldoc?' (whoever he is) is respectfully
informed that there is not a printer's devil in our office
who is not in the daily habit of composing better lines.
Those of 'Oppodeldoc' will not scan. 'Oppodeldoc'
should learn to count. But why he should have
conceived the idea that we (of all others, we!) would
disgrace our pages with his ineffable nonsense is
utterly beyond comprehension. Why, the absurd
twattle is scarcely good enough for the 'Hum–Drum,'
the 'Rowdy–Dow,' the 'Goosetherumfoodle,'– things
that are in the practice of publishing 'Mother Gooses
Melodies' as original lyrics. And 'Oppodeldoc'

(whoever he is) has even the assurance to demand pay for this drivel. Does 'Oppodeldoc' (whoever he is) know– is he aware that we could not be paid to insert it?"

As I perused this I felt myself growing gradually smaller and smaller, and when I came to the point at which the editor sneered at the poem as "verses," there was little more than an ounce of me left. As for "Oppodeldoc," I began to experience compassion for the poor fellow. But the "Goosetherumfoodle" showed, if possible, less mercy than the "Lollipop." It was the "Goosetherumfoodle" that said–

"A wretched poetaster, who signs himself 'Oppodeldoc,' is silly enough to fancy that we will print and pay for a medley of incoherent and ungrammatical bombast which he has transmitted to us, and which commences with the following most intelligible line:–

'Hail Holy Light! Offspring of Heaven, first born.'

"We say, 'most intelligible.' 'Oppodeldoc' (whoever he is) will be kind enough to tell us, perhaps, how 'hail' can be 'holy light.' We always regarded it as frozen rain. Will he inform us, also, how frozen rain can be, at one and the same time, both 'holy light' (whatever that is) and an 'off–spring'?– which latter term (if we understand anything about English) is only employed, with propriety, in reference to small babies of about six weeks old. But it is preposterous to descant upon such absurdity– although 'Oppodeldoc' (whoever he is) has the unparalled effrontery to suppose that we will not only 'insert' his ignorant ravings, but (absolutely) pay for them?

"Now this is fine– it is rich!– and we have half a mind to punish this young scribbler for his egotism by really publishing his effusion verbatim et literatim, as he has written it. We could inflict no punishment so severe, and we would inflict it, but for the boredom which we should cause our readers in so doing.

"Let 'Oppodeldoc' (whoever he is) send any future composition of like character to the 'Hum–Drum,' the 'Lollipop,' or the 'Rowdy–Dow: They will 'insert' it. They 'insert' every month just such stuff. Send it to them. WE are not to be insulted with impunity."

This made an end of me, and as for the "Hum–Drum," the "Rowdy–Dow," and the "Lollipop," I never could comprehend how they survived it. The putting them in the smallest possible minion (that was the rub– thereby insinuating their lowness– their baseness,) while WE stood looking upon them in gigantic capitals!– oh it was too bitter!– it was wormwood– it was gall. Had I been either of these periodicals I would have spared no pains to have the "Goosetherumfoodle" prosecuted. It might have been done under the Act for the "Prevention of Cruelty to Animals." for Oppodeldoc (whoever he was), I had by this time lost all patience with the fellow, and sympathized with him no longer. He was a fool, beyond doubt, (whoever he was,) and got not a kick more than he deserved.

The result of my experiment with the old books convinced me, in the first place, that "honesty is the best policy," and, in the second, that if I could not write better than Mr. Dante, and the two blind men, and the rest of the old set, it would, at least, be a difficult matter to write worse. I took heart, therefore, and determined to prosecute the "entirely original" (as they say on the covers of the magazines), at whatever cost of study and pains. I again placed before my eyes, as a model, the brilliant stanzas on "The Oil–of–Bob" by the editor of the "Gad–Fly" and resolved to construct an ode on the same sublime theme, in rivalry of what had already been done.

With my first line I had no material difficulty. It ran thus:

> "To pen an Ode upon the 'Oil-of-Bob.'"

Having carefully looked out, however, all the legitimate rhymes to "Bob," I found it impossible to proceed. In this dilemma I had recourse to paternal aid; and, after some hours of mature thought, my father and myself thus constructed the poem:

> "To pen an Ode upon the 'Oil-of-Bob'
> Is all sorts of a job.
>
> (Signed)   Snob."

To be sure, this composition was of no very great length,– but I "have yet to learn," as they say in the "Edinburgh Review," that the mere extent of a literary work has anything to do with its merit. As for the Quarterly cant about "sustained effort," it is impossible to see the sense of it. Upon the whole, therefore, I was satisfied with the success of my maiden attempt, and now the only question regarded the disposal I should make of it. My father suggested that I should send it to the "Gad–Fly,"– but there were two reasons which operated to prevent me from so doing. I dreaded the jealousy of the editor– and I had ascertained that he did not pay for original contributions. I therefore, after due deliberation, consigned the article to the more dignified pages of the "Lollipop" and awaited the event in anxiety, but with resignation.

In the very next published number I had the proud satisfaction of seeing my poem printed at length, as the leading article, with the following significant words, prefixed in italics and between brackets:

[We call the attention of our readers to the subjoined admirable on "The Oil–of–Bob." We need say nothing of their sublimity, or of their pathos.– it is impossible to peruse them without tears. Those who have been nauseated with a sad dose on the same august topic from the goose–quill of the editor of the "Gad–Fly," will do well to compare the two compositions.

P. S.– We are consumed with anxiety to probe the mystery which envelops the evident pseudonym "Snob" May we hope for a personal interview?]

All this was scarcely more than justice, but it was, I confess, rather more than I had expected:– I acknowledge this, be it observed, to the everlasting disgrace of my country and of mankind. I lost no time, however, in calling upon the editor of the "Lollipop" and had the good fortune to find this gentleman at home. He saluted me with an air of profound respect, slightly blended with a fatherly and patronizing admiration, wrought in him, no doubt, by my appearance of extreme youth and inexperience. Begging me to be seated, he entered at once upon the subject of my poem;– but modesty will ever forbid me to repeat the thousand compliments which he lavished upon me. The eulogies of Mr. Crab (such was the editor's name) were, however, by no means fulsomely indiscriminate. He analyzed my composition with much freedom and great ability– not hesitating to point out a few trivial defects– a circumstance which elevated him highly in my esteem. The "Gad–Fly" was, of course, brought upon the tapis, and I hope never to be subjected to a criticism so searching, or to rebukes so withering, as were bestowed by Mr. Crab upon that unhappy effusion. I had been accustomed to regard the editor of the "Gad–Fly" as something superhuman; but Mr. Crab soon disabused me of that idea. He set the literary as well as the personal character of the Fly (so Mr. C. satirically designated the rival editor), in its true light. He, the Fly, was very little better than he should be. He had written infamous things. He was a penny–a–liner, and a buffoon. He was a villain. He had composed a tragedy which set the whole country in a guffaw, and a farce which deluged the universe in tears. Besides all this, he had the impudence to pen what he meant for a lampoon upon himself (Mr. Crab), and the temerity to style him "an ass." Should I at any time wish to express my opinion of Mr. Fly, the pages of the "Lollipop," Mr. Crab assured me, were at my unlimited disposal. In the meantime, as it was very certain that I would be attacked in the "Fly" for my attempt at composing a rival poem on the "Oil–of–Bob," he (Mr. Crab) would take it upon himself to attend, pointedly, to my private and personal interests. If I were not made a man of at once, it should not be the fault of himself (Mr. Crab).

Mr. Crab having now paused in his discourse (the latter portion of which I found it impossible to comprehend), I ventured to suggest something about the remuneration which I had been taught to expect for my poem, by an announcement on the cover of the "Lollipop," declaring that it (the "Lollipop") "insisted upon being permitted to pay exorbitant prices for all accepted contributions,– frequently expending more money for a single brief poem than the whole annual cost of the 'Hum–Drum,' the 'Rowdy–Dow,' and the 'Goosetherumfoodle' combined."

As I mentioned the word "remuneration," Mr. Crab first opened his eyes, and then his mouth, to quite a remarkable extent, causing his personal appearance to resemble that of a highly agitated elderly duck in the act of quacking; and in this condition he remained (ever and anon pressing his hinds tightly to his forehead, as if in a state of desperate bewilderment) until I had nearly made an end of what I had to say.

Upon my conclusion, he sank back into his seat, as if much overcome, letting his arms fall lifelessly by his side, but keeping his mouth still rigorously open, after the fashion of the duck. While I remained in speechless astonishment at behavior so alarming he suddenly leaped to his feet and made a rush at the bell–rope; but just as he reached this, he appeared to have altered his intention, whatever it was, for he dived under a table and immediately re–appeared with a cudgel. This he was in the act of uplifting (for what purpose I am at a loss to imagine), when all at once, there came a benign smile over his features, and he sank placidly back in his chair.

"Mr. Bob," he said, (for I had sent up my card before ascending myself,) "Mr. Bob, you are a young man, I presume– very?"

I assented; adding that I had not yet concluded my third lustrum.

"Ah!" he replied, "very good! I see how it is– say no more! Touching this matter of compensation, what you observe is very just,– in fact it is excessively so. But ah– ah– the first contribution– the first, I say– it is never the Magazine custom to pay for,– you comprehend, eh? The truth is, we are usually the recipients in such case." [Mr. Crab smiled blandly as he emphasized the word "recipients."] "for the most part, we are paid for the insertion of a maiden attempt– especially in verse. In the second place, Mr. Bob, the Magazine rule is never to disburse what we term in France the argent comptant:– I have no doubt you understand. In a quarter or two after publication of the article– or in a year or two– we make no objection to giving our note at nine months; provided, always, that we can so arrange our affairs as to be quite certain of a 'burst up' in six. I really do hope, Mr. Bob, that you will look upon this explanation as satisfactory." Here Mr. Crab concluded, and the tears stood in his eyes.

Grieved to the soul at having been, however innocently, the cause of pain to so eminent and so sensitive a man, I hastened to apologize, and to reassure him, by expressing my perfect coincidence with his views, as well as my entire appreciation of the delicacy of his position. Having done all this in a neat speech, I took leave.

One fine morning, very shortly afterwards, "I awoke and found myself famous." The extent of my renown will be best estimated by reference to the editorial opinions of the day. These opinions, it will be seen, were embodied in critical notices of the number of the "Lollipop" containing my poem, and are perfectly satisfactory, conclusive, and clear with the exception, perhaps, of the hieroglyphical marks, "Sep. 15– 1 t," appended to each of the critiques.

The "Owl" a journal of profound sagacity, and well known for the deliberate gravity of its literary decisions– the "Owl," I say, spoke as follows:

"The LOLLIPOP! The October number of this delicious Magazine surpasses its predecessors, and sets competition at defiance. In the beauty of its typography and paper– in the number and excellence of its steel plates– as well as in the literary merit of its contributions– the 'Lollipop' compares with its slow–paced rivals as Hyperion with Satyr. The 'Hum–Drum,' the 'Rowdy–Dow,' and the 'Goosetherumfoodle,' excel, it is true, in braggadocio, but in all other points, give us the 'Lollipop'! How this celebrated journal can sustain its evidently tremendous expenses, is more than we can understand. To be sure, it has a circulation of 100,000 and its subscription list has increased one fourth during the last month; but, on the other hand, the sums it disburses constantly for contributions are incon-ceivable. It is reported that Mr. Slyass received no less than thirty–seven and a half cents for his inimitable paper on 'Pigs.' With Mr. Crab, as editor, and with such names upon the list of contributors as SNOB and Slyass, there can be no such word as 'fail' for the 'Lollipop.' Go and subscribe. Sep. 15– 1 t."

I must say that I was gratified with this high–toned notice from a paper so respectable as the "Owl." The placing my name– that is to say, my nom de guerre– in priority of station to that of the great Slyass, was a compliment as happy as I felt it to be deserved.

My attention was next arrested by these paragraphs in the "Toad"– print highly distinguished for its uprightness and independence– for its entire freedom from sycophancy and subservience to the givers of dinners:

"The 'Lollipop' for October is out in advance of all its contemporaries, and infinitely surpasses them, of course, in the splendor of its embellishments, as well as in the richness of its contents. The 'Hum–Drum,' the 'Rowdy–Dow,' and the 'Goosetherumfoodle' excel, we admit, in braggadocio, but, in all other points, give us the 'Lollipop.' How this celebrated Magazine can sustain its evidently tremendous expenses is more than we can understand. To be sure, it has a circulation of 200,000 and its subscription list has increased one third during the last fortnight, but, on the other hand, the sums it disburses, monthly, for contributions, are fearfully great. We learn that Mr. Mumblethumb received no less than fifty cents for his late 'Monody in a Mud–Puddle.'

"Among the original contributors to the present number we notice (besides the eminent editor, Mr. Crab), such men as SNOB, Slyass, and Mumblethumb. Apart from the editorial matter, the most valuable paper, nevertheless, is, we think, a poetical gem by Snob, on the 'Oil–of–Bob.'–but our readers must not suppose, from the title of this incomparable bijou, that it bears any similitude to some balderdash on the same subject by a certain contemptible individual whose name is unmentionable to ears polite. The present poem 'On the Oil–of–Bob,' has excited universal anxiety and curiosity in respect to the owner of the evident pseudonym, 'Snob,'– a curiosity which, happily, we have it in our power to satisfy. 'Snob' is the nom de plume of Mr. Thingum Bob, of this city, a relative of the great Mr. Thingum, (after whom he is named), and otherwise connected with the most illustrious families of the State. His father, Thomas Bob, Esq., is an opulent merchant in Smug. Sep. 15– 1 t."

This generous approbation touched me to the heart– the more especially as it emanated from a source so avowedly– so proverbially pure as the "Toad." The word "balderdash," as applied to the "Oil–of–Bob" of the Fly, I considered singularly pungent and appropriate. The words "gem" and "bijou," however, used in reference to my composition, struck me as being, in some degree, feeble. They seemed to me to be deficient in force. They were not sufficiently prononces (as we have it in France).

I had hardly finished reading the "Toad," when a friend placed in my hands a copy of the "Mole," a daily, enjoying high reputation for the keenness of its perception about matters in general, and for the open, honest, above–ground style of its editorials. The "Mole" spoke of the "Lollypop" as follows:

"We have just received the 'Lollipop' for October, and must say that never before have we perused any single number of any periodical which afforded us a felicity so supreme. We speak advisedly. The 'Hum–Drum.' the 'Rowdy–Dow,' and the 'Goosetherumfoodle' must look well to their laurels. These prints, no doubt, surpass everything in loudness of pretension, but, in all other points, give us the 'Lollipop'! How this celebrated Magazine can sustain its evidently tremendous expenses, is more than we can comprehend. To be sure, it has a circulation of 300,000; and its subscription list has increased one half within the last week, but then the sum it disburses, monthly, for contributions, is astoundingly enormous. We have it upon good authority that Mr. Fatquack received no less than sixty–two cents and a half for his late Domestic Nouvellette, the 'Dish–Clout.'

"The contributors to the number before us are Mr. CRAB (the eminent editor), SNOB, Mumblethumb, Fatquack, and others; but, after the inimitable compositions of the editor himself, we prefer a diamond– like effusion from the pen of a rising poet who writes over the signature 'Snob'– a nom de guerre which we predict will one day extinguish the radiance of 'BOZ.' 'SNOB,' we learn, is a Mr. THINGUM BOB, Esq., sole heir of a wealthy merchant of this city, Thomas Bob, Esq., and a near relative of the distinguished Mr. Thingum. The title of Mr. B.'s admirable poem is the 'Oil–of–Bob'– a somewhat unfortunate name, by–the–bye, as some contemptible vagabond connected with the penny press has already disgusted the town with a great deal of drivel upon the same topic. There will be no danger, however, of confounding the compositions. Sep. 15– 1 t.

The generous approbation of so clear–sighted a journal as the "Mole" penetrated my soul with delight. The only objection which occurred to me was, that the terms "contemptible vagabond" might have been better written "odious and contemptible wretch, villain, and vagabond." This would have sounded more graceful, I think. "Diamond–like," also, was scarcely, it will be admitted, of sufficient intensity to express what the "Mole" evidently thought of the brilliancy of the "Oil–of–Bob."

On the same afternoon in which I saw these notices in the "Owl," the "Toad" and the "Mole," I happened to meet with a copy of the "Daddy–Long–Legs," a periodical proverbial for the extreme extent of its understanding. And it was the "Daddy–Long–Legs" which spoke thus:

"The 'Lollipop'! This gorgeous Magazine is already before the public for October. The question of pre–eminence is forever put to rest, and hereafter it will be preposterous in the 'Hum–Drum,' the 'Rowdy–Dow,' or the 'Goosetherumfoodle' to make any further spasmodic attempts at competition. These journals may excel the 'Lollipop' in outcry, but, in all other points, give us the 'Lollipop'! How this celebrated Magazine can sustain its evidently tremendous expenses, is past comprehension. To be sure it has a circulation of precisely half a million, and its subscription list has increased seventy–five per cent. within the last couple of days, but then the sums it disburses, monthly, for contributions, are scarcely credible; we are cognizant of the fact, that Mademoiselle Cribalittle received no less than eighty–seven cents and a half for her late valuable Revolutionary Tale, entitled 'The York–Town Katy–Did, and the Bunker–Hill Katy–Didn't.'

"The most able papers in the present number are, of course, those furnished by the editor (the eminent Mr. CRAB), but there are numerous magnificent contributions from such names as SNOB, Mademoiselle Cribalittle, Slyass, Mrs. Fibalittle, Mumblethumb, Mrs. Squibalittle, and last, though not least, Fatquack. The world may well be challenged to produce so rich a galaxy of genius.

"The poem over the signature, "SNOB" is, we find, attracting universal commendation, and, we are constrained to say, deserves, if possible, even more applause than it has received. The 'Oil–of–Bob' is the title of this masterpiece of eloquence and art. One or two of our readers may have a very faint, although sufficiently disgusting recollection of a poem (?) similarly entitled, the perpetration of a miserable penny–a–liner, mendicant, and cut–throat, connected in the capacity of scullion, we believe, with one of the indecent prints about the purlieus of the city, we beg them, for God's sake, not to confound the compositions. The author of the 'Oil–of–Bob' is, we hear, Thingum Bob, Esq, a gentleman of high genius, and a scholar. 'Snob' is merely a nom de guerre. Sep. 15– 1 t."

I could scarcely restrain my indignation while I perused the concluding portions of this diatribe. It was clear to me that the yea–nay manner– not to say the gentleness,– the positive forbearance– with which the "Daddy–Long–Legs" spoke of that pig, the editor of the "Gad–Fly,"– it was evident to me, I say, that this gentleness of speech could proceed from nothing else than a partiality for the "Fly"– whom it was clearly the intention of the "Daddy–Long–Legs" to elevate into reputation at my expense. Any one, indeed, might perceive, with half an eye, that, had the real design of the "Daddy" been what it wished to appear, it (the "Daddy") might have expressed itself in terms more direct, more pungent, and altogether more to the purpose. The words "penny–a–liner," "mendicant," "scullion," and "cut–throat," were epithets so intentionally inexpressive and equivocal, as to be worse than nothing when applied to the author of the very worst stanzas ever penned by one of the human race. We all know what is meant by "damning with faint praise," and, on the other hand, who could fail seeing through the covert purpose of the "Daddy,"–

that of glorifying with feeble abuse?

What the "Daddy" chose to say to the "Fly," however, was no business of mine. What it said of myself was. After the noble manner in which the "Owl," the "Toad," the "Mole," had expressed themselves in respect to my ability, it was rather too much to be coolly spoken of by a thing like the "Daddy–Long–Legs," as merely "a gentleman of high genius and scholar." Gentleman indeed! I made up my mind at once either to get written apology from the "Daddy–Long–Legs," or to call it out.

Full of this purpose, I looked about me to find a friend whom I could entrust with a message to his "Daddy"ship, and as the editor of the "Lollipop" had given me marked tokens of regard, I at length concluded to seek assistance upon the present occasion.

I have never yet been able to account, in a manner satisfactory to my own understanding, for the very peculiar countenance and demeanor with which Mr. Crab listened to me, as I unfolded to him my design. He again went through the scene of the bell–rope and cudgel, and did not omit the duck. At one period I thought he really intended to quack. His fit, nevertheless, finally subsided as before, and he began to act and speak in a rational way. He declined bearing the cartel, however, and in fact, dissuaded me from sending it at all; but was candid enough to admit that the "Daddy–Long–Legs" had been disgracefully in the wrong– more especially in what related to the epithets "gentleman and scholar."

Toward the end of this interview with Mr. Crab, who

really appeared to take a paternal interest in my welfare, he suggested to me that I might turn an honest penny, and at the same time, advance my reputation, by occasionally playing Thomas Hawk for the "Lollypop."

I begged Mr. Crab to inform me who was Mr. Thomas Hawk, and how it was expected that I should play him.

Here Mr. Crab again "made great eyes" (as we say in Germany), but at length, recovering himself from a profound attack of astonishment, he assured me that he employed the words "Thomas Hawk" to avoid the colloquialism, Tommy, which was low– but that the true idea was Tommy Hawk– or tomahawk– and that by "playing tomahawk" he referred to scalping, brow–beating, and otherwise using– up the herd of poor–devil authors.

I assured my patron that, if this was all, I was perfectly resigned to the task of playing Thomas Hawk. Hereupon Mr. Crab desired me to use up the editor of the "Gad–Fly" forthwith, in the fiercest style within the scope of my ability, and as a specimen of my powers. This I did, upon the spot, in a review of the original "Oil–of–Bob," occupying thirty–six pages of the "Lollipop." I found playing Thomas Hawk, indeed, a far less onerous occupation than poetizing; for I went upon system altogether, and thus it was easy to do the thing thoroughly well. My practice was this. I bought auction copies (cheap) of "Lord Brougham's speeches," "Cobbett's Complete Works," the "New Slang–Syllabus," the "Whole Art of Snubbing," "Prentice's Billingsgate" (folio edition), and "Lewis G. Clarke on Tongue." These works I cut up thoroughly with a curry–comb, and then, throwing the shreds into a sieve, sifted out carefully all that might be thought decent (a mere trifle); reserving the hard phrases, which I threw into a large tin pepper–castor with longitudinal holes, so that an entire sentence could get through without material injury. The mixture was then ready for use. When called upon to play Thomas Hawk, I anointed a sheet of foolscap with the white of a gander's egg; then, shredding the thing to be reviewed as I had previously shredded the books– only with more care, so as to get every word separate– I threw the latter shreds in with the former, screwed on the lid of the castor, gave it a shake, and so dusted out the mixture upon the egged foolscap; where it stuck. The effect was beautiful to behold. It was captivating. Indeed, the reviews I brought to pass by this simple expedient have never been approached, and were the wonder of the world. At first, through bashfulness– the result of inexperience– I was a little put out by a certain inconsistency– a certain air of the bizarre (as we say in France), worn by the composition as a whole. All the phrases did not fit (as we say in the Anglo–Saxon). Many were quite awry. Some, even, were upside–down; and there were none of them which were not in some measure, injured in regard to effect, by this latter species of accident, when it occurred– with the exception of Mr. Lewis Clarkes paragraphs, which were so vigorous and altogether stout, that they seemed not particularly disconcerted by any extreme of position, but looked equally happy and satisfactory, whether on their heads, or on their heels.

What became of the editor of the "Gad–Fly" after the publication of my criticism on his "Oil–of–Bob," it is somewhat difficult to determine. The most reasonable conclusion is, that he wept himself to death. At all events he disappeared instantaneously from the face of the earth, and no man has seen even the ghost of him since.

This matter having been properly accomplished, and the Furies appeased, I grew at once into high favor with Mr. Crab. He took me into his confidence, gave me a permanent situation as Thomas Hawk of the "Lollipop," and, as for the present, he could afford me no salary, allowed me to profit, at discretion, by his advice.

"My dear Thingum," said he to me one day after dinner, "I respect your abilities and love you as a son. You shall be my heir. When I die I will bequeath you the "Lollipop." In the meantime I will make a man of you– I will– provided always that you follow my counsel. The first thing to do is to get rid of the old bore."

"Boar?" said I inquiringly– "pig, eh?– aper? (as we say in Latin)– who?– where?"

"Your father," said he.

"Precisely," I replied– "pig."

"You have your fortune to make, Thingum," resumed Mr. Crab, "and that governor of yours is a millstone about your neck. We must cut him at once." [Here I took out my knife.] "We must cut him," continued Mr. Crab, "decidedly and forever. He won't do– he won't. Upon second thoughts, you had better kick him, or cane him, or something of that kind."

"What do you say," I suggested modestly, "to my kicking him in the first instance, caning him afterward, and winding up by tweaking his nose?"

Mr. Crab looked at me musingly for some moments, and then answered:

"I think, Mr. Bob, that what you propose would answer sufficiently well– indeed remarkably well– that is to say, as far as it went– but barbers are exceedingly hard to cut, and I think, upon the whole, that, having performed upon Thomas Bob the operations you suggest, it would be advisable to blacken, with your fists, both his eyes, very carefully and thoroughly, to prevent his ever seeing you again in fashionable promenades. After doing this, I really do not perceive that you can do any more. However– it might be just as well to roll him once or twice in the gutter, and then put him in charge of the police. Any time the next morning you can call at the watch–house and swear an assault."

I was muc affected by the kindness of feeling toward me personally, which was evinced in this excellent advice of Mr. Crab, and I did not fail to profit by it forthwith. The result was, that I got rid of the old bore, and began to feel a little independent and gentleman–like. The want of money, however, was, for a few weeks, a source of some discomfort; but at length, by carefully putting to use my two eyes, and observing how matters went just in front of my nose, I perceived how the thing was to be brought about. I say "thing"– be it observed– for they tell me in the Latin for it is rem. By the way, talking of Latin, can any one tell me the meaning of quocunque– or what is the meaning of modo?

My plan was exceedingly simple. I bought, for a song,

a sixteenth of the "Snapping–Turtle":– that was all. The thing was done, and I put money in my purse. There were some trivial arrangements afterward, to be sure, but these formed no portion of the plan. They were a consequence– a result. For example, I bought pen, ink, and paper, and put them into furious activity. Having thus completed a Magazine article, I gave it, for appellation, "Fol Lol, by the Author of 'THE OIL–OF–BOB,'" and enveloped it to the "Goosetherumfoodle." That journal, however, having pronounced it "twattle" in the "Monthly Notices to Correspondents," I reheaded the paper "Hey–Diddle–Diddle," by Thigum BOB, Esq., Author of the Ode on 'The Oil–of–Bob,' and Editor of the 'Snapping Turtle.'" With this amendment, I re–enclosed it to the "Goosetherumfoodle," and, while I awaited a reply, published daily, in the "Turtle," six columns of what may be termed philosophical and analytical investigation of the literary merits of the "Goosetherumfoodle," as well as of the personal character of the editor of the "Goosetherumfoodle." At the end of a week the "Goosetherumfoodle," discovered that it had, by some odd mistake, "confounded a stupid article, headed 'Hey–Diddle–Diddle,' and composed by some unknown ignoramus, with a gem of resplendent lustre similarly entitled, the work of Thingum Bob, Esq, the celebrated author of 'The Oil–of–Bob.'" The "Goosetherumfoodle" deeply "regretted this very natural accident," and promised, moreover, an insertion of the genuine "Hey–Diddle–Diddle" in the very next number of the Magazine.

The fact is, I thought– I really thought– I thought at the time– I thought then– and have no reason for thinking otherwise now– that the "Goosetherumfoodle" did make a mistake. With the best intentions in the world, I never knew any thing that made as many singular mistakes as the "Goosetherumfoodle." From that day I took a liking to the "Goosetherumfoodle" and the result was I soon saw into the very depths of its literary merits, and did not fail to expatiate upon them, in the "Turtle," whenever a fitting opportunity occurred. And it is to be regarded as a very peculiar coincidence– as one of those positively remarkable coincidences which set a man to serious thinking– that just such a total revolution of opinion– just such entire bouleversement (as we say in French)– just such thorough topsiturviness (if I may be permitted to employ a rather forcible term of the Choctaws), as happened, pro and con, between myself on the one part, and the "Goosetherumfoodle" on the other, did actually again happen, in a brief period afterwards, and with precisely similar circumstances, in the case of myself and the "Rowdy–Dow," and in the case of myself and the "Hum–Drum."

Thus it was that, by a master–stroke of genius, I at length consummated my triumphs by "putting money in my purse," and thus may be said really and fairly to have commenced that brilliant and eventful career which rendered me illustrious, and which now enables me to say with Chateaubriand: "I have made history"– J'ai fait l'histoire."

I have indeed "made history." From the bright epoch which I now record, my actions– my works– are the property of mankind. They are familiar to the world. It is, then, needless for me to detail how, soaring rapidly, I fell heir to the "Lollipop"– how I merged this journal in the "Hum–Drum"– how again I made purchase of the "Rowdy–Dow," thus combining the three periodicals– how lastly, I effected a bargain for the sole remaining rival, and united all the literature of the country in one magnificent Magazine known everywhere as the–

Rowdy-Dow, Lollipop, Hum-Drum,
and
GOOSETHERUMFOODLE.

Yes, I have made history. My fame is universal. It extends to the uttermost ends of the earth. You cannot take up a common newspaper in which you shall not see some allusion to the immortal Thigum Bob. It is Mr. Thingum Bob said so, and Mr. Thingum Bob wrote this, and Mr. Thingum Bob did that. But I am meek and expire with an humble heart. After all, what is it?– this indescribable something which men will persist in terming "genius"? I agree with Buffon– with Hogarth– it is but diligence after all.

Look at me!– how I labored– how I toiled– how I wrote! Ye Gods, did I not write? I knew not the word "ease." By day I adhered to my desk, and at night, a pale student, I consumed the midnight oil. You should have seen me– you should. I leaned to the right. I leaned to the left. I sat forward. I sat backward. I sat tete baissee (as they have it in the Kickapoo), bowing my head close to the alabaster page. And, through all, I– wrote. Through joy and through sorrow, I–wrote. Through hunger and through thirst, I–wrote. Through good report and through ill report– I wrote. Through sunshine and through moonshine, I–wrote. What I wrote it is unnecessary to say. The style!– that was the thing. I caught it from Fatquack– whizz!– fizz!– and I am giving you a specimen of it now.

HOW TO WRITE A BLACKWOOD ARTICLE

"In the name of the prophets- figs!!"

Cry of Turkish fig-peddler.

I PRESUME everybody has heard of me. My name is the Signora Psyche Zenobia. This I know to be a fact.Nobody but my enemies ever calls me Suky Snobbs. I have been assured that Suky is but a vulgar corruption of Psyche, which is good Greek, and means "the soul" (that's me, I'm all soul) and sometimes "a butterfly," which latter meaning undoubtedly alludes to my appearance in my new crimson satin dress, with the sky–blue Arabian mantelet, and the trimmings of green agraffas, and the seven flounces of orange–colored auriculas. As for Snobbs– any person who should look at me would be instantly aware that my name wasn't Snobbs. Miss Tabitha Turnip propagated that report through sheer envy. Tabitha Turnip indeed! Oh the little wretch! But what can we expect from a turnip? Wonder if she remembers the old adage about "blood out of a turnip," &c.? [Mem. put her in mind of it the first opportunity.] [Mem. again– pull her nose.] Where was I? Ah! I have been assured that Snobbs is a mere corruption of Zenobia, and that Zenobia was a queen– (So am I. Dr. Moneypenny always calls me the Queen of the Hearts)– and that Zenobia, as well as Psyche, is good Greek, and that my father was "a Greek," and that consequently I have a right to our patronymic, which is Zenobia and not by any means Snobbs. Nobody but Tabitha Turnip calls me Suky Snobbs. I am the Signora Psyche Zenobia.

As I said before, everybody has heard of me. I am that very Signora Psyche Zenobia, so justly celebrated as corresponding secretary to the "Philadelphia, Regular, Exchange, Tea, Total, Young, Belles, Lettres, Universal, Experimental, Bibliographical, Association, To, Civilize, Humanity." Dr. Moneypenny made the title for us, and says he chose it because it sounded big like an empty rum–puncheon. (A vulgar man that sometimes– but he's deep.) We all sign the initials of the society after our names, in the fashion of the R. S. A., Royal Society of Arts– the S. D. U. K., Society for the Diffusion of Useful Knowledge, &c, &c. Dr. Moneypenny says that S. stands for stale, and that D. U. K. spells duck, (but it don't,) that S. D. U. K. stands for Stale Duck and not for Lord Brougham's society– but then Dr. Moneypenny is such a queer man that I am never sure when he is telling me the truth. At any rate we always add to our names the initials P. R. E. T. T. Y. B. L. U. E. B. A. T. C. H.– that is to say, Philadelphia, Regular, Exchange, Tea, Total, Young, Belles, Lettres, Universal, Experimental, Bibliogra-phical, Associa-tion, To, Civilize, Humanity– one letter for each word, which is a decided improvement upon Lord Brougham. Dr. Moneypenny will have it that our initials give our true character– but for my life I can't see what he means.

Notwithstanding the good offices of the Doctor, and the strenuous exertions of the association to get itself into notice, it met with no very great success until I joined it. The truth is, the members indulged in too flippant a tone of discussion. The papers read every Saturday evening were characterized less by depth than buffoonery. They were all whipped syllabub. There was no investigation of first causes, first principles. There was no investigation of any thing at all. There was no attention paid to that great point, the "fitness of things." In short there was no fine writing like this. It was all low– very! No profundity, no reading, no metaphysics– nothing which the learned call spirituality, and which the unlearned choose to stigmatize as cant. [Dr. M. says I ought to spell "cant" with a capital K– but I know better.]

When I joined the society it was my endeavor to introduce a better style of thinking and writing, and all the world knows how well I have succeeded. We get up as good papers now in the P. R. E. T. T. Y. B. L. U. E. B. A. T. C. H. as any to be found even in Blackwood. I say, Blackwood, because I have been assured that the finest writing, upon every subject, is to be discovered in the pages of that justly celebrated Magazine. We now take it for our model upon all themes, and are getting into rapid notice accordingly. And, after all, it's not so very difficult a matter to compose an article of the genuine Blackwood stamp, if one only goes properly about it. Of course I don't speak of the political articles. Everybody knows how they are managed, since Dr. Moneypenny explained it. Mr. Blackwood has a pair of tailor's–shears, and three apprentices who stand by him for orders. One hands him the "Times," another the "Examiner" and a third a "Culley's New Compendium of Slang–Whang." Mr. B. merely cuts out and intersperses. It is soon done– nothing but "Examiner," "Slang–Whang," and "Times"– then "Times," "Slang–Whang," and

"Examiner" – and then "Times," " Examiner," and"Slang–Whang."

But the chief merit of the Magazine lies in its miscellaneous articles; and the best of these come under the head of what Dr. Moneypenny calls the bizarreries (whatever that may mean) and what everybody else calls the intensities. This is a species of writing which I have long known how to appreciate, although it is only since my late visit to Mr. Blackwood (deputed by the society) that I have been made aware of the exact method of composition. This method is very simple, but not so much so as the politics. Upon my calling at Mr. B.'s, and making known to him the wishes of the society, he received me with great civility, took me into his study, and gave me a clear explanation of the whole process.

"My dear madam," said he, evidently struck with my majestic appearance, for I had on the crimson satin, with the green agraffas, and orange–colored auriclas. "My dear madam," said he, "sit down. The matter stands thus: In the first place your writer of intensities must have very black ink, and a very big pen, with a very blunt nib. And, mark me, Miss Psyche Zenobia!" he continued, after a pause, with the most expressive energy and solemnity of manner, "mark me!– that pen– must– never be mended! Herein, madam, lies the secret, the soul, of intensity. I assume upon myself to say, that no individual, of however great genius ever wrote with a good pen– understand me,– a good article. You may take, it for granted, that when manuscript can be read it is never worth reading. This is a leading principle in our faith, to which if you cannot readily assent, our conference is at an end."

He paused. But, of course, as I had no wish to put an end to the conference, I assented to a proposition so very obvious, and one, too, of whose truth I had all along been sufficiently aware. He seemed pleased, and went on with his instructions.

"It may appear invidious in me, Miss Psyche Zenobia, to refer you to any article, or set of articles, in the way of model or study, yet perhaps I may as well call your attention to a few cases. Let me see. There was 'The Dead Alive,' a capital thing!– the record of a gentleman's sensations when entombed before the breath was out of his body– full of tastes, terror, sentiment, metaphysics, and erudition. You would have sworn that the writer had been born and brought up in a coffin. Then we had the 'Confessions of an Opium–eater'– fine, very fine!– glorious imagination– deep philosophy acute speculation– plenty of fire and fury, and a good spicing of the decidedly unintelligible. That was a nice bit of flummery, and went down the throats of the people delightfully. They would have it that Coleridge wrote the paper– but not so. It was composed by my pet baboon, Juniper, over a rummer of Hollands and water, 'hot, without sugar.'" [This I could scarcely have believed had it been anybody but Mr. Blackwood, who assured me of it.] "Then there was 'The Involuntary Experimentalist,' all about a gentleman who got baked in an oven, and came out alive and well, although certainly done to a turn. And then there was 'The Diary of a Late Physician,' where the merit lay in good rant, and indifferent Greek– both of them taking things with the public. And then there was 'The Man in the Bell,' a paper by– the–by, Miss Zenobia, which I cannot sufficiently recommend to your attention. It is the history of a young person who goes to sleep under the clapper of a church bell, and is awakened by its tolling for a funeral. The sound drives him mad, and, accordingly, pulling out his tablets, he gives a record of his sensations. Sensations are the great things after all. Should you ever be drowned or hung, be sure and make a note of your sensations– they will be worth to you ten guineas a sheet. If you wish to write forcibly, Miss Zenobia, pay minute attention to the sensations."

"That I certainly will, Mr. Blackwood," said I.

"Good!" he replied. "I see you are a pupil after my own heart. But I must put you au fait to the details necessary in composing what may be denominated a genuine Blackwood article of the sensation stamp– the kind which you will understand me to say I consider the best for all purposes.

"The first thing requisite is to get yourself into such a scrape as no one ever got into before. The oven, for instance,– that was a good hit. But if you have no oven or big bell, at hand, and if you cannot conveniently tumble out of a balloon, or be swallowed up in an earthquake, or get stuck fast in a chimney, you will have to be contented with simply imagining some similar misadventure. I should prefer, however, that you have the actual fact to bear you out. Nothing so well assists the fancy, as an experimental knowledge of the matter in hand. 'Truth is strange,' you know, 'stranger than fiction'– besides being more to the purpose."

Here I assured him I had an excellent pair of garters, and would go and hang myself forthwith.

"Good!" he replied, "do so;– although hanging is

somewhat hacknied. Perhaps you might do better. Take a dose of Brandreth's pills, and then give us your sensations. However, my instructions will apply equally well to any variety of misadventure, and in your way home you may easily get knocked in the head, or run over by an omnibus, or bitten by a mad dog, or drowned in a gutter. But to proceed.

"Having determined upon your subject, you must next consider the tone, or manner, of your narration. There is the tone didactic, the tone enthusiastic, the tone natural– all common– place enough. But then there is the tone laconic, or curt, which has lately come much into use. It consists in short sentences. Somehow thus: Can't be too brief. Can't be too snappish. Always a full stop. And never a paragraph.

"Then there is the tone elevated, diffusive, and interjectional. Some of our best novelists patronize this tone. The words must be all in a whirl, like a humming–top, and make a noise very similar, which answers remarkably well instead of meaning. This is the best of all possible styles where the writer is in too great a hurry to think.

"The tone metaphysical is also a good one. If you know any big words this is your chance for them. Talk of the Ionic and Eleatic schools– of Archytas, Gorgias, and Alcmaeon. Say something about objectivity and subjectivity. Be sure and abuse a man named Locke. Turn up your nose at things in general, and when you let slip any thing a little too absurd, you need not be at the trouble of scratching it out, but just add a footnote and say that you are indebted for the above profound observation to the 'Kritik der reinem Vernunft,' or to

Edgar Allan Poe

the 'Metaphysithe Anfongsgrunde der Noturwiss-enchaft.' This would look erudite and– and– and frank.

"There are various other tones of equal celebrity, but I shall mention only two more– the tone transcendental and the tone heterogeneous. In the former the merit consists in seeing into the nature of affairs a very great deal farther than anybody else. This second sight is very efficient when properly managed. A little reading of the 'Dial' will carry you a great way. Eschew, in this case, big words; get them as small as possible, and write them upside down. Look over Channing's poems and quote what he says about a 'fat little man with a delusive show of Can.' Put in something about the Supernal Oneness. Don't say a syllable about the Infernal Twoness. Above all, study innuendo. Hint everything– assert nothing. If you feel inclined to say 'bread and butter,' do not by any means say it outright. You may say any thing and every thing approaching to 'bread and butter.' You may hint at buck–wheat cake, or you may even go so far as to insinuate oat–meal porridge, but if bread and butter be your real meaning, be cautious, my dear Miss Psyche, not on any account to say 'bread and butter!'

I assured him that I should never say it again as long as I lived. He kissed me and continued:

"As for the tone heterogeneous, it is merely a judicious mixture, in equal proportions, of all the other tones in the world, and is consequently made up of every thing deep, great, odd, piquant, pertinent, and pretty.

"Let us suppose now you have determined upon your incidents and tone. The most important portion– in fact, the soul of the whole business, is yet to be attended to– I allude to the filling up. It is not to be supposed that a lady, or gentleman either, has been leading the life of a book worm. And yet above all things it is necessary that your article have an air of erudition, or at least afford evidence of extensive general reading. Now I'll put you in the way of accomplishing this point. See here!" (pulling down some three or four ordinary–looking volumes, and opening them at random). "By casting your eye down almost any page of any book in the world, you will be able to perceive at once a host of little scraps of either learning or bel–espritism, which are the very thing for the spicing of a Blackwood article. You might as well note down a few while I read them to you. I shall make two divisions: first, Piquant Facts for the Manufacture of Similes, and, second, Piquant Expressions to be introduced as occasion may require. Write now!"– and I wrote as he dictated.

"PIQUANT FACTS FOR SIMILES. 'There were originally but three Muses– Melete, Mneme, Aoede– meditation, memory, and singing.' You may make a good deal of that little fact if properly worked. You see it is not generally known, and looks recherche. You must be careful and give the thing with a downright improviso air.

"Again. 'The river Alpheus passed beneath the sea, and emerged without injury to the purity of its waters.' Rather stale that, to be sure, but, if properly dressed and dished up, will look quite as fresh as ever.

"Here is something better. 'The Persian Iris appears to some persons to possess a sweet and very powerful perfume, while to others it is perfectly scentless.' Fine that, and very delicate! Turn it about a little, and it will do wonders. We'll have some thing else in the botanical line. There's nothing goes down so well, especially with the help of a little Latin. Write!

"'The Epidendrum Flos Aeris, of Java, bears a very beautiful flower, and will live when pulled up by the roots. The natives suspend it by a cord from the ceiling, and enjoy its fragrance for years.' That's capital! That will do for the similes. Now for the Piquant Expressions.

"PIQUANT EXPRESSIONS. 'The Venerable Chinese novel Ju–Kiao–Li.' Good! By introducing these few words with dexterity you will evince your intimate acquaintance with the language and literature of the Chinese. With the aid of this you may either get along without either Arabic, or Sanscrit, or Chickasaw. There is no passing muster, however, without Spanish, Italian, German, Latin, and Greek. I must look you out a little specimen of each. Any scrap will answer, because you must depend upon your own ingenuity to make it fit into your article. Now write!

"'Aussi tendre que Zaire'– as tender as Zaire–French. Alludes to the frequent repetition of the phrase, la tendre Zaire, in the French tragedy of that name. Properly introduced, will show not only your knowledge of the language, but your general reading and wit. You can say, for instance, that the chicken you were eating (write an article about being choked to death by a chicken–bone) was not altogether aussi tendre que Zaire. Write!

> 'Van muerte tan escondida,
> Que no te sienta venir,
> Porque el plazer del morir,

No mestorne a dar la vida.'

"That's Spanish– from Miguel de Cervantes. 'Come quickly, O death! but be sure and don't let me see you coming, lest the pleasure I shall feel at your appearance should unfortunately bring me back again to life.' This you may slip in quite a propos when you are struggling in the last agonies with the chicken–bone. Write!

> Il pover 'huomo che non se'n era accorto,
> Andava combattendo, e era morto.'

That's Italian, you perceive– from Ariosto. It means that a great hero, in the heat of combat, not perceiving that he had been fairly killed, continued to fight valiantly, dead as he was. The application of this to your own case is obvious– for I trust, Miss Psyche, that you will not neglect to kick for at least an hour and a half after you have been choked to death by that chicken–bone. Please to write!

> 'Und sterb'ich doch, no sterb'ich denn
> Durch sie- durch sie!'

That's German– from Schiller. 'And if I die, at least I die– for thee– for thee!' Here it is clear that you are apostrophizing the cause of your disaster, the chicken. Indeed what gentleman (or lady either) of sense, wouldn't die, I should like to know, for a well fattened capon of the right Molucca breed, stuffed with capers and mushrooms, and served up in a salad–bowl, with orange–jellies en mosaiques. Write! (You can get them that way at Tortoni's)– Write, if you please!

"Here is a nice little Latin phrase, and rare too, (one

can't be too recherche or brief in one's Latin, it's getting so common– ignoratio elenchi. He has committed an ignoratio elenchi– that is to say, he has understood the words of your proposition, but not the idea. The man was a fool, you see. Some poor fellow whom you address while choking with that chicken–bone, and who therefore didn't precisely understand what you were talking about. Throw the ignoratio elenchi in his teeth, and, at once, you have him annihilated. If he dares to reply, you can tell him from Lucan (here it is) that speeches are mere anemonae verborum, anemone words. The anemone, with great brilliancy, has no smell. Or, if he begins to bluster, you may be down upon him with insomnia Jovis, reveries of Jupiter– a phrase which Silius Italicus (see here!) applies to thoughts pompous and inflated. This will be sure and cut him to the heart. He can do nothing but roll over and die. Will you be kind enough to write?

"In Greek we must have some thing pretty– from Demosthenes, for example.

Anerh o pheugoen kai palin makesetai

There is a tolerably good translation of it in Hudibras

> 'For he that flies may fight again,
> Which he can never do that's slain.'

In a Blackwood article nothing makes so fine a show as your Greek. The very letters have an air of profundity about them. Only observe, madam, the astute look of that Epsilon! That Phi ought certainly to be a bishop! Was ever there a smarter fellow than that Omicron? Just twig that Tau! In short, there is nothing like Greek for a genuine sensation–paper. In the present case your application is the most obvious thing in the world. Rap out the sentence, with a huge oath, and by way of ultimatum at the good–for–nothing dunder–headed villain who couldn't understand your plain English in relation to the chicken–bone. He'll take the hint and be off, you may depend upon it."

These were all the instructions Mr. B. could afford me upon the topic in question, but I felt they would be entirely sufficient. I was, at length, able to write a genuine Blackwood article, and determined to do it forthwith. In taking leave of me, Mr. B. made a proposition for the purchase of the paper when written; but as he could offer me only fifty guineas a sheet, I thought it better to let our society have it, than sacrifice it for so paltry a sum. Notwithstanding this niggardly spirit, however, the gentleman showed his consideration for me in all other respects, and indeed treated me with the greatest civility. His parting words made a deep impression upon my heart, and I hope I shall always remember them with gratitude.

"My dear Miss Zenobia," he said, while the tears stood in his eyes, "is there anything else I can do to promote the success of your laudable undertaking? Let me reflect! It is just possible that you may not be able, so soon as convenient, to– to– get yourself drowned, or– choked with a chicken–bone, or– or hung,– or– bitten by a– but stay! Now I think me of it, there are a couple of very excellent bull–dogs in the yard– fine fellows, I assure you– savage, and all that– indeed just the thing for your money– they'll have you eaten up, auricula and all, in less than five minutes (here's my watch!)– and then only think of the sensations! Here! I say– Tom!– Peter!– Dick, you villain!– let out those"– but as I was really in a great hurry, and had not another moment to spare, I was reluctantly forced to expedite my departure, and accordingly took leave at once– somewhat more abruptly, I admit, than strict courtesy would have otherwise allowed.

It was my primary object upon quitting Mr. Blackwood, to get into some immediate difficulty, pursuant to his advice, and with this view I spent the greater part of the day in wandering about Edinburgh, seeking for desperate adventures– adventures adequate to the intensity of my feelings, and adapted to the vast character of the article I intended to write. In this excursion I was attended by one negro– servant, Pompey, and my little lap–dog Diana, whom I had brought with me from Philadelphia. It was not, however, until late in the afternoon that I fully succeeded in my arduous undertaking. An important event then happened of which the following Blackwood article, in the tone heterogeneous, is the substance and result.

A PREDICAMENT

What chance, good lady, hath bereft you thus?

—COMUS.

IT was a quiet and still afternoon when I strolled forth in the goodly city of Edina. The confusion and bustle in the streets were terrible. Men were talking. Women were screaming. Children were choking. Pigs were whistling. Carts they rattled. Bulls they bellowed. Cows they lowed. Horses they neighed. Cats they caterwauled. Dogs they danced. Danced! Could it then be possible? Danced! Alas, thought I, my dancing days are over! Thus it is ever. What a host of gloomy recollections will ever and anon be awakened in the mind of genius and imaginative contemplation, especially of a genius doomed to the everlasting and eternal, and continual, and, as one might say, the– continued– yes, the continued and continuous, bitter, harassing, disturbing, and, if I may be allowed the expression, the very disturbing influence of the serene, and godlike, and heavenly, and exalted, and elevated, and purifying effect of what may be rightly termed the most enviable, the most truly enviable– nay! the most benignly beautiful, the most deliciously ethereal, and, as it were, the most pretty (if I may use so bold an expression) thing (pardon me, gentle reader!) in the world– but I am always led away by my feelings. In such a mind, I repeat, what a host of recollections are stirred up by a trifle! The dogs danced! I– I could not! They frisked– I wept. They capered– I sobbed aloud. Touching circumstances! which cannot fail to bring to the recollection of the classical reader that exquisite passage in relation to the fitness of things, which is to be found in the commencement of the third volume of that admirable and venerable Chinese novel the Jo–Go–Slow.

In my solitary walk through, the city I had two humble but faithful companions. Diana, my poodle! sweetest of creatures! She had a quantity of hair over her one eye, and a blue ribband tied fashionably around her neck. Diana was not more than five inches in height, but her head was somewhat bigger than her body, and her tail being cut off exceedingly close, gave an air of injured innocence to the interesting animal which rendered her a favorite with all.

And Pompey, my negro!– sweet Pompey! how shall I ever forget thee? I had taken Pompey's arm. He was three feet in height (I like to be particular) and about seventy, or perhaps eighty, years of age. He had bow–legs and was corpulent. His mouth should not be called small, nor his ears short. His teeth, however, were like pearl, and his large full eyes were deliciously white. Nature had endowed him with no neck, and had placed his ankles (as usual with that race) in the middle of the upper portion of the feet. He was clad with a striking simplicity. His sole garments were a stock of nine inches in height, and a nearly– new drab overcoat which had formerly been in the service of the tall, stately, and illustrious Dr. Moneypenny. It was a good overcoat. It was well cut. It was well made. The coat was nearly new. Pompey held it up out of the dirt with both hands.

There were three persons in our party, and two of them have already been the subject of remark. There was a third– that person was myself. I am the Signora Psyche Zenobia. I am not Suky Snobbs. My appearance is commanding. On the memorable occasion of which I speak I was habited in a crimson satin dress, with a sky–blue Arabian mantelet. And the dress had trimmings of green agraffas, and seven graceful flounces of the orange–colored auricula. I thus formed the third of the party. There was the poodle. There was Pompey. There was myself. We were three. Thus it is said there were originally but three Furies– Melty, Nimmy, and Hetty– Meditation, Memory, and Fiddling.

Leaning upon the arm of the gallant Pompey, and attended at a respectable distance by Diana, I proceeded down one of the populous and very pleasant streets of the now deserted Edina. On a sudden, there presented itself to view a church– a Gothic cathedral– vast, venerable, and with a tall steeple, which towered into the sky. What madness now possessed me? Why did I rush upon my fate? I was seized with an uncontrollable desire to ascend the giddy pinnacle, and then survey the immense extent of the city. The door of the cathedral stood invitingly open. My destiny prevailed. I entered the ominous archway. Where then was my guardian angel?– if indeed such angels there be. If! Distressing monosyllable! what world of mystery, and meaning, and doubt, and uncertainty is there involved in thy two letters! I entered the ominous archway! I entered; and, without injury to my orange–colored auriculas, I passed beneath the portal, and emerged within the vestibule. Thus it is said the immense river Alfred passed, unscathed, and unwetted, beneath the sea.

I thought the staircase would never have an end. Round! Yes, they went round and up, and round and up and round and up, until I could not help surmising, with the sagacious Pompey, upon whose supporting arm I leaned in all the confidence of early affection– I could not help surmising that the upper end of the continuous spiral ladder had been accidentally, or perhaps designedly, removed. I paused for breath; and, in the meantime, an accident occurred of too momentous a nature in a moral, and also in a metaphysical point of view, to be passed over without notice. It appeared to me– indeed I was quite confident of the fact– I could not be mistaken– no! I had, for some moments, carefully and anxiously observed the motions of my Diana– I say that I could not be mistaken– Diana smelt a rat! At once I called Pompey's attention to the subject, and he– he agreed with me. There was then no longer any reasonable room for doubt. The rat had been smelled– and by Diana. Heavens! shall I ever forget the intense excitement of the moment? Alas! what is the boasted intellect of man? The rat!– it was there– that is to say, it was somewhere. Diana smelled the rat. I– I could not! Thus it is said the Prussian Isis has, for some persons, a sweet and very powerful perfume, while to others it is perfectly scentless.

The stair case had been surmounted, and there were now only three or four more upward steps intervening between us and the summit. We still ascended, and now only one step remained. One step! One little, little step! Upon one such little step in the great staircase of human life how vast a sum of human happiness or misery depends! I thought of myself, then of Pompey, and then of the mysterious and inexplicable destiny which surrounded us. I thought of Pompey!– alas, I thought of love! I thought of my many false steps which have been taken, and may be taken again. I resolved to be more cautious, more reserved. I abandoned the arm of Pompey, and, without his assistance, surmounted the one remaining step, and gained the chamber of the belfry. I was followed immediately afterward by my poodle. Pompey alone remained behind. I stood at the head of the staircase, and encouraged him to ascend. He stretched forth to me his hand, and unfortunately in so doing was forced to abandon his firm hold upon the overcoat. Will the gods never cease their persecution? The overcoat is dropped, and, with one of his feet, Pompey stepped upon the long and trailing skirt of the overcoat. He stumbled and fell– this consequence was inevitable. He fell forward, and, with his accursed head, striking me full in the– in the breast, precipitated me headlong, together with himself, upon the hard, filthy, and detestable floor of the belfry. But my revenge was sure, sudden, and complete. Seizing him furiously by the wool with both hands, I tore out a vast quantity of black, and crisp, and curling material, and tossed it from me with every manifestation of disdain. It fell among the ropes of the belfry and remained. Pompey arose, and said no word. But he regarded me piteously with his large eyes and– sighed. Ye Gods– that sigh! It sunk into my heart. And the hair– the wool! Could I have reached that wool I would have bathed it with my tears, in testimony of regret. But alas! it was now far beyond my grasp. As it dangled among the cordage of the bell, I fancied it alive. I fancied that it stood on end with indignation. Thus the happy–dandy Flos Aeris of Java bears, it is said, a beautiful flower, which will live when pulled up by the roots. The natives suspend it by a cord from the ceiling and enjoy its fragrance for years.

Our quarrel was now made up, and we looked about the room for an aperture through which to survey the city of Edina. Windows there were none. The sole light admitted into the gloomy chamber proceeded from a square opening, about a foot in diameter, at a height of about seven feet from the floor. Yet what will the energy of true genius not effect? I resolved to clamber up to this hole. A vast quantity of wheels, pinions, and other cabalistic– looking machinery stood opposite the hole, close to it; and through the hole there passed an iron rod from the machinery. Between the wheels and the wall where the hole lay there was barely room for my body– yet I was desperate, and determined to persevere. I called Pompey to my side.

"You perceive that aperture, Pompey. I wish to look through it. You will stand here just beneath the hole– so. Now, hold out one of your hands, Pompey, and let me step upon it– thus. Now, the other hand, Pompey, and with its aid I will get upon your shoulders."

He did every thing I wished, and I found, upon getting up, that I could easily pass my head and neck through the aperture. The prospect was sublime. Nothing could be more magnificent. I merely paused a moment to bid Diana behave herself, and assure Pompey that I would be considerate and bear as lightly as possible upon his shoulders. I told him I would be tender of his feelings– ossi tender que beefsteak. Having done this justice to my faithful friend, I gave myself up with great zest and enthusiasm to the enjoyment of the scene which so obligingly spread itself out before my eyes.

Upon this subject, however, I shall forbear to dilate. I will not describe the city of Edinburgh. Every one has been to the city of Edinburgh. Every one has been to Edinburgh– the classic Edina. I will confine myself to the momentous details of my own lamentable adventure. Having, in some measure, satisfied my curiosity in regard to the extent, situation, and general appearance of the city, I had leisure to survey the church in which I was, and the delicate architecture of the steeple. I observed that the aperture through which I had thrust my head was an opening in the dial–plate of a gigantic clock, and must have appeared, from the street, as a large key–hole, such as we see in the face of the French watches. No doubt the true object was to admit the arm of an attendant, to adjust, when necessary, the hands of the clock from within. I observed also, with surprise, the immense size of these hands, the longest of which could not have been less than ten feet in length, and, where broadest, eight or nine inches in breadth. They were of solid steel apparently, and their edges appeared to be sharp. Having noticed these particulars, and some others, I again turned my eyes upon the glorious prospect below, and soon became absorbed in contemplation.

From this, after some minutes, I was aroused by the voice of Pompey, who declared that he could stand it no longer, and requested that I would be so kind as to come down. This was unreasonable, and I told him so in a speech of some length. He replied, but with an evident misunderstanding of my ideas upon the subject. I accordingly grew angry, and told him in plain words, that he was a fool, that he had committed an ignoramus e–clench–eye, that his notions were mere insommary Bovis, and his words little better than an ennemywerrybor'em. With this he appeared satisfied,

Edgar Allan Poe

and I resumed my contemplations.

It might have been half an hour after this altercation when, as I was deeply absorbed in the heavenly scenery beneath me, I was startled by something very cold which pressed with a gentle pressure on the back of my neck. It is needless to say that I felt inexpressibly alarmed. I knew that Pompey was beneath my feet, and that Diana was sitting, according to my explicit directions, upon her hind legs, in the farthest corner of the room. What could it be? Alas! I but too soon discovered. Turning my head gently to one side, I perceived, to my extreme horror, that the huge, glittering, scimetar–like minute–hand of the clock had, in the course of its hourly revolution, descended upon my neck. There was, I knew, not a second to be lost. I pulled back at once– but it was too late. There was no chance of forcing my head through the mouth of that terrible trap in which it was so fairly caught, and which grew narrower and narrower with a rapidity too horrible to be conceived. The agony of that moment is not to be imagined. I threw up my hands and endeavored, with all my strength, to force upward the ponderous iron bar. I might as well have tried to lift the cathedral itself. Down, down, down it came, closer and yet closer. I screamed to Pompey for aid; but he said that I had hurt his feelings by calling him 'an ignorant old squint–eye:' I yelled to Diana; but she only said 'bow–wow–wow,' and that I had told her 'on no account to stir from the corner.' Thus I had no relief to expect from my associates.

Meantime the ponderous and terrific Scythe of Time (for I now discovered the literal import of that classical phrase) had not stopped, nor was it likely to stop, in its career. Down and still down, it came. It had already buried its sharp edge a full inch in my flesh, and my sensations grew indistinct and confused. At one time I fancied myself in Philadelphia with the stately Dr. Moneypenny, at another in the back parlor of Mr. Blackwood receiving his invaluable instructions. And then again the sweet recollection of better and earlier times came over me, and I thought of that happy period when the world was not all a desert, and Pompey not altogether cruel.

The ticking of the machinery amused me. Amused me, I say, for my sensations now bordered upon perfect happiness, and the most trifling circumstances afforded me pleasure. The eternal click–clak, click–clak, click–clak of the clock was the most melodious of music in my ears, and occasionally even put me in mind of the graceful sermonic harangues of Dr. Ollapod. Then there were the great figures upon the dial–plate– how intelligent how intellectual, they all looked! And presently they took to dancing the Mazurka, and I think it was the figure V. who performed the most to my satisfaction. She was evidently a lady of breeding. None of your swaggerers, and nothing at all indelicate in her motions. She did the pirouette to admiration– whirling round upon her apex. I made an endeavor to hand her a chair, for I saw that she appeared fatigued with her exertions– and it was not until then that I fully perceived my lamentable situation. Lamentable indeed! The bar had buried itself two inches in my neck. l was aroused to a sense of exquisite pain. I prayed for death, and, in the agony of the moment, could not help repeating those exquisite verses of the poet Miguel De Cervantes:

> Vanny Buren, tan escondida
> Query no te senty venny

> Pork and pleasure, delly morry
> Nommy, torny, darry, widdy!

But now a new horror presented itself, and one indeed sufficient to startle the strongest nerves. My eyes, from the cruel pressure of the machine, were absolutely starting from their sockets. While I was thinking how I should possibly manage without them, one actually tumbled out of my head, and, rolling down the steep side of the steeple, lodged in the rain gutter which ran along the eaves of the main building. The loss of the eye was not so much as the insolent air of independence and contempt with which it regarded me after it was out. There it lay in the gutter just under my nose, and the airs it gave itself would have been ridiculous had they not been disgusting. Such a winking and blinking were never before seen. This behavior on the part of my eye in the gutter was not only irritating on account of its manifest insolence and shameful ingratitude, but was also exceedingly inconvenient on account of the sympathy which always exists between two eyes of the same head, however far apart. I was forced, in a manner, to wink and to blink, whether I would or not, in exact concert with the scoundrelly thing that lay just under my nose. I was presently relieved, however, by the dropping out of the other eye. In falling it took the same direction (possibly a concerted plot) as its fellow. Both rolled out of the gutter together, and in truth I was very glad to get rid of them.

The bar was now four inches and a half deep in my neck, and there was only a little bit of skin to cut through. My sensations were those of entire happiness, for I felt that in a few minutes, at farthest, I should be relieved from my disagreeable situation. And in this expectation I was not at all deceived. At twenty–five minutes past five in the afternoon, precisely, the huge minute–hand had proceeded sufficiently far on its terrible revolution to sever the small remainder of my neck. I was not sorry to see the head which had occasioned me so much embarrassment at length make a final separation from my body. It first rolled down the side of the steeple, then lodge, for a few seconds, in the gutter, and then made its way, with a plunge, into the middle of the street.

I will candidly confess that my feelings were now of the most singular– nay, of the most mysterious, the most perplexing and incomprehensible character. My senses were here and there at one and the same moment. With my head I imagined, at one time, that I, the head, was the real Signora Psyche Zenobia– at another I felt convinced that myself, the body, was the proper identity. To clear my ideas on this topic I felt in my pocket for my snuff–box, but, upon getting it, and endeavoring to apply a pinch of its grateful contents in the ordinary manner, I became immediately aware of my peculiar deficiency, and threw the box at once down to my head. It took a pinch with great satisfaction, and smiled me an acknowledgement in return. Shortly afterward it made me a speech, which I could hear but indistinctly without ears. I gathered enough, however, to know that it was astonished at my wishing to remain alive under such circumstances. In the concluding sentences it quoted the noble words of Ariosto–

> Il pover hommy che non sera corty
> And have a combat tenty erry morty;

thus comparing me to the hero who, in the heat of the

combat, not perceiving that he was dead, continued to contest the battle with inextinguishable valor. There was nothing now to prevent my getting down from my elevation, and I did so. What it was that Pompey saw so very peculiar in my appearance I have never yet been able to find out. The fellow opened his mouth from ear to ear, and shut his two eyes as if he were endeavoring to crack nuts between the lids. Finally, throwing off his overcoat, he made one spring for the staircase and disappeared. I hurled after the scoundrel these vehement words of Demosthenes–

Andrew O'Phlegethon, you really make haste to fly,

and then turned to the darling of my heart, to the one–eyed! the shaggy–haired Diana. Alas! what a horrible vision affronted my eyes? Was that a rat I saw skulking into his hole? Are these the picked bones of the little angel who has been cruelly devoured by the monster? Ye gods! and what do I behold– is that the departed spirit, the shade, the ghost, of my beloved puppy, which I perceive sitting with a grace so melancholy, in the corner? Hearken! for she speaks, and, heavens! it is in the German of Schiller–

> "Unt stubby duk, so stubby dun
> Duk she! duk she!"

Alas! and are not her words too true?

> "And if I died, at least I died
> For thee- for thee."

Sweet creature! she too has sacrificed herself in my behalf. Dogless, niggerless, headless, what now remains for the unhappy Signora Psyche Zenobia? Alas– nothing! I have done.

X–ING A PARAGRAB

AS it is well known that the 'wise men' came 'from the East,' and as Mr. Touch–and–go Bullet–head came from the East, it follows that Mr. Bullet–head was a wise man; and if collateral proof of the matter be needed, here we have it– Mr. B. was an editor. Irascibility was his sole foible, for in fact the obstinacy of which men accused him was anything but his foible, since he justly considered it his forte. It was his strong point– his virtue; and it would have required all the logic of a Brownson to convince him that it was 'anything else.'

I have shown that Touch–and–go Bullet–head was a wise man; and the only occasion on which he did not prove infallible, was when, abandoning that legitimate home for all wise men, the East, he migrated to the city of Alexander–the–Great–o–nopolis, or some place of a similar title, out West.

I must do him the justice to say, however, that when he made up his mind finally to settle in that town, it was under the impression that no newspaper, and consequently no editor, existed in that particular section of the country. In establishing 'The Tea–Pot' he expected to have the field all to himself. I feel confident he never would have dreamed of taking up his residence in Alexander–the–Great–o–nopolis had he been aware that, in Alexander–the–Great–o–

nopolis, there lived a gentleman named John Smith (if I rightly remember), who for many years had there quietly grown fat in editing and publishing the 'Alexander–the–Great–o–nopolis Gazette.' It was solely, therefore, on account of having been misinformed, that Mr. Bullet–head found himself in Alex–suppose we call it Nopolis, 'for short'– but, as he did find himself there, he determined to keep up his character for obst– for firmness, and remain. So remain he did; and he did more; he unpacked his press, type, etc., etc., rented an office exactly opposite to that of the 'Gazette,' and, on the third morning after his arrival, issued the first number of 'The Alexan'– that is to say, of 'The Nopolis Tea–Pot'– as nearly as I can recollect, this was the name of the new paper.

The leading article, I must admit, was brilliant– not to say severe. It was especially bitter about things in general– and as for the editor of 'The Gazette,' he was torn all to pieces in particular. Some of Bullethead's remarks were really so fiery that I have always, since that time, been forced to look upon John Smith, who is still alive, in the light of a salamander. I cannot pretend to give all the 'Tea–Pot's' paragraphs verbatim, but one of them runs thus:

'Oh, yes!– Oh, we perceive! Oh, no doubt! The editor over the way is a genius– O, my! Oh, goodness, gracious!– what is this world coming to? Oh, tempora! Oh, Moses!'

A philippic at once so caustic and so classical, alighted like a bombshell among the hitherto peaceful citizens of Nopolis. Groups of excited individuals gathered at the corners of the streets. Every one awaited, with heartfelt anxiety, the reply of the dignified Smith. Next morning it appeared as follows:

'We quote from "The Tea–Pot" of yesterday the subjoined paragraph: "Oh, yes! Oh, we perceive! Oh, no doubt! Oh, my! Oh, goodness! Oh, tempora! Oh, Moses!" Why, the fellow is all O! That accounts for his reasoning in a circle, and explains why there is neither beginning nor end to him, nor to anything he says. We really do not believe the vagabond can write a word that hasn't an O in it. Wonder if this O–ing is a habit of his? By–the–by, he came away from Down–East in a great hurry. Wonder if he O's as much there as he does here? "O! it is pitiful."'

The indignation of Mr. Bullet–head at these scandalous insinuations, I shall not attempt to describe. On the eel–skinning principle, however, he did not seem to be so much incensed at the attack upon his integrity as one might have imagined. It was the sneer at his style that drove him to desperation. What!– he Touch–and–go Bullet–head!– not able to write a word without an O in it! He would soon let the jackanapes see that he was mistaken. Yes! he would let him see how much he was mistaken, the puppy! He, Touch–and–go Bullet–head, of Frogpondium, would let Mr. John Smith perceive that he, Bullet–head, could indite, if it so pleased him, a whole paragraph– aye! a whole article– in which that contemptible vowel should not once– not even once– make its appearance. But no;– that would be yielding a point to the said John Smith. He, Bullet–head, would make no alteration in his style, to suit the caprices of any Mr. Smith in Christendom. Perish so vile a thought! The O forever; He would persist in the O. He would be as O–wy as O–wy could be.

Burning with the chivalry of this determination, the

great Touch–and–go, in the next 'Tea–Pot,' came out merely with this simple but resolute paragraph, in reference to this unhappy affair:

'The editor of the "Tea–Pot" has the honor of advising the editor of the "Gazette" that he (the "Tea–Pot") will take an opportunity in tomorrow morning's paper, of convincing him (the "Gazette") that he (the "Tea–Pot") both can and will be his own master, as regards style; he (the "Tea–Pot") intending to show him (the "Gazette") the supreme, and indeed the withering contempt with which the criticism of him (the "Gazette") inspires the independent bosom of him (the "TeaPot") by composing for the especial gratification (?) of him (the "Gazette") a leading article, of some extent, in which the beautiful vowel– the emblem of Eternity– yet so offensive to the hyper–exquisite delicacy of him (the "Gazette") shall most certainly not be avoided by his (the "Gazette's") most obedient, humble servant, the "Tea–Pot." "So much for Buckingham!"'

In fulfilment of the awful threat thus darkly intimated rather than decidedly enunciated, the great Bullet–head, turning a deaf ear to all entreaties for 'copy,' and simply requesting his foreman to 'go to the d–l,' when he (the foreman) assured him (the 'Tea–Pot'!) that it was high time to 'go to press': turning a deaf ear to everything, I say, the great Bullet–head sat up until day–break, consuming the midnight oil, and absorbed in the composition of the really unparalleled paragraph, which follows:–

'So ho, John! how now? Told you so, you know. Don't crow, another time, before you're out of the woods! Does your mother know you're out? Oh, no, no!– so go home at once, now, John, to your odious old woods of Concord! Go home to your woods, old owl– go! You won't! Oh, poh, poh, don't do so! You've got to go, you know! So go at once, and don't go slow, for nobody owns you here, you know! Oh! John, John, if you don't go you're no homo– no! You're only a fowl, an owl, a cow, a sow,– a doll, a poll; a poor, old, good–for–nothing–to–nobody, log, dog, hog, or frog, come out of a Concord bog. Cool, now– cool! Do be cool, you fool! None of your crowing, old cock! Don't frown so– don't! Don't hollo, nor howl nor growl, nor bow–wow–wow! Good Lord, John, how you do look! Told you so, you know– but stop rolling your goose of an old poll about so, and go and drown your sorrows in a bowl!'

Exhausted, very naturally, by so stupendous an effort, the great Touch–and–go could attend to nothing farther that night. Firmly, composedly, yet with an air of conscious power, he handed his MS. to the devil in waiting, and then, walking leisurely home, retired, with ineffable dignity to bed.

Meantime the devil, to whom the copy was entrusted, ran up stairs to his 'case,' in an unutterable hurry, and forthwith made a commencement at 'setting' the MS. 'up.'

In the first place, of course,– as the opening word was 'So,'– he made a plunge into the capital S hole and came out in triumph with a capital S. Elated by this success, he immediately threw himself upon the little–o box with a blindfold impetuosity– but who shall describe his horror when his fingers came up without the anticipated letter in their clutch? who shall paint his astonishment and rage at perceiving, as he rubbed his knuckles, that he had been only thumping them to no purpose, against the bottom of an empty box. Not a single little–o was in the little–o hole; and, glancing fearfully at the capital–O partition, he found that to his extreme terror, in a precisely similar predicament. Awe– stricken, his first impulse was to rush to the foreman.

'Sir!' said he, gasping for breath, 'I can't never set up nothing without no o's.'

'What do you mean by that?' growled the foreman, who was in a very ill humor at being kept so late.

'Why, sir, there beant an o in the office, neither a big un nor a little un!'

'What– what the d–l has become of all that were in the case?'

'I don't know, sir,' said the boy, 'but one of them ere "G'zette" devils is bin prowling 'bout here all night, and I spect he's gone and cabbaged 'em every one.'

'Dod rot him! I haven't a doubt of it,' replied the foreman, getting purple with rage 'but I tell you what you do, Bob, that's a good boy– you go over the first chance you get and hook every one of their i's and (d–n them!) their izzards.'

'Jist so,' replied Bob, with a wink and a frown– 'I'll be into 'em, I'll let 'em know a thing or two; but in de meantime, that ere paragrab? Mus go in to–night, you know– else there'll be the d–l to pay, and–'

'And not a bit of pitch hot,' interrupted the foreman, with a deep sigh, and an emphasis on the 'bit.' 'Is it a long paragraph, Bob?'

'Shouldn't call it a wery long paragrab,' said Bob.

'Ah, well, then! do the best you can with it! We must get to press," said the foreman, who was over head and ears in work; 'just stick in some other letter for o; nobody's going to read the fellow's trash anyhow.'

'Wery well,' replied Bob, 'here goes it!' and off he hurried to his case, muttering as he went: 'Considdeble vell, them ere expressions, perticcler for a man as doesn't swar. So I's to gouge out all their eyes, eh? and d–n all their gizzards! Vell! this here's the chap as is just able for to do it.' The fact is that although Bob was but twelve years old and four feet high, he was equal to any amount of fight, in a small way.

The exigency here described is by no means of rare occurrence in printing–offices; and I cannot tell how to account for it, but the fact is indisputable, that when the exigency does occur, it almost always happens that x is adopted as a substitute for the letter deficient. The true reason, perhaps, is that x is rather the most superabundant letter in the cases, or at least was so in the old times– long enough to render the substitution in question an habitual thing with printers. As for Bob, he would have considered it heretical to employ any other character, in a case of this kind, than the x to which he had been accustomed.

'I shell have to x this ere paragrab,' said he to himself, as he read it over in astonishment, 'but it's jest about the awfulest o–wy paragrab I ever did see': so x it he did, unflinchingly, and to press it went x–ed.

Next morning the population of Nopolis were taken all aback by reading in 'The Tea–Pot,' the following extraordinary leader:

'Sx hx, Jxhn! hxw nxw? Txld yxu sx, yxu knxw. Dxn't crxw, anxther time, befxre yxu're xut xf the wxxds! Dxes yxur mxther knxw yxu're xut? Xh, nx, nx!– sx gx hxme at xnce, nxw, Jxhn, tx yxur xdixus xld wxxds xf Cxncxrd! Gx hxme tx yxur wxxds, xld xwl,– gx! Yxu wxn't? Xh, pxh, pxh, Jxhn, dxn't dx sx! Yxu've gxt tx gx, yxu knxw, sx gx at xnce, and dxn't gx slxw; fxr nxbxdy xwns yxu here, yxu knxw. Xh, Jxhn, Jxhn, Jxhn, if yxu dxn't gx yxu're nx hxmx– nx! Yxu're xnly a fxwl, an xwl; a cxw, a sxw; a dxll, a pxll; a pxxr xld gxxd–fxr–nxthing–tx–nxbxdy, lxg, dxg, hxg, xr frxg, cxme xut xf a Cxncxrd bxg. Cxxl, nxw– cxxl! Dx be cxxl, yxu fxxl! Nxne xf yxur crxwing, xld cxck! Dxn't frxwn sx– dxn't! Dxn't hxllx, nxr hxwl, nxr grxwl, nxr bxw–wxw–wxw! Gxxd Lxrd, Jxhn, hxw yxu dx lxxk! Txld yxu sx, yxu knxw,– but stxp rxlling yxur gxxse xf an xld pxll abxut sx, and gx and drxwn yxur sxrrxws in a bxwl!'

The uproar occasioned by this mystical and cabalistical article, is not to be conceived. The first definite idea entertained by the populace was, that some diabolical treason lay concealed in the hieroglyphics; and there was a general rush to Bullet–head's residence, for the purpose of riding him on a rail; but that gentleman was nowhere to be found. He had vanished, no one could tell how; and not even the ghost of him has ever been seen since.

Unable to discover its legitimate object, the popular fury at length subsided; leaving behind it, by way of sediment, quite a medley of opinion about this

Edgar Allan Poe

unhappy affair.

One gentleman thought the whole an X–ellent joke.

Another said that, indeed, Bullet–head had shown much X–uberance of fancy.

A third admitted him X–entric, but no more.

A fourth could only suppose it the Yankee's design to X–press, in a general way, his X–asperation.

'Say, rather, to set an X–ample to posterity,' suggested a fifth.

That Bullet–head had been driven to an extremity, was clear to all; and in fact, since that editor could not be found, there was some talk about lynching the other one.

The more common conclusion, however, was that the affair was, simply, X–traordinary and in–X–plicable. Even the town mathematician confessed that he could make nothing of so dark a problem. X, every. body knew, was an unknown quantity; but in this case (as he properly observed), there was an unknown quantity of X.

The opinion of Bob, the devil (who kept dark about his having 'X–ed the paragrab'), did not meet with so much attention as I think it deserved, although it was very openly and very fearlessly expressed. He said that, for his part, he had no doubt about the matter at all, that it was a clear case, that Mr. Bullet–head 'never could be persuaded fur to drink like other folks, but vas continually a–svigging o' that ere blessed XXX ale,

and as a naiteral consekvence, it just puffed him up
savage, and made him X (cross) in the X–treme.'

Edgar Allan Poe

DIDDLING

Considered as One of the Exact Sciences

Hey, diddle diddle
The cat and the fiddle

SINCE the world began there have been two Jeremys. The one wrote a Jeremiad about usury, and was called Jeremy Bentham. He has been much admired by Mr. John Neal, and was a great man in a small way. The other gave name to the most important of the Exact Sciences, and was a great man in a great way– I may say, indeed, in the very greatest of ways.

Diddling– or the abstract idea conveyed by the verb to diddle– is sufficiently well understood. Yet the fact, the deed, the thing diddling, is somewhat difficult to define. We may get, however, at a tolerably distinct conception of the matter in hand, by defining– not the thing, diddling, in itself– but man, as an animal that diddles. Had Plato but hit upon this, he would have been spared the affront of the picked chicken.

Very pertinently it was demanded of Plato, why a picked chicken, which was clearly "a biped without feathers," was not, according to his own definition, a man? But I am not to be bothered by any similar query. Man is an animal that diddles, and there is no animal that diddles but man. It will take an entire hen–coop of picked chickens to get over that.

What constitutes the essence, the nare, the principle of diddling is, in fact, peculiar to the class of creatures that wear coats and pantaloons. A crow thieves; a fox cheats; a weasel outwits; a man diddles. To diddle is his destiny. "Man was made to mourn," says the poet. But not so:– he was made to diddle. This is his aim– his object– his end. And for this reason when a man's diddled we say he's "done."

Diddling, rightly considered, is a compound, of which the ingredients are minuteness, interest, perseverance, ingenuity, audacity, nonchalance, originality, imper-tinence, and grin.

Minuteness:– Your diddler is minute. His operations are upon a small scale. His business is retail, for cash, or approved paper at sight. Should he ever be tempted into magnificent speculation, he then, at once, loses his distinctive features, and becomes what we term "financier." This latter word conveys the diddling idea in every respect except that of magnitude. A diddler may thus be regarded as a banker in petto– a "financial operation," as a diddle at Brobdignag. The one is to the other, as Homer to "Flaccus"– as a Mastodon to a mouse– as the tail of a comet to that of a pig.

Interest:– Your diddler is guided by self–interest. He scorns to diddle for the mere sake of the diddle. He has an object in view– his pocket– and yours. He regards always the main chance. He looks to Number One. You are Number Two, and must look to yourself.

Perseverance:– Your diddler perseveres. He is not

readily discouraged. Should even the banks break, he cares nothing about it. He steadily pursues his end, and

Ut canis a corio nunquam absterrebitur uncto.

so he never lets go of his game.

Ingenuity:– Your diddler is ingenious. He has constructiveness large. He understands plot. He invents and circumvents. Were he not Alexander he would be Diogenes. Were he not a diddler, he would be a maker of patent rat–traps or an angler for trout.

Audacity:– Your diddler is audacious.– He is a bold man. He carries the war into Africa. He conquers all by assault. He would not fear the daggers of Frey Herren. With a little more prudence Dick Turpin would have made a good diddler; with a trifle less blarney, Daniel O'Connell; with a pound or two more brains Charles the Twelfth.

Nonchalance:– Your diddler is nonchalant. He is not at all nervous. He never had any nerves. He is never seduced into a flurry. He is never put out– unless put out of doors. He is cool– cool as a cucumber. He is calm– "calm as a smile from Lady Bury." He is easy– easy as an old glove, or the damsels of ancient Baiae.

Originality:– Your diddler is original– conscientiously so. His thoughts are his own. He would scorn to employ those of another. A stale trick is his aversion. He would return a purse, I am sure, upon discovering that he had obtained it by an unoriginal diddle.

Impertinence.– Your diddler is impertinent. He swaggers. He sets his arms a–kimbo. He thrusts. his hands in his trowsers' pockets. He sneers in your face. He treads on your corns. He eats your dinner, he drinks your wine, he borrows your money, he pulls your nose, he kicks your poodle, and he kisses your wife.

Grin:– Your true diddler winds up all with a grin. But this nobody sees but himself. He grins when his daily work is done– when his allotted labors are accomplished– at night in his own closet, and altogether for his own private entertainment. He goes home. He locks his door. He divests himself of his clothes. He puts out his candle. He gets into bed. He places his head upon the pillow. All this done, and your diddler grins. This is no hypothesis. It is a matter of course. I reason a priori, and a diddle would be no diddle without a grin.

The origin of the diddle is referrable to the infancy of the Human Race. Perhaps the first diddler was Adam. At all events, we can trace the science back to a very remote period of antiquity. The moderns, however, have brought it to a perfection never dreamed of by our thick–headed progenitors. Without pausing to speak of the "old saws," therefore, I shall content myself with a compendious account of some of the more "modern instances."

A very good diddle is this. A housekeeper in want of a sofa, for instance, is seen to go in and out of several cabinet warehouses. At length she arrives at one offering an excellent variety. She is accosted, and invited to enter, by a polite and voluble individual at the door. She finds a sofa well adapted to her views, and upon inquiring the price, is surprised and delighted to hear a sum named at least twenty per cent. lower than her expectations. She hastens to make the purchase, gets a bill and receipt, leaves her address, with a request that the article be sent home as speedily as possible, and retires amid a profusion of bows from the shopkeeper. The night arrives and no sofa. A servant is sent to make inquiry about the delay. The whole transaction is denied. No sofa has been sold– no money received– except by the diddler, who played shop–keeper for the nonce.

Our cabinet warehouses are left entirely unattended, and thus afford every facility for a trick of this kind. Visiters enter, look at furniture, and depart unheeded and unseen. Should any one wish to purchase, or to inquire the price of an article, a bell is at hand, and this is considered amply sufficient.

Again, quite a respectable diddle is this. A well–dressed individual enters a shop, makes a purchase to the value of a dollar; finds, much to his vexation, that he has left his pocket–book in another coat pocket; and so says to the shopkeeper–

"My dear sir, never mind; just oblige me, will you, by sending the bundle home? But stay! I really believe that I have nothing less than a five dollar bill, even there. However, you can send four dollars in change with the bundle, you know."

"Very good, sir," replies the shop–keeper, who entertains, at once, a lofty opinion of the high–mindedness of his customer. "I know fellows," he says to himself, "who would just have put the goods under their arm, and walked off with a promise to call and pay the dollar as they came by in the afternoon."

A boy is sent with the parcel and change. On the route,

quite accidentally, he is met by the purchaser, who exclaims:

"Ah! This is my bundle, I see– I thought you had been home with it, long ago. Well, go on! My wife, Mrs. Trotter, will give you the five dollars– I left instructions with her to that effect. The change you might as well give to me– I shall want some silver for the Post Office. Very good! One, two, is this a good quarter?– three, four– quite right! Say to Mrs. Trotter that you met me, and be sure now and do not loiter on the way."

The boy doesn't loiter at all– but he is a very long time in getting back from his errand– for no lady of the precise name of Mrs. Trotter is to be discovered. He consoles himself, however, that he has not been such a fool as to leave the goods without the money, and re–entering his shop with a self–satisfied air, feels sensibly hurt and indignant when his master asks him what has become of the change.

A very simple diddle, indeed, is this. The captain of a ship, which is about to sail, is presented by an official looking person with an unusually moderate bill of city charges. Glad to get off so easily, and confused by a hundred duties pressing upon him all at once, he discharges the claim forthwith. In about fifteen minutes, another and less reasonable bill is handed him by one who soon makes it evident that the first collector was a diddler, and the original collection a diddle.

And here, too, is a somewhat similar thing. A steamboat is casting loose from the wharf. A traveller, portmanteau in hand, is discovered running toward the wharf, at full speed. Suddenly, he makes a dead halt, stoops, and picks up something from the ground in a very agitated manner. It is a pocket–book, and– "Has any gentleman lost a pocketbook?" he cries. No one can say that he has exactly lost a pocket–book; but a great excitement ensues, when the treasure trove is found to be of value. The boat, however, must not be detained.

"Time and tide wait for no man," says the captain.

"For God's sake, stay only a few minutes," says the finder of the book– "the true claimant will presently appear."

"Can't wait!" replies the man in authority; "cast off there, d'ye hear?"

"What am I to do?" asks the finder, in great tribulation. "I am about to leave the country for some years, and I cannot conscientiously retain this large amount in my possession. I beg your pardon, sir," [here he addresses a gentleman on shore,] "but you have the air of an honest man. Will you confer upon me the favor of taking charge of this pocket–book– I know I can trust you– and of advertising it? The notes, you see, amount to a very considerable sum. The owner will, no doubt, insist upon rewarding you for your trouble–

"Me!– no, you!– it was you who found the book."

"Well, if you must have it so– I will take a small reward– just to satisfy your scruples. Let me see– why these notes are all hundreds– bless my soul! a hundred is too much to take– fifty would be quite enough, I am sure–

"Cast off there!" says the captain.

"But then I have no change for a hundred, and upon the whole, you had better–

"Cast off there!" says the captain.

"Never mind!" cries the gentleman on shore, who has been examining his own pocket–book for the last minute or so– "never mind! I can fix it– here is a fifty on the Bank of North America– throw the book."

And the over–conscientious finder takes the fifty with marked reluctance, and throws the gentleman the book, as desired, while the steamboat fumes and fizzes on her way. In about half an hour after her departure, the "large amount" is seen to be a "counterfeit presentment," and the whole thing a capital diddle.

A bold diddle is this. A camp–meeting, or something similar, is to be held at a certain spot which is accessible only by means of a free bridge. A diddler stations himself upon this bridge, respectfully informs all passers by of the new county law, which establishes a toll of one cent for foot passengers, two for horses and donkeys, and so forth, and so forth. Some grumble but all submit, and the diddler goes home a wealthier man by some fifty or sixty dollars well earned. This taking a toll from a great crowd of people is an excessively troublesome thing.

A neat diddle is this. A friend holds one of the diddler's promises to pay, filled up and signed in due form, upon the ordinary blanks printed in red ink. The diddler purchases one or two dozen of these blanks, and every day dips one of them in his soup, makes his dog jump for it, and finally gives it to him as a bonne bouche. The note arriving at maturity, the diddler, with the diddler's dog, calls upon the friend, and the promise to pay is made the topic of discussion. The friend produces it from his escritoire, and is in the act of reaching it to the diddler, when up jumps the diddler's dog and devours it forthwith. The diddler is not only surprised but vexed and incensed at the absurd behavior of his dog, and expresses his entire readiness to cancel the obligation at any moment when the evidence of the obligation shall be forthcoming.

A very mean diddle is this. A lady is insulted in the street by a diddler's accomplice. The diddler himself flies to her assistance, and, giving his friend a comfortable thrashing, insists upon attending the lady to her own door. He bows, with his hand upon his heart, and most respectfully bids her adieu. She entreats him, as her deliverer, to walk in and be introduced to her big brother and her papa. With a sigh, he declines to do so. "Is there no way, then, sir," she murmurs, "in which I may be permitted to testify my gratitude?"

"Why, yes, madam, there is. Will you be kind enough to lend me a couple of shillings?"

In the first excitement of the moment the lady decides upon fainting outright. Upon second thought, however, she opens her purse–strings and delivers the specie. Now this, I say, is a diddle minute– for one entire moiety of the sum borrowed has to be paid to the gentleman who had the trouble of performing the insult, and who had then to stand still and be thrashed for performing it.

Rather a small but still a scientific diddle is this. The diddler approaches the bar of a tavern, and demands a couple of twists of tobacco. These are handed to him, when, having slightly examined them, he says:

"I don't much like this tobacco. Here, take it back, and give me a glass of brandy and water in its place." The brandy and water is furnished and imbibed, and the diddler makes his way to the door. But the voice of the tavern–keeper arrests him.

"I believe, sir, you have forgotten to pay for your brandy and water."

"Pay for my brandy and water!– didn't I give you the tobacco for the brandy and water? What more would you have?"

"But, sir, if you please, I don't remember that you paid me for the tobacco."

What do you mean by that, you scoundrel?– Didn't I give you back your tobacco? Isn't that your tobacco lying there? Do you expect me to pay for what I did not take?"

"But, sir," says the publican, now rather at a loss what to say, "but sir–"

"But me no buts, sir," interrupts the diddler, apparently in very high dudgeon, and slamming the door after him, as he makes his escape.– "But me no buts, sir, and none of your tricks upon travellers."

Here again is a very clever diddle, of which the simplicity is not its least recommendation. A purse, or pocket–book, being really lost, the loser inserts in one of the daily papers of a large city a fully descriptive advertisement.

Whereupon our diddler copies the facts of this advertisement, with a change of heading, of general phraseology and address. The original, for instance, is long, and verbose, is headed "A Pocket–Book Lost!" and requires the treasure, when found, to be left at No. 1 Tom Street. The copy is brief, and being headed with "Lost" only, indicates No. 2 Dick, or No. 3 Harry Street, as the locality at which the owner may be seen. Moreover, it is inserted in at least five or six of the daily papers of the day, while in point of time, it makes its appearance only a few hours after the original. Should it be read by the loser of the purse, he would hardly suspect it to have any reference to his own misfortune. But, of course, the chances are five or six to one, that the finder will repair to the address given by the diddler, rather than to that pointed out by the rightful proprietor. The former pays the reward, pockets the treasure and decamps.

Quite an analogous diddle is this. A lady of ton has dropped, some where in the street, a diamond ring of very unusual value. For its recovery, she offers some forty or fifty dollars reward– giving, in her advertisement, a very minute description of the gem, and of its settings, and declaring that, on its restoration at No. so and so, in such and such Avenue, the reward would be paid instanter, without a single question being asked. During the lady's absence from home, a day or two afterwards, a ring is heard at the door of No. so and so, in such and such Avenue; a servant appears; the lady of the house is asked for and is declared to be out, at which astounding information, the visitor expresses the most poignant regret. His business is of importance and concerns the lady herself. In fact, he had the good fortune to find her diamond ring. But perhaps it would be as well that he should call again. "By no means!" says the servant; and "By no means!" says the lady's sister and the lady's sister–in–law, who are summoned forthwith. The ring is clamorously identified, the reward is paid, and the finder nearly thrust out of doors. The lady returns and expresses some little dissatisfaction with her sister and sister–in–law, because they happen to have paid forty or fifty dollars for a fac–simile of her diamond ring– a fac–simile made out of real pinch–beck and unquestionable paste.

But as there is really no end to diddling, so there would be none to this essay, were I even to hint at half the variations, or inflections, of which this science is susceptible. I must bring this paper, perforce, to a conclusion, and this I cannot do better than by a summary notice of a very decent, but rather elaborate diddle, of which our own city was made the theatre, not very long ago, and which was subsequently repeated with success, in other still more verdant localities of the Union. A middle–aged gentleman arrives in town from parts unknown. He is remarkably precise, cautious, staid, and deliberate in his demeanor. His dress is scrupulously neat, but plain,unostentatious. He wears a white cravat, an ample waistcoat, made with an eye to comfort alone; thick–soled cosy–looking shoes, and pantaloons without straps. He has the whole air, in fact, of your well–to–do, sober–sided, exact, and respectable "man of business," Par excellence– one of the stern and outwardly hard, internally soft, sort of people that we see in the crack high comedies– fellows whose words are so many bonds, and who are noted for giving away guineas, in charity, with the one hand, while, in the way of mere bargain, they exact the uttermost fraction of a farthing with the other.

He makes much ado before he can get suited with a boarding house. He dislikes children. He has been accustomed to quiet. His habits are methodical– and then he would prefer getting into a private and respectable small family, piously inclined. Terms, however, are no object– only he must, insist upon settling his bill on the first of every month, (it is now the second) and begs his landlady, when he finally obtains one to his mind, not on any account to forget his instructions upon this point– but to send in a bill, and receipt, precisely at ten o'clock, on the first day of every month, and under no circumstances to put it off to the second.

These arrangements made, our man of business rents an office in a reputable rather than a fashionable quarter of the town. There is nothing he more despises than pretense. "Where there is much show," he says, "there is seldom any thing very solid behind"– an observation which so profoundly impresses his landlady's fancy, that she makes a pencil memorandum of it forthwith, in her great family Bible, on the broad margin of the Proverbs of Solomon.

The next step is to advertise, after some such fashion as this, in the principal business six–pennies of the city– the pennies are eschewed as not "respectable"– and as demanding payment for all advertisements in advance. Our man of business holds it as a point of his faith that work should never be paid for until done.

"WANTED– The advertisers, being about to commence extensive business operations in this city, will require the services of three or four intelligent and competent clerks, to whom a liberal salary will be paid. The very best recommendations, not so much for capacity, as for integrity, will be expected. Indeed, as the duties to be performed involve high responsibilities, and large amounts of money must necessarily pass through the hands of those engaged, it is deemed advisable to demand a deposit of fifty dollars from each clerk employed. No person need apply, therefore, who is not prepared to leave this sum in the possession of the advertisers, and who cannot furnish the most satisfactory testimonials of morality. Young gentlemen piously inclined will be preferred. Application should be made between the hours of ten and eleven A. M., and four and five P. M., of Messrs.

"Bogs, Hogs Logs, Frogs & Co.,
"No. 110 Dog Street"

By the thirty–first day of the month, this advertisement has brought to the office of Messrs. Bogs, Hogs, Logs, Frogs, and Company, some fifteen or twenty young gentlemen piously inclined. But our man of business is in no hurry to conclude a contract with any– no man of business is ever precipitate– and it is not until the most rigid catechism in respect to the piety of each young gentleman's inclination, that his services are engaged and his fifty dollars receipted for, just by way of proper precaution, on the part of the respectable firm of Bogs, Hogs, Logs, Frogs, and Company. On the morning of the first day of the next month, the landlady does not present her bill, according to promise– a piece of neglect for which the comfortable head of the house ending in ogs would no doubt have chided her severely, could he have been prevailed upon to remain in town a day or two for that purpose.

As it is, the constables have had a sad time of it, running hither and thither, and all they can do is to declare the man of business most emphatically, a "hen knee high"– by which some persons imagine them to imply that, in fact, he is n. e. i.– by which again the very classical phrase non est inventus, is supposed to be understood. In the meantime the young gentlemen, one and all, are somewhat less piously inclined than before, while the landlady purchases a shilling's worth of the Indian rubber, and very carefully obliterates the pencil memorandum that some fool has made in her great family Bible, on the broad margin of the Proverbs of Solomon.

VON KEMPELEN AND HIS DISCOVERY

AFTER THE very minute and elaborate paper by
Arago, to say nothing of the summary in 'Silliman's
Journal,' with the detailed statement just published by
Lieutenant Maury, it will not be supposed, of course,
that in offering a few hurried remarks in reference to
Von Kempelen's discovery, I have any design to look
at the subject in a scientific point of view. My object is
simply, in the first place, to say a few words of Von
Kempelen himself (with whom, some years ago, I had
the honor of a slight personal acquaintance), since
every thing which concerns him must necessarily, at
this moment, be of interest; and, in the second place, to
look in a general way, and speculatively, at the results
of the discovery.

It may be as well, however, to premise the cursory
observations which I have to offer, by denying, very
decidedly, what seems to be a general impression
(gleaned, as usual in a case of this kind, from the
newspapers), viz.: that this discovery, astounding as it
unquestionably is, is unanticipated.

By reference to the 'Diary of Sir Humphrey Davy'
(Cottle and Munroe, London, pp. 150), it will be seen
at pp. 53 and 82, that this illustrious chemist had not
only conceived the idea now in question, but had
actually made no inconsiderable progress, experi-
mentally, in the very identical analysis now so

triumphantly brought to an issue by Von Kempelen, who although he makes not the slightest allusion to it, is, without doubt (I say it unhesitatingly, and can prove it, if required), indebted to the 'Diary' for at least the first hint of his own undertaking.

The paragraph from the 'Courier and Enquirer,' which is now going the rounds of the press, and which purports to claim the invention for a Mr. Kissam, of Brunswick, Maine, appears to me, I confess, a little apocryphal, for several reasons; although there is nothing either impossible or very improbable in the statement made. I need not go into details. My opinion of the paragraph is founded principally upon its manner. It does not look true. Persons who are narrating facts, are seldom so particular as Mr. Kissam seems to be, about day and date and precise location. Besides, if Mr. Kissam actually did come upon the discovery he says he did, at the period designated– nearly eight years ago– how happens it that he took no steps, on the instant, to reap the immense benefits which the merest bumpkin must have known would have resulted to him individually, if not to the world at large, from the discovery? It seems to me quite incredible that any man of common understanding could have discovered what Mr. Kissam says he did, and yet have subsequently acted so like a baby– so like an owl– as Mr. Kissam admits that he did. By–the–way, who is Mr. Kissam? and is not the whole paragraph in the 'Courier and Enquirer' a fabrication got up to 'make a talk'? It must be confessed that it has an amazingly moon–hoaxy–air. Very little dependence is to be placed upon it, in my humble opinion; and if I were not well aware, from experience, how very easily men of science are mystified, on points out of their usual range of inquiry, I should be profoundly astonished at finding so eminent a chemist as Professor Draper, discussing Mr. Kissam's (or is it Mr. Quizzem's?) pretensions to the discovery, in so serious a tone.

But to return to the 'Diary' of Sir Humphrey Davy. This pamphlet was not designed for the public eye, even upon the decease of the writer, as any person at all conversant with authorship may satisfy himself at once by the slightest inspection of the style. At page 13, for example, near the middle, we read, in reference to his researches about the protoxide of azote: 'In less than half a minute the respiration being continued, diminished gradually and were succeeded by analogous to gentle pressure on all the muscles.' That the respiration was not 'diminished,' is not only clear by the subsequent context, but by the use of the plural, 'were.' The sentence, no doubt, was thus intended: 'In less than half a minute, the respiration [being continued, these feelings] diminished gradually, and were succeeded by [a sensation] analogous to gentle pressure on all the muscles.' A hundred similar instances go to show that the MS. so inconsiderately published, was merely a rough note–book, meant only for the writer's own eye, but an inspection of the pamphlet will convince almost any thinking person of the truth of my suggestion. The fact is, Sir Humphrey Davy was about the last man in the world to commit himself on scientific topics. Not only had he a more than ordinary dislike to quackery, but he was morbidly afraid of appearing empirical; so that, however fully he might have been convinced that he was on the right track in the matter now in question, he would never have spoken out, until he had every thing ready for the most practical demonstration. I verily believe that his last moments would have been rendered wretched, could he have suspected that his wishes in regard to burning this 'Diary' (full of crude speculations) would have been unattended to; as, it seems, they were. I say 'his wishes,' for that he meant to include this note–book among the miscellaneous papers directed 'to be burnt,' I think there can be no manner of doubt. Whether it escaped the flames by good fortune or by bad, yet remains to be seen. That the passages quoted above, with the other similar ones referred to, gave Von Kempelen the hint, I do not in the slightest degree question; but I repeat, it yet remains to be seen whether this momentous discovery itself (momentous under any circumstances) will be of service or disservice to mankind at large. That Von Kempelen and his immediate friends will reap a rich harvest, it would be folly to doubt for a moment. They will scarcely be so weak as not to 'realize,' in time, by large purchases of houses and land, with other property of intrinsic value.

In the brief account of Von Kempelen which appeared in the 'Home Journal,' and has since been extensively copied, several misapprehensions of the German original seem to have been made by the translator, who professes to have taken the passage from a late number of the Presburg 'Schnellpost.' 'Viele' has evidently been misconceived (as it often is), and what the translator renders by 'sorrows,' is probably 'lieden,' which, in its true version, 'sufferings,' would give a totally different complexion to the whole account; but, of course, much of this is merely guess, on my part.

Von Kempelen, however, is by no means 'a misan-thrope,' in appearance, at least, whatever he may be in fact. My acquaintance with him was casual altogether; and I am scarcely warranted in saying that I know him at all; but to have seen and conversed with a man of so prodigious a notoriety as he has attained, or will attain in a few days, is not a small matter, as times go.

'The Literary World' speaks of him, confidently, as a native of Presburg (misled, perhaps, by the account in 'The Home Journal') but I am pleased in being able to state positively, since I have it from his own lips, that he was born in Utica, in the State of New York, although both his parents, I believe, are of Presburg descent. The family is connected, in some way, with Maelzel, of Automaton–chess–player memory. In person, he is short and stout, with large, fat, blue eyes, sandy hair and whiskers, a wide but pleasing mouth, fine teeth, and I think a Roman nose. There is some defect in one of his feet. His address is frank, and his whole manner noticeable for bonhomie. Altogether, he looks, speaks, and acts as little like 'a misanthrope' as any man I ever saw. We were fellow–sojouners for a week about six years ago, at Earl's Hotel, in Providence, Rhode Island; and I presume that I conversed with him, at various times, for some three or four hours altogether. His principal topics were those of the day, and nothing that fell from him led me to suspect his scientific attainments. He left the hotel before me, intending to go to New York, and thence to Bremen; it was in the latter city that his great discovery was first made public; or, rather, it was there that he was first suspected of having made it. This is about all that I personally know of the now immortal Von Kempelen; but I have thought that even these few details would have interest for the public.

There can be little question that most of the marvellous rumors afloat about this affair are pure inventions, entitled to about as much credit as the story of Aladdin's lamp; and yet, in a case of this kind, as in the case of the discoveries in California, it is clear that the truth may be stranger than fiction. The following anecdote, at least, is so well authenticated, that we may receive it implicitly.

Von Kempelen had never been even tolerably well off during his residence at Bremen; and often, it was well known, he had been put to extreme shifts in order to raise trifling sums. When the great excitement occurred about the forgery on the house of Gutsmuth & Co., suspicion was directed toward Von Kempelen, on account of his having purchased a considerable property in Gasperitch Lane, and his refusing, when questioned, to explain how he became possessed of the purchase money. He was at length arrested, but nothing decisive appearing against him, was in the end set at liberty. The police, however, kept a strict watch upon his movements, and thus discovered that he left home frequently, taking always the same road, and invariably giving his watchers the slip in the neighborhood of that labyrinth of narrow and crooked passages known by the flash name of the 'Dondergat.' Finally, by dint of great perseverance, they traced him to a garret in an old house of seven stories, in an alley called Flatzplatz,– and, coming upon him suddenly, found him, as they imagined, in the midst of his counterfeiting operations. His agitation is represented as so excessive that the officers had not the slightest doubt of his guilt. After hand–cuffing him, they searched his room, or rather rooms, for it appears he occupied all the mansarde.

Opening into the garret where they caught him, was a closet, ten feet by eight, fitted up with some chemical apparatus, of which the object has not yet been ascertained. In one corner of the closet was a very small furnace, with a glowing fire in it, and on the fire a kind of duplicate crucible– two crucibles connected by a tube. One of these crucibles was nearly full of lead in a state of fusion, but not reaching up to the aperture of the tube, which was close to the brim. The other crucible had some liquid in it, which, as the officers entered, seemed to be furiously dissipating in vapor. They relate that, on finding himself taken, Kempelen seized the crucibles with both hands (which were encased in gloves that afterwards turned out to be asbestic), and threw the contents on the tiled floor. It was now that they hand–cuffed him; and before proceeding to ransack the premises they searched his person, but nothing unusual was found about him, excepting a paper parcel, in his coat–pocket, containing what was afterward ascertained to be a mixture of antimony and some unknown substance, in nearly, but not quite, equal proportions. All attempts at analyzing the unknown substance have, so far, failed, but that it will ultimately be analyzed, is not to be doubted.

Passing out of the closet with their prisoner, the officers went through a sort of ante–chamber, in which nothing material was found, to the chemist's sleeping–room. They here rummaged some drawers and boxes, but discovered only a few papers, of no importance, and some good coin, silver and gold. At length, looking under the bed, they saw a large, common hair trunk, without hinges, hasp, or lock, and with the top lying carelessly across the bottom portion. Upon attempting to draw this trunk out from under the bed, they found that, with their united strength (there were three of them, all powerful men), they 'could not stir it one inch.' Much astonished at this, one of them crawled under the bed, and looking into the trunk, said:

'No wonder we couldn't move it– why it's full to the brim of old bits of brass!'

Putting his feet, now, against the wall so as to get a good purchase, and pushing with all his force, while his companions pulled with an theirs, the trunk, with much difficulty, was slid out from under the bed, and its contents examined. The supposed brass with which it was filled was all in small, smooth pieces, varying from the size of a pea to that of a dollar; but the pieces were irregular in shape, although more or less flat– looking, upon the whole, 'very much as lead looks when thrown upon the ground in a molten state, and there suffered to grow cool.' Now, not one of these officers for a moment suspected this metal to be any thing but brass. The idea of its being gold never entered their brains, of course; how could such a wild fancy have entered it? And their astonishment may be well conceived, when the next day it became known, all over Bremen, that the 'lot of brass' which they had carted so contemptuously to the police office, without putting themselves to the trouble of pocketing the smallest scrap, was not only gold– real gold– but gold far finer than any employed in coinage–gold, in fact, absolutely pure, virgin, without the slightest appreciable alloy.

I need not go over the details of Von Kempelen's confession (as far as it went) and release, for these are familiar to the public. That he has actually realized, in spirit and in effect, if not to the letter, the old chimaera of the philosopher's stone, no sane person is at liberty to doubt. The opinions of Arago are, of course, entitled to the greatest consideration; but he is by no means infallible; and what he says of bismuth, in his report to the Academy, must be taken cum grano salis. The simple truth is, that up to this period all analysis has failed; and until Von Kempelen chooses to let us have the key to his own published enigma, it is more than probable that the matter will remain, for years, in statu quo. All that as yet can fairly be said to be known is, that 'Pure gold can be made at will, and very readily from lead in connection with certain other substances, in kind and in proportions, unknown.'

Speculation, of course, is busy as to the immediate and ultimate results of this discovery– a discovery which few thinking persons will hesitate in referring to an increased interest in the matter of gold generally, by the late developments in California; and this reflection brings us inevitably to another– the exceeding inopportuneness of Von Kempelen's analysis. If many were prevented from adventuring to California, by the mere apprehension that gold would so materially diminish in value, on account of its plentifulness in the mines there, as to render the speculation of going so far in search of it a doubtful one– what impression will be wrought now, upon the minds of those about to emigrate, and especially upon the minds of those actually in the mineral region, by the announcement of this astounding discovery of Von Kempelen? a discovery which declares, in so many words, that beyond its intrinsic worth for manufacturing purposes (whatever that worth may be), gold now is, or at least soon will be (for it cannot be supposed that Von Kempelen can long retain his secret), of no greater value than lead, and of far inferior value to silver. It is, indeed, exceedingly difficult to speculate prospectively upon the consequences of the discovery, but one thing may be positively maintained– that the announcement of the discovery six months ago would have had material influence in regard to the settlement of California.

In Europe, as yet, the most noticeable results have been a rise of two hundred per cent. in the price of lead, and nearly twenty–five per cent. that of silver.

MELLONTA TAUTA

To The Editors of The Lady's Book:

I have the honor of sending you, for your magazine, an article which I hope you will be able to comprehend rather more distinctly than I do myself. It is a translation, by my friend, Martin Van Buren Mavis, (sometimes called the "Toughkeepsie Seer") of an odd–looking MS. which I found, about a year ago, tightly corked up in a jug floating in the Mare Tenebrarum– a sea well described by the Nubian geographer, but seldom visited now–a–days, except for the transcendentalists and divers for crotchets.

Truly yours,

Edgar A. Poe

On Board Balloon "Skylark", April, 1, 2848

NOW, my dear friend– now, for your sins, you are to suffer the infliction of a long gossiping letter. I tell you distinctly that I am going to punish you for all your impertinences by being as tedious, as discursive, as incoherent and as unsatisfactory as possible. Besides, here I am, cooped up in a dirty balloon, with some one or two hundred of the canaille, all bound on a pleasure excursion, (what a funny idea some people have of pleasure!) and I have no prospect of touching terra firma for a month at least. Nobody to talk to. Nothing to do. When one has nothing to do, then is the time to correspond with ones friends. You perceive, then, why it is that I write you this letter– it is on account of my ennui and your sins.

Get ready your spectacles and make up your mind to be annoyed. I mean to write at you every day during this odious voyage.

Heigho! when will any Invention visit the human pericranium? Are we forever to be doomed to the thousand inconveniences of the balloon? Will nobody contrive a more expeditious mode of progress? The jog–trot movement, to my thinking, is little less than positive torture. Upon my word we have not made more than a hundred miles the hour since leaving home! The very birds beat us– at least some of them. I assure you that I do not exaggerate at all. Our motion, no doubt, seems slower than it actually is– this on account of our having no objects about us by which to estimate our velocity, and on account of our going with the wind. To be sure, whenever we meet a balloon we have a chance of perceiving our rate, and then, I admit, things do not appear so very bad. Accustomed as I am to this mode of travelling, I cannot get over a kind of giddiness whenever a balloon passes us in a current directly overhead. It always seems to me like an immense bird of prey about to pounce upon us and carry us off in its claws. One went over us this morning about sunrise, and so nearly overhead that its drag–rope actually brushed the network suspending our car, and caused us very serious apprehension. Our captain said that if the material of the bag had been the trumpery varnished "silk" of five hundred or a thousand years ago, we should inevitably have been damaged. This silk, as he explained it to me, was a fabric composed of the entrails of a species of earth–worm. The worm was carefully fed on mulberries–kind of fruit resembling a water–melon– and, when sufficiently fat, was crushed in a mill. The paste thus arising was called papyrus in its primary state, and went through a variety of processes until it finally became "silk." Singular to relate, it was once much admired as an article of female dress! Balloons were also very generally constructed from it. A better kind of material, it appears, was subsequently found in the down surrounding the seed–vessels of a plant vulgarly called euphorbium, and at that time botanically termed milk–weed. This latter kind of silk was designated as silk–buckingham, on account of its superior durability, and was usually prepared for use by being varnished with a solution of gum caoutchouc– a substance which in some respects must have resembled the gutta percha now in common use. This caoutchouc was occasi-onally called Indian rubber or rubber of twist, and was no doubt one of the numerous fungi. Never tell me again that I am not at heart an antiquarian.

Talking of drag–ropes– our own, it seems, has this moment knocked a man overboard from one of the small magnetic propellers that swarm in ocean below us– a boat of about six thousand tons, and, from all accounts, shamefully crowded. These diminutive barques should be prohibited from carrying more than a definite number of passengers. The man, of course, was not permitted to get on board again, and was soon out of sight, he and his life–preserver. I rejoice, my dear friend, that we live in an age so enlightened that no such a thing as an individual is supposed to exist. It is the mass for which the true Humanity cares. By–the–by, talking of Humanity, do you know that our immortal Wiggins is not so original in his views of the Social Condition and so forth, as his contemporaries are inclined to suppose? Pundit assures me that the same ideas were put nearly in the same way, about a thousand years ago, by an Irish philosopher called Furrier, on account of his keeping a retail shop for cat peltries and other furs. Pundit knows, you know; there can be no mistake about it. How very wonderfully do we see verified every day, the profound observation of the Hindoo Aries Tottle (as quoted by Pundit)– "Thus must we say that, not once or twice, or a few times, but with almost infinite repetitions, the same opinions come round in a circle among men."

April 2.– Spoke to–day the magnetic cutter in charge of the middle section of floating telegraph wires. I learn that when this species of telegraph was first put into operation by Horse, it was considered quite impossible to convey the wires over sea, but now we are at a loss to comprehend where the difficulty lay! So wags the world. Tempora mutantur– excuse me for quoting the Etruscan. What would we do without the Atalantic telegraph? (Pundit says Atlantic was the ancient adjective.) We lay to a few minutes to ask the cutter some questions, and learned, among other glorious news, that civil war is raging in Africa, while the plague is doing its good work beautifully both in Yurope and Ayesher. Is it not truly remarkable that, before the magnificent light shed upon philosophy by Humanity, the world was accustomed to regard War and Pestilence as calamities? Do you know that prayers were actually offered up in the ancient temples to the end that these evils (!) might not be visited upon mankind? Is it not really difficult to comprehend upon what principle of interest our forefathers acted? Were they so blind as not to perceive that the destruction of a myriad of individuals is only so much positive advantage to the mass!

April 3.– It is really a very fine amusement to ascend the rope–ladder leading to the summit of the balloon–bag, and thence survey the surrounding world. From the car below you know the prospect is not so comprehensive– you can see little vertically. But seated here (where I write this) in the luxuriously–cushioned open piazza of the summit, one can see everything that is going on in all directions. Just now there is quite a crowd of balloons in sight, and they present a very animated appearance, while the air is resonant with the hum of so many millions of human voices. I have heard it asserted that when Yellow or (Pundit will have it) Violet, who is supposed to have been the first aeronaut, maintained the practicability of traversing the atmosphere in all directions, by merely ascending or descending until a favorable current was attained, he was scarcely hearkened to at all by his contemporaries, who looked upon him as merely an ingenious sort of madman, because the philosophers (?) of the day declared the thing impossible. Really now it does seem to me quite unaccountable how any thing so obviously feasible could have escaped the sagacity of the ancient savans. But in all ages the great obstacles to advancement in Art have been opposed by the so–called men of science. To be sure, our men of science are not quite so bigoted as those of old:– oh, I have something so queer to tell you on this topic. Do you know that it is not more than a thousand years ago since the metaphysicians consented to relieve the people of the singular fancy that there existed but two possible roads for the attainment of Truth! Believe it if you can! It appears that long, long ago, in the night of Time, there lived a Turkish philosopher (or Hindoo possibly) called Aries Tottle. This person introduced, or at all events propagated what was termed the deductive or a priori mode of investigation. He started with what he maintained to be axioms or "self–evident truths," and thence proceeded "logically" to results. His greatest disciples were one Neuclid, and one Cant. Well, Aries Tottle flourished supreme until advent of one Hog, surnamed the "Ettrick Shepherd," who preached an entirely different system, which he called the a posteriori or inductive. His plan referred altogether to Sensation. He proceeded by observing, analyzing, and classifying facts–instantiae naturae, as they were affectedly called– into general laws. Aries Tottle's mode, in a word, was based on noumena; Hog's on phenomena. Well, so great was the admiration excited by this latter system that, at its first introduction, Aries Tottle fell into disrepute; but finally he recovered ground and was permitted to divide the realm of Truth with his more modern rival. The savans now maintained the Aristotelian and Baconian roads were the sole possible avenues to knowledge. "Baconian," you must know, was an adjective invented as equivalent to Hog–ian and more euphonious and dignified.

Now, my dear friend, I do assure you, most positively, that I represent this matter fairly, on the soundest authority and you can easily understand how a notion so absurd on its very face must have operated to retard the progress of all true knowledge– which makes its advances almost invariably by intuitive bounds. The ancient idea confined investigations to crawling; and for hundreds of years so great was the infatuation about Hog especially, that a virtual end was put to all thinking, properly so called. No man dared utter a truth to which he felt himself indebted to his Soul alone. It mattered not whether the truth was even demonstrably a truth, for the bullet–headed savans of the time regarded only the road by which he had attained it. They would not even look at the end. "Let us see the means," they cried, "the means!" If, upon investigation of the means, it was found to come under neither the category Aries (that is to say Ram) nor under the category Hog, why then the savans went no farther, but pronounced the "theorist" a fool, and would have nothing to do with him or his truth.

Now, it cannot be maintained, even, that by the crawling system the greatest amount of truth would be attained in any long series of ages, for the repression of imagination was an evil not to be compensated for by any superior certainty in the ancient modes of investigation. The error of these Jurmains, these Vrinch, these Inglitch, and these Amriccans (the latter, by the way, were our own immediate progenitors), was an error quite analogous with that of the wiseacre who fancies that he must necessarily see an object the better the more closely he holds it to his eyes. These people blinded themselves by details. When they proceeded Hoggishly, their "facts" were by no means always facts– a matter of little consequence had it not been for assuming that they were facts and must be facts because they appeared to be such. When they proceeded on the path of the Ram, their course was scarcely as straight as a ram's horn, for they never had an axiom which was an axiom at all. They must have been very blind not to see this, even in their own day; for even in their own day many of the long "established" axioms had been rejected. For example– "Ex nihilo nihil fit"; "a body cannot act where it is not"; "there cannot exist antipodes"; "darkness cannot come out of light"– all these, and a dozen other similar propositions, formerly admitted without hesitation as axioms, were, even at the period of which I speak, seen to be untenable. How absurd in these people, then, to persist in putting faith in "axioms" as immutable bases of Truth! But even out of the mouths of their soundest reasoners it is easy to demonstrate the futility, the impalpability of their axioms in general. Who was the soundest of their logicians? Let me see! I will go and ask Pundit and be back in a minute.... Ah, here we have it! Here is a book written nearly a thousand years ago and lately translated from the Inglitch– which, by the way, appears to have been the rudiment of the Amriccan. Pundit says it is decidedly the cleverest ancient work on its topic, Logic. The author (who was much thought of in his day) was one Miller, or Mill; and we find it recorded of him, as a point of some importance, that he had a mill–horse called Bentham. But let us glance at the treatise!

Ah!– "Ability or inability to conceive," says Mr. Mill, very properly, "is in no case to be received as a criterion of axiomatic truth." What modern in his senses would ever think of disputing this truism? The only wonder with us must be, how it happened that Mr. Mill conceived it necessary even to hint at any thing so obvious. So far good– but let us turn over another paper. What have we here?– "Contradictories cannot both be true– that is, cannot co–exist in nature." Here Mr. Mill means, for example, that a tree must be either a tree or not a tree– that it cannot be at the same time a tree and not a tree. Very well; but I ask him why. His reply is this– and never pretends to be any thing else than this– "Because it is impossible to conceive that contradictories can both be true." But this is no answer at all, by his own showing, for has he not just admitted as a truism that "ability or inability to conceive is in no case to be received as a criterion of axiomatic truth."

Now I do not complain of these ancients so much because their logic is, by their own showing, utterly baseless, worthless and fantastic altogether, as because of their pompous and imbecile proscription of all other roads of Truth, of all other means for its attainment than the two preposterous paths– the one of creeping and the one of crawling– to which they have dared to confine the Soul that loves nothing so well as to soar.

By the by, my dear friend, do you not think it would have puzzled these ancient dogmaticians to have determined by which of their two roads it was that the most important and most sublime of all their truths was, in effect, attained? I mean the truth of Gravitation. Newton owed it to Kepler. Kepler admitted that his three laws were guessed at– these three laws of all laws which led the great Inglitch mathematician to his principle, the basis of all physical principle– to go behind which we must enter the Kingdom of Metaphysics. Kepler guessed– that is to say imagined. He was essentially a "theorist"– that word now of so much sanctity, formerly an epithet of contempt. Would it not have puzzled these old moles too, to have explained by which of the two "roads" a cryptographist unriddles a cryptograph of more than usual secrecy, or by which of the two roads Champollion directed mankind to those enduring and almost innumerable truths which resulted from his deciphering the Hieroglyphics.

One word more on this topic and I will be done boring you. Is it not passing strange that, with their eternal

Edgar Allan Poe

prattling about roads to Truth, these bigoted people missed what we now so clearly perceive to be the great highway– that of Consistency? Does it not seem singular how they should have failed to deduce from the works of God the vital fact that a perfect consistency must be an absolute truth! How plain has been our progress since the late announcement of this proposition! Investigation has been taken out of the hands of the ground–moles and given, as a task, to the true and only true thinkers, the men of ardent imagination. These latter theorize. Can you not fancy the shout of scorn with which my words would be received by our progenitors were it possible for them to be now looking over my shoulder? These men, I say, theorize; and their theories are simply corrected, reduced, systematized– cleared, little by little, of their dross of inconsistency– until, finally, a perfect consistency stands apparent which even the most stolid admit, because it is a consistency, to be an absolute and an unquestionable truth.

April 4.– The new gas is doing wonders, in conjunction with the new improvement with gutta percha. How very safe, commodious, manageable, and in every respect convenient are our modern balloons! Here is an immense one approaching us at the rate of at least a hundred and fifty miles an hour. It seems to be crowded with people– perhaps there are three or four hundred passengers– and yet it soars to an elevation of nearly a mile, looking down upon poor us with sovereign contempt. Still a hundred or even two hundred miles an hour is slow travelling after all. Do you remember our flight on the railroad across the Kanadaw continent?– fully three hundred miles the hour– that was travelling. Nothing to be seen though– nothing to be done but flirt, feast and dance in the magnificent saloons. Do you remember what an odd sensation was experienced when, by chance, we caught a glimpse of external objects while the cars were in full flight? Every thing seemed unique– in one mass. For my part, I cannot say but that I preferred the travelling by the slow train of a hundred miles the hour. Here we were permitted to have glass windows– even to have them open– and something like a distinct view of the country was attainable.... Pundit says that the route for the great Kanadaw railroad must have been in some measure marked out about nine hundred years ago! In fact, he goes so far as to assert that actual traces of a road are still discernible– traces referable to a period quite as remote as that mentioned. The track, it appears was double only; ours, you know, has twelve paths; and three or four new ones are in preparation. The ancient rails were very slight, and placed so close together as to be, according to modern notions, quite frivolous, if not dangerous in the extreme. The present width of track– fifty feet– is considered, indeed, scarcely secure enough. For my part, I make no doubt that a track of some sort must have existed in very remote times, as Pundit asserts; for nothing can be clearer, to my mind, than that, at some period– not less than seven centuries ago, certainly– the Northern and Southern Kanadaw continents were united; the Kanawdians, then, would have been driven, by necessity, to a great railroad across the continent.

April 5.– I am almost devoured by ennui. Pundit is the only conversible person on board; and he, poor soul! can speak of nothing but antiquities. He has been occupied all the day in the attempt to convince me that the ancient Amriccans governed themselves!– did ever anybody hear of such an absurdity?– that they existed in a sort of every–man–for–himself confederacy, after the fashion of the "prairie dogs" that we read of in fable. He says that they started with the queerest idea conceivable, viz: that all men are born free and equal– this in the very teeth of the laws of gradation so visibly impressed upon all things both in the moral and physical universe. Every man "voted," as they called it– that is to say meddled with public affairs– until at length, it was discovered that what is everybody's business is nobody's, and that the "Republic" (so the absurd thing was called) was without a government at all. It is related, however, that the first circumstance which disturbed, very particularly, the self– complacency of the philosophers who constructed this "Republic," was the startling discovery that universal suffrage gave opportunity for fraudulent schemes, by means of which any desired number of votes might at any time be polled, without the possibility of prevention or even detection, by any party which should be merely villainous enough not to be ashamed of the fraud. A little reflection upon this discovery sufficed to render evident the consequences, which were that rascality must predominate– in a word, that a republican government could never be any thing but a rascally one. While the philosophers, however, were busied in blushing at their stupidity in not having foreseen these inevitable evils, and intent upon the invention of new theories, the matter was put to an abrupt issue by a fellow of the name of Mob, who took every thing into his own hands and set up a despotism, in comparison with which those of the fabulous Zeros and Hellofagabaluses were respectable and delectable. This Mob (a foreigner, by–the–by), is said to have been the most odious of all men that ever encumbered the earth. He was a giant in stature– insolent, rapacious, filthy, had the gall of a bullock with the heart of a hyena and the brains of a peacock. He died, at length, by dint of his own energies, which exhausted him. Nevertheless, he had his uses, as every thing has, however vile, and taught mankind a lesson which to this day it is in no danger of forgetting– never to run directly contrary to the natural analogies. As for Republicanism, no analogy could be found for it upon the face of the earth– unless we except the case of the "prairie dogs," an exception which seems to demonstrate, if anything, that democracy is a very admirable form of government– for dogs.

April 6.– Last night had a fine view of Alpha Lyrae, whose disk, through our captain's spy–glass, subtends an angle of half a degree, looking very much as our sun does to the naked eye on a misty day. Alpha Lyrae, although so very much larger than our sun, by the by, resembles him closely as regards its spots, its atmosphere, and in many other particulars. It is only within the last century, Pundit tells me, that the binary relation existing between these two orbs began even to be suspected. The evident motion of our system in the heavens was (strange to say!) referred to an orbit about a prodigious star in the centre of the galaxy. About this star, or at all events about a centre of gravity common to all the globes of the Milky Way and supposed to be near Alcyone in the Pleiades, every one of these globes was declared to be revolving, our own performing the circuit in a period of 117,000,000 of years! We, with our present lights, our vast telescopic improvements, and so forth, of course find it difficult to comprehend the ground of an idea such as this. Its first propagator was one Mudler. He was led, we must presume, to this wild hypothesis by mere analogy in the first instance; but, this being the case, he should have at least adhered to analogy in its development. A great central orb was, in fact, suggested; so far Mudler was consistent. This central orb, however, dynamically, should have been greater than all its surrounding orbs taken together. The question might then have been asked– "Why do we not see it?"– we, especially, who occupy the mid region of the cluster– the very locality near which, at least, must be situated this inconceivable central sun. The astronomer, perhaps, at this point, took refuge in the suggestion of non–luminosity; and here analogy was suddenly let fall. But even admitting the central orb non–luminous, how did he manage to explain its failure to be rendered visible by the incalculable host of glorious suns glaring in all directions about it? No doubt what he finally maintained was merely a centre of gravity common to all the revolving orbs– but here again analogy must have been let fall. Our system revolves, it is true, about a common centre of gravity, but it does this in connection with and in consequence of a material sun whose mass more than counterbalances the rest of the system. The mathematical circle is a curve composed of an infinity of straight lines; but this idea of the circle– this idea of it which, in regard to all earthly geometry, we consider as merely the mathematical, in contradistinction from the practical, idea– is, in sober fact, the practical conception which alone we have any right to entertain in respect to those Titanic circles with which we have to deal, at least in fancy, when we suppose our system, with its fellows, revolving about a point in the centre of the galaxy. Let the most vigorous of human imaginations but attempt to take a single step toward the comprehension of a circuit so unutterable! I would scarcely be paradoxical to say that a flash of lightning itself, travelling forever upon the circumference of this inconceivable circle, would still forever be travelling in a straight line. That the path of our sun along such a circumference– that the direction of our system in such an orbit– would, to any human perception, deviate in the slightest degree from a straight line even in a million of years, is a proposition not to be entertained; and yet these ancient astronomers were absolutely cajoled, it appears, into believing that a decisive curvature had become apparent during the brief period of their astronomical history– during the mere point– during the utter nothingness of two or three thousand years! How incomprehensible, that considerations such as this did not at once indicate to them the true state of affairs– that of the binary revolution of our sun and Alpha Lyrae around a common centre of gravity!

April 7.– Continued last night our astronomical amusements. Had a fine view of the five Neptunian asteroids, and watched with much interest the putting up of a huge impost on a couple of lintels in the new temple at Daphnis in the moon. It was amusing to think that creatures so diminutive as the lunarians, and bearing so little resemblance to humanity, yet evinced a mechanical ingenuity so much superior to our own. One finds it difficult, too, to conceive the vast masses which these people handle so easily, to be as light as our own reason tells us they actually are.

April 8.– Eureka! Pundit is in his glory. A balloon from Kanadaw spoke us to–day and threw on board several late papers; they contain some exceedingly curious information relative to Kanawdian or rather Amriccan antiquities. You know, I presume, that laborers have for some months been employed in preparing the ground for a new fountain at Paradise, the Emperor's principal pleasure garden. Paradise, it appears, has been, literally speaking, an island time out of mind– that is to say, its northern boundary was always (as far back as any record extends) a rivulet, or rather a very narrow arm of the sea. This arm was gradually widened until it attained its present breadth– a mile. The whole length of the island is nine miles; the breadth varies materially. The entire area (so Pundit says) was, about eight hundred years ago, densely packed with houses, some of them twenty stories high; land (for some most unaccountable reason) being considered as especially precious just in this vicinity. The disastrous earthquake, however, of the year 2050, so totally uprooted and overwhelmed the town (for it was almost too large to be called a village) that the most indefatigable of our antiquarians have never yet been able to obtain from the site any sufficient data (in the shape of coins, medals or inscriptions) wherewith to build up even the ghost of a theory concerning the manners, customs, &c., &c., &c., of the aboriginal inhabitants. Nearly all that we have hitherto known of them is, that they were a portion of the Knickerbocker tribe of savages infesting the continent at its first discovery by Recorder Riker, a knight of the Golden Fleece. They were by no means uncivilized, however, but cultivated various arts and even sciences after a fashion of their own. It is related of them that they were acute in many respects, but were oddly afflicted with monomania for building what, in the ancient Amriccan, was denominated "churches"– a kind of pagoda instituted for the worship of two idols that went by the names of Wealth and Fashion. In the end, it is said, the island became, nine tenths of it, church. The women, too, it appears, were oddly deformed by a natural protuberance of the region just below the small of the back– although, most unaccountably, this deformity was looked upon altogether in the light of a beauty. One or two pictures of these singular women have in fact, been miracu- lously preserved. They look very odd, very – like something between a turkey–cock and a dromedary.

Well, these few details are nearly all that have descended to us respecting the ancient Knickerbockers. It seems, however, that while digging in the centre of the emperors garden, (which, you know, covers the whole island), some of the workmen unearthed a cubical and evidently chiseled block of granite, weighing several hundred pounds. It was in good preservation, having received, apparently, little injury from the convulsion which entombed it. On one of its surfaces was a marble slab with (only think of it!) an inscription– a legible inscription. Pundit is in ecstacies. Upon detaching the slab, a cavity appeared, containing a leaden box filled with various coins, a long scroll of names, several documents which appear to resemble newspapers, with other matters of intense interest to the antiquarian! There can be no doubt that all these are genuine Amriccan relics belonging to the tribe called Knickerbocker. The papers thrown on board our balloon are filled with fac–similes of the coins, MSS., typography, &c., &c. I copy for your amusement the Knickerbocker inscription on the marble slab:–

> This Corner Stone of a Monument to
> The Memory of George Washington
>
> Was Laid With Appropriate Ceremonies
> on the 19th Day of October, 1847
> The Anniversary of the Surrender of
> Lord Cornwallis to General Washington
> at Yorktown A. D. 1781
>
> Under the Auspices of the Washington
> Monument Association of the City of
> New York.

This, as I give it, is a verbatim translation done by Pundit himself, so there can be no mistake about it. From the few words thus preserved we glean several important items of knowledge, not the least interesting of which is the fact that a thousand years ago actual monuments had fallen into disuse — as was all very proper — the people contenting themselves, as we do now, with a mere indication of the design to erect a monument at some future time; a corner–stone being cautiously laid by itself "solitary and alone" (excuse me for quoting the great Amriccan poet Benton) as a guarantee of the magnanimous intention. We ascertain, too, very distinctly, from this admirable inscription, the how, as well as the where and the what, of the great surrender in question. As to the where, it was Yorktown (wherever that was), and as to the what, it was General Cornwallis (no doubt some wealthy dealer in corn). He was surrendered. The inscription comme-morates the surrender of — what? — why, "of Lord Cornwallis." The only question is what could the savages wish him surrendered for. But when we remember that these savages were undoubtedly cannibals, we are led to the conclusion that they intended him for sausage. As to the how of the surrender, no language can be more explicit. Lord Cornwallis was surrendered (for sausage) "under the auspices of the Washington Monument Association," no doubt a charitable institution for the depositing of corner–stones. — But, Heaven, bless me! what is the matter? Ah, I see — the balloon has collapsed, and we shall have a tumble into the sea. I have, therefore, only time enough to add that, from a hasty inspection of the fac–similes of newspapers, etc., etc., I find that the great men in those days among the Amriccans were one John, a smith, and one Zacchary, a tailor.

Good–by, until I see you again. Whether you ever get this letter or not is a point of little importance, as I write altogether for my own amusement. I shall cork the MS. up in a bottle however, and throw it into the sea.

Yours everlastingly,

PUNDITA.

CPSIA information can be obtained
at www.ICGtesting.com
Printed in the USA
LVHW040904050323
740959LV00001B/167

9 781595 404237